THE AMBIGUITY OF PLAY

THE AMBIGUITY OF PLAY

Brian Sutton-Smith

■ ▲ ■ ▲ ■ ▲

HARVARD UNIVERSITY PRESS

Cambridge, Massachusetts
London, England
1997

Library of Congress Cataloging-in-Publication Data

Sutton-Smith, Brian.
    The ambiguity of play / Brian Sutton-Smith.
        p.   cm.
    Includes bibliographical references and index.
    ISBN 0–674–01733–1 (alk. paper)
    1. Play—Psychological aspects. I. Title.
BF717.S93 1997
155—dc21   97-21713

CONTENTS

PREFACE

He cometh unto you with a tale which holdeth children from play, and old men from the chimney corner.

Sir Philip Sidney

In forty years of pursuing the meaning of play, it has become apparent to me that an understanding of play's ambiguity requires the help of multiple disciplines. But it has also become apparent that it is difficult to approach the subject matter of play directly when there is so much implicit ideological rhetoric that comes with these disciplines. The procedure to be adopted, therefore, is like that of Umberto Eco in his novel *The Name of the Rose* (1983), in which he describes the activity of a group of medieval monks who, having realized that it is impossible to say what God is, have devoted themselves to revealing what God is *not*. And so the margins of their hand-printed Bibles are replete with artistic playfulness exhibiting nonsensical creatures that could not have existed and actions that are impossible. In the present book I attempt to arrive at the meaning of play in a sometimes similarly indirect and nonsensical fashion. I contend that one can conduct a serious examination of the rhetorics that are marginal to play and that this will illuminate our understanding of it. An earlier title of this book was, indeed, "The Rhetorics of Adult and Child Play Theory," which reveals the marginality of the present approach. The chapter epigraphs indicate that it is possible to go even further in pursuing play as marginal. Contrarily, as I have dealt with my own reflexive involvement elsewhere, I treat it as some-what marginal here and confine it to a footnote.*

In general terms, although this work wallows in the mystifications of rhetoric and theory, its intention is to clarify the science of play as well as to celebrate its authenticity.

*The reflexive issue of how my own scholarship is itself a personal rhetoric of relevance to this volume is too complicated for treatment here. References that are directly relevant are: Chick, 1991; Lee, 1994; Sutton-Smith, 1993a, 1994b, 1994c. The rest of the bibliography under Sutton-Smith and coauthors is at least indirectly relevant.

ACKNOWLEDGMENTS

The modern use of a rhetorical approach to matters of scholarship and science probably owes the most, ultimately, to two great scholars of rhetoric, Kenneth Burke, whom I had the good fortune to meet, and Ludwig Wittgenstein, whom I did not. My more immediate debt is to the three truly great twentieth-century play theorists, J. Huizinga, M. Spariosu, and R. Fagen, who have, wittingly or otherwise, contributed to our playful illusion that the time of the "ludic turn" in Western culture is about to arrive. In addition I must thank the universities that over the years have allowed me, a psychologist, to indulge myself by teaching courses in play, games, toys and sports, the psychology of childlore, and children's folklore: Bowling Green State University in Ohio (1956–1967), Teachers College, Columbia University, in New York City (1967–1977), the University of Pennsylvania in Philadelphia (1977–1990), and the New College of the University of Southern Florida (1995). Long before that, the University of New Zealand gave me one of its first doctoral fellowships (1949–1950) to pursue my studies of the games of the children in that country. Thanks also to the Fulbright Foundation, which permitted me to continue the same ludic insouciance in the United States (1952–53) and later in Yugoslavia (1984). In addition, thanks to my colleagues for two Festschrifts about play (Chick, 1991: Pellegrini, 1995a) and two toy research awards (Brio, Sweden, 1994; Halmstad, Sweden, 1996), and to the American Folklore Society for a Life Achievement Award in Children's folklore, as well as the Opie book award.

Beyond that, I wish to thank all those scholars of play, some ten of whom were my own doctoral students, who have also attempted to discover what it is that we have all been studying (cited in Pellegrini, 1995a). I am indebted as well to those who are cited in the text here and whose works appear in the bibliography. In particular my thanks go to those who read and reflected on all or part of the present work: Gary Chick, Greta Fein, Felicia McMahon, Tony Pellegrini, and Kevin Sheehan and my sixteen students at New College. I must give special thanks to Peter R. Huttenlocher for providing me with a copy of his "Synaptogenesis in Human Cerebral Cortex" (in Geraldine Dawson and Kurt W. Fischer, eds. 1994. *Human Behavior and the Developing Brain*. New York: Guilford Press, pp. 137–152.) which I draw upon in my Conclusion.

Finally thanks to my father, Ernest James, for confronting our family with a dialectic of order and disorder in his life roles as post office bureaucrat and actor, and to my elder brother, Vaughan, for presenting satirical metadisorders of my father's fabulations, as a result of which most respectable things in my life came to appear as very funny. I thank my mother, Nita Katherine, in turn, for making all of this virtuality appear quite authentic. And I thank my wife, Shirley, and children, Katherine, Mark, Leslie, Mary, and Emily, for being kind and playful about all of this, which is as good as you can get.

My soul, sit thou a patient looker-on;
Judge not the play before the play is done:
Her plot hath many changes; every day
Speaks a new scene; the last act crowns the play.
Francis Quarles

Play and Ambiguity

A nip is but a nip
And a boojum
Is but a buttercup.
after Lewis Carroll

We all play occasionally, and we all know what playing feels like. But when it comes to making theoretical statements about what play is, we fall into silliness. There is little agreement among us, and much ambiguity. Some of the most outstanding scholars of children's play have been concerned by this ambiguity. For example, classical scholar Mihail Spariosu (1989) calls play "amphibolous," which means it goes in two directions at once and is not clear. Victor Turner (1969), the anthropologist, calls play "liminal" or "liminoid," meaning that it occupies a threshold between reality and unreality, as if, for example, it were on the beach between the land and the sea. Geoffrey Bateson (1955), biologist, suggests that play is a paradox because it both is and is not what it appears to be. Animals at play bite each other playfully, knowing that the playful nip connotes a bite, but not what a bite connotes. In turn, Richard Schechner (1988), dramaturge, suggests that a playful nip is not only not a bite, it is also *not* not a bite. That is, it is a positive, the sum of two negatives. Which is again to say that the playful nip may not be a bite, but it is indeed what a bite means.

Kenneth Burke's works suggest that play is probably what he terms a "dramatistic negative," which means that for animals who do not have any way of saying "no," it is a way of indicating the negative through an affirmative action that is clearly not the same as that which it represents (thus, again, nipping rather than biting). He says

1

that prior to the evolutionary emergence of words, the negative could be dramatized only by the presentation of stylized and gestural forms of the positive (Burke, 1966, p. 423). "The most irritating feature of play," says Robert Fagen (1981), leading animal play theorist, "is not the perceptual incoherence, as such, but rather that play taunts us with its inaccessibility. We feel that something is behind it all, but we do not know, or have forgotten how to see it."

If we seek greater definitional clarity by analyzing the meaning of ambiguity itself, following William Empson's classic *Seven Types of Ambiguity* (1955), then we can say that play involves all of his seven types, which are as follows, with the play examples in parentheses:

1. the ambiguity of reference (is that a pretend gun sound, or are you choking?);
2. the ambiguity of the referent (is that an object or a toy?);
3. the ambiguity of intent (do you mean it, or is it pretend?);
4. the ambiguity of sense (is this serious, or is it nonsense?);
5. the ambiguity of transition (you said you were only playing);
6. the ambiguity of contradiction (a man playing at being a woman);
7. the ambiguity of meaning (is it play or playfighting?).

And finally, as if all these paradoxes were not enough, Stephen Jay Gould, evolutionist, says that there are some human traits that are just side effects of more fundamental genetic functions and really deserve no functional explanation themselves. The quotation that heads this chapter, and those in the chapters that follow, would suggest that, if that is the case, there are nevertheless many interesting things about our so-called junk genes. The quotations at the beginning of each chapter also often bring up interesting rhetorics from much earlier times. Many authors use children's play as a metaphor for the ephemerality of life, for what quickly passes, or for what is innocent, infantile, or foolish. Others who are quoted render adult life as a very serious mortal game in which foul play is possible. The diversity of this metaphoric playfulness would seem to suggest that, whether junk or not, play takes on multiple forms in somber discourse.*

*Play-related quotations here and throughout the rest of this work are, for the most part, from *Barlett's Familiar Quotations*, 16th ed. (Boston: Little, Brown, 1992) Playful quotes, noted as "after" are of fictional status. Dr. Frech is frivolous.

This chapter is a search for some of the more obvious possible reasons for the ambiguity, as well as an introduction to the particular focus of the volume as a whole: the ideological underpinnings of play theories, and what an understanding of them can contribute to clearing up these confusions. The ambiguity is most obvious, however, in the multiple forms of play and the diversity of the kinds of play scholarship they have instigated. Obviously the word *play* stands for a category of very diverse happenings, though the same could be said about most omnibus categories, such as, for example, religion, art, war, politics, and culture.

The Diversity of Play Forms and Experiences

The diversity of play is well illustrated by the varied kinds of play that are to be found within the larger menagerie of the "play" sphere. Almost anything can allow play to occur within its boundaries, as is illustrated, for example, by works on tourism as play (McCannell, 1976), television as play (Stephenson, 1967), daydreaming as play (Caughey, 1984), sexual intimacy as play (Betcher, 1987), and even gossip as play (Spack, 1986). Travel can be a playful competition to see who can go to the most places or have the most authentic encounters. "Have you done London, the Eiffel Tower, Ayres Rock, Palmer Station, and Easter Island?" Watching television can be watching and identifying with other people at play, whether in fiction or in real life—and, after all, one can turn it off or on, which makes it like play and not like real life. Viewers can control their involvement just as if the "play" belongs to them, as in "playing" with the channels. Even the news, which is "live at five," is only an account from a studio with theatric backdrops. All of us carry dozens of characters around in our daydreams with whom we carry on imaginary encounters and conversations, none of which are real in the usual sense. Many of the characters in our heads are also people on television or in films, but most are everyday acquaintances. Sexual intimates are said to play with each other in innumerable ways, painting each other's bodies, eating food off of each other, playing hide the thimble with bodily crevices, communicating in public with their own esoteric vocabulary, and, in general, teasing and testing each other with playful impropriety. Gossip, by contrast, can be a playfully irreverent game of denigrating those who are not present.

A list of activities that are often said to be play forms or play experiences themselves is presented below. The terms illustrate the great diversity of play phenomena, although they do not indicate the even wider extension of informal play through all other spheres of life. This list itself awaits both adequate description and adequate play theorizing, because the items that it contains are often typically called by other names, such as entertainments, recreations, pastimes, and hobbies, as if it would be an embarrassment to admit that they can also be called play. Each of these states of mind, activities, or events could be described as has I have described with travel and gossip, above. The boundaries between them are never as discrete as listing them here might imply. They are arranged in order from the mostly more private to the mostly more public.

Mind or subjective play: dreams, daydreams, fantasy, imagination, ruminations, reveries, Dungeons and Dragons, metaphors of play, and playing with metaphors.

Solitary play: hobbies, collections, (model trains, model airplanes, model power boats, stamps), writing to pen pals, building models, listening to records and compact discs, constructions, art projects, gardening, flower arranging, using computers, watching videos, reading and writing, novels, toys, travel, Civil War reenactments, music, pets, reading, woodworking, yoga, antiquing, flying, auto racing, collecting and rebuilding cars, sailing, diving, astrology, bicycling, handicrafts, photography, shopping, backpacking, fishing, needlework, quilting, bird watching, crosswords, and cooking.

Playful behaviors: playing tricks, playing around, playing for time, playing up to someone, playing a part, playing down to someone, playing upon words, making a play for someone, playing upon others as in tricking them, playing hob, putting something into play, bringing it into play, holding it in play, playing fair, playing by the rules, being played out, playing both ends against the middle, playing one's cards well, playing second fiddle.

Informal social play: joking, parties, cruising, travel, leisure, dancing, roller-skating, losing weight, dinner play, getting laid, potlucks, malls, hostessing, babysitting, Saturday night fun, rough and tumble, creative anachronism, amusement parks, intimacy, speech play (riddles, stories, gossip, jokes, nonsense), singles clubs, bars and taverns, magic, ham radio, restaurants, and the Internet.

Vicarious audience play: television, films, cartoons, concerts, fantasylands, spectator sports, theater, jazz, rock music, parades (Rose Bowl, mummers', Thanksgiving), beauty contests, stock-car racing, Renaissance festivals, national parks, comic books, folk festivals, museums, and virtual reality.

Performance play: playing the piano, playing music, being a play actor, playing the game for the game's sake, playing New York, playing the fishes, playing the horses, playing Iago, play voices, play gestures, playbills, playback, play by play, player piano, playgoing, playhouses, playlets.

Celebrations and festivals: birthdays, Christmas, Easter, Mother's Day, Halloween, gifting, banquets, roasts, weddings, carnivals, initiations, balls, Mardi Gras, Fastnacht, Odunde.

Contests (games and sports): athletics, gambling, casinos, horses, lotteries, pool, touch football, kite fighting, golf, parlor games, drinking, the Olympics, bullfights, cockfights, cricket, Buzkashi, poker, gamesmanship, strategy, physical skill, chance, animal contests, archery, arm wrestling, board games, card games, martial arts, gymnastics.

Risky or deep play: Caving, hang gliding, kayaking, rafting, snowmobiling, orienteering, snowballing, and extreme games such as bungee jumping, windsurfing, sport climbing, skateboarding, mountain biking, kite skiing, street luge, ultrarunning, and sky jumping.

The Diversity of Players, Play Agencies, and Play Scenarios

The ambiguity of play, as well as lying in this great diversity of play forms, owes some of its force to the parallel diversity of the players. There are infant, preschool, childhood, adolescent, and adult players, all of whom play somewhat differently. There are male and female players. There are gamblers, gamesters, sports, and sports players, and there are playboys and playgirls, playfellows, playful people, playgoers, playwrights, playmakers, and playmates. There are performers who play music and act in plays and perhaps play when they paint, sing, or sculpt. There are dilettantes, harlequins, clowns, tricksters, comedians, and jesters who represent a kind of characterological summit of playfulness. There are even playful scholars, such as Paul Feyerabend (1995), Jacques Derrida (1980), and Mikhail Bakhtin (1981). Playful persons in literature and the arts are countless.

Then there is the diversity of multiple kinds of play equipment, such as balls, bats, goals, cards, checkers, roulettes, and toys. Practically anything can become an agency for some kind of play. The scenarios of play vary widely also, from playpens, playrooms, playhouses, and playgrounds to sports fields, circuses, parade grounds, and casinos. Again, while some playfulness is momentary, other kinds, with their attendant preparations, can last throughout a season (as in many festivals and team sports) and, in some cases, over periods of years, as in the World Cup and the Olympics. Play has temporal diversity as well as spatial diversity.

The Diversity of Play Scholarship

Although most people throughout history have taken for granted their own play, and in some places have not even had a word for it, since about 1800 in Western society, intellectuals of various kinds have talked more or less systematically and more or less scientifically about play, and have discovered that they have immense problems in conceptualizing it. Presumably this is in part because there are multiple kinds of play and multiple kinds of players, as described above. Different academic disciplines also have quite different play interests. Some study the body, some study behavior, some study thinking, some study groups or individuals, some study experience, some study language—and they all use the word *play* for these quite different things. Furthermore their play theories, which are the focus of this present work, rather than play itself, come to reflect these various diversities and make them even more variable.

For example, biologists, psychologists, educators, and sociologists tend to focus on how play is adaptive or contributes to growth, development, and socialization. Communication theorists tell us that play is a form of metacommunication far preceding language in evolution because it is also found in animals. Sociologists say that play is an imperial social system that is typically manipulated by those with power for their own benefit. Mathematicians focus on war games and games of chance, important in turn because of the data they supply about strategy and probability. Thermonuclear war games, it appears, can be either a hobby or deadly serious. Anthropologists pursue the relationships between ritual and play as these are found in customs and festivals, while folklorists add an interest in play and game traditions. Art and literature, by contrast, have a major focus on play as a spur to creativity. In some mythology scholarship, play is said to be the sphere of the gods, while in the physical sciences it is sometimes another name for the indeterminacy or chaos of basic matter. In psychiatry, play offers a way to diagnose and provide therapy for the inner conflicts of young and old patients alike. And in the leisure sciences, play is about qualities of personal experience, such as intrinsic motivation, fun, relaxation, escape, and so on. No discipline is, however, so homogeneous that all its members are funneled into only one such way of theorizing. Nevertheless the diversity exists, and it makes reconciliation difficult.

Finally there are the ambiguities that seem particularly problematic in Western society, such as why play is seen largely as what children do but not what adults do; why children play but adults only recreate; why play is said to be important for children's growth but is merely a diversion for adults. The most reviled form of play, gambling, is also the largest part of the national play budget. How can it be that such ecstatic adult play experiences, which preoccupy so much emotional time, are only diversions? And why do these adult play preoccupations, which seem like some vast cultural, even quasi-religious subconsciousness, require us to deny that this kind of play may have the same meaning for children?

The Rhetorical Solution

It is the intent of the present work to bring some coherence to the ambiguous field of play theory by suggesting that some of the chaos to be found there is due to the lack of clarity about the popular cultural rhetorics that underlie the various play theories and play terms. The word *rhetoric* is used here in its modern sense, as being a persuasive discourse, or an implicit narrative, wittingly or unwittingly adopted by members of a particular affiliation to persuade others of the veracity and worthwhileness of their beliefs. In a sense, whenever identification is made with a belief or a cause or a science or an ideology, that identification reveals itself by the words that are spoken about it, by the clothes and insignia worn to celebrate it, by the allegiances adopted to sustain it, and by the hard work and scholarly devotion to it, as well as by the theories that are woven within it (Burke, 1950). Authors seek to persuade us in innumerable ways that their choice and their direction of research or study is sound. These identifications of theirs, and their persuasiveness, implicit or otherwise, are the intellectual odor that is to be known here as their rhetoric. It needs to be stressed that what is to be talked about here as rhetoric, therefore, is not so much the substance of play or of its science or of its theories, but rather the way in which the underlying ideological values attributed to these matters are both subsumed by the theorists and presented persuasively to the rest of us. As the term is used here, the rhetorics of play express the way play is placed in context within broader value systems, which are assumed by the theorists of play rather than studied directly by them. Having said that, however, it must be admitted that it is still almost impossible to suppress the desire to ask the question: "Yes, all right, but what is play itself?"—an impulse that the reader needs to stifle for now, though it will not go untrifled with before this work is played out.

It follows that all the sciences, physical and social, whatever their empirical virtues, are presented here as being maintained by rhetorical means, whether these be seen optimistically, for example, as the "scientific attitude," or somewhat more cynically, as the way in which disciplines, through controlling a knowledge base, enhance their own political power (Foucault, 1973). In what follows, the rhetorics that are the focus of this work will be called popular ideological rhetorics, and where necessary, these will be distinguished from what are called scientific or scholarly rhetorics, as well as from disciplinary rhetorics and personal rhetorics. The popular rhetorics are large-scale cultural "ways of thought" in which most of us participate in one way or another, although some specific groups will be more strongly advocates for this or that particular rhetoric. The larger play rhetorics are part of the multiple broad symbolic systems—political, religious, social, and educational—through which we construct the meaning of the cultures in which we live. It should be made clear that I do not assume these value presuppositions to be necessarily in vain or negative, nor to be without considerable value to those committed to them. In fact, it is impossible to live without them. The issue is only whether, by becoming confused with our play theories, they set us in pursuit of false explanations or false grandiosity. One promise of such an analysis as I propose is that, by revealing these rhetorical underpinnings of the apparently diverse theoretical approaches to play, there is the possibility of bridging them within some more unifying discourse. *The Recovery of Rhetoric* (Roberts and Good, 1993) offers much optimism for the possibilities of a more genuinely interdisciplinary organization of any subject matter, not excluding that of play. However, opinion has to be reserved on the integrating promise of rhetorical analysis until there is an examination of the present popular rhetorics specific to play and their interaction with the scholarly studies that have arisen around them. It is just as possible that the rhetorics, when explicated, will be revealed to be themselves a deceptive gloss over other, far more fundamental cultural disagreements. For example, play's supposed frivolity may itself be a mask for play's use in more widespread systems for denigrating the play of other groups, as has been done characteristically throughout history by those of higher status against the recreations of those of lower status (Armitage, 1977).

Seven Rhetorics

The seven rhetorics to be presented in this work are characterized as follows.

The rhetoric of play as progress, usually applied to children's play, is the advocacy of the notion that animals and children, but not adults, adapt and develop through their play (Chapters 2 and 3). This belief in play as progress is something that most Westerners cherish, but its relevance to play has been more often assumed than demonstrated. Most educators over the past two hundred years seem to have so needed to represent playful imitation as a form of children's socialization and moral, social, and cognitive growth that they have seen play as being primarily about development rather than enjoyment.

The rhetoric of play as fate (Chapter 4) is usually applied to gambling and games of chance, and it contrasts totally with the prior rhetoric. It is probably the oldest of all of the rhetorics, resting as it does on the belief that human lives and play are controlled by destiny, by the gods, by atoms or neurons, or by luck, but very little by ourselves, except perhaps through the skillful use of magic or astrology. This rhetoric enjoys only an underground advocacy in the modern world. It is no longer a widespread and conscious value system among the intellectual elites, though it remains popular among lower socioeconomic groups. It contrasts most strongly also with those modern theories of leisure that argue that the distinguishing feature of play is that it is an exercise of free choice.

The rhetoric of play as power (Chapter 5), usually applied to sports, athletics, and contests, is—like fate, community identity, and frivolity—a rhetoric of ancient hue. These four all predate modern times and advocate collectively held community values rather than individual experiences. Recently these ancient rhetorics have been given much less philosophical attention than the modern three, progress, the imaginary, and the self, though they are more deep seated as cultural ideologies. The rhetoric of play as power is about the use of play as the representation of conflict and as a way to fortify the status of those who control the play or are its heroes. This rhetoric is as ancient as warfare and patriarchy. It is an anathema to many modern progress- and leisure-oriented play theorists.

The rhetoric of play as identity, usually applied to traditional and community celebrations and festivals, occurs when the play tradition is seen as a means of confirming, maintaining, or advancing the power and identity of the community of players (Chapter 6). Chapter 7, in turn, deals with the place of the rhetorics of both power and identity in children's play. Because so much twentieth-century attention has been given to children's play as a form of progress, I have found it valuable to present a more balanced rhetorical advocacy of the character of their play from the point of view of these other rhetorics, power and fantasy, both in Chapter 7 and later in Chapter 9 on child phantasmagoria.

The rhetoric of play as the imaginary (Chapter 8), usually applied to playful improvisation of all kinds in literature and elsewhere, idealizes the imagination, flexibility, and creativity of the animal and human play worlds. This rhetoric is sustained by modern positive attitudes toward creativity and innovation. Chapter 9, on child phantasmagoria, attempts to moderate some of this idealization by indicating the large amounts of inversion and irrationality that are also a typical part of play's flexibility. The rhetoric of progress, the rhetoric of the self, and the rhetoric of the imaginary constitute the modern set of rhetorics, with a history largely elaborated ideologically only in the past two hundred years.

The rhetoric of the self (Chapter 10) is usually applied to solitary activities like hobbies or high-risk phenomena like bungee jumping, but it need not be so proscribed. These are forms of play in which play is idealized by attention to the desirable experiences of the players—their fun, their relaxation, their escape—and the intrinsic or the aesthetic satisfactions of the play performances. Here the central advocacies of the secular and consumerist manner of modern life invade the interpretations of play and are questioned because of their twentieth-century relativity.

The rhetoric of play as frivolous (Chapter 11) is usually applied to the activities of the idle or the foolish. But in modern times, it inverts the classic "work ethic" view of play, against which all the other rhetorics exist as rhetorics of rebuttal. But frivolity, as used here, is not just the puritanic negative, it is also a term to be applied more to historical trickster figures and fools, who were once the central and carnivalesque persons who enacted playful protest against the orders of the ordained world. This chapter is placed last in this work because of its largely reflexive character, as commentary on all the other rhetorics. Historically frivolity belongs with the ancient set that includes fate, power, and identity.

I should note that although each of these rhetorics is discussed in the singular, there are multiple variants within each category, so that it might be more proper to speak of the plural *rhetorics* throughout. To repeat, each is called a rhetoric because its ideological values are something that the holders like to persuade others to believe in and to live by. Much of the time such values do not even reach a level of conscious awareness. People simply take it for granted, for example, that children develop as a result of their playing; or that sports are a part of the way in which different states and nations compete with each other; or that festivals are a way in which groups are bonded together; or that play is a desirable modern form of creativity or personal choice; or that, contrary to all of these, play is a waste of time. By seeing how the play descriptions and play theories can be tied in with such broad patterns of ideological value, one has greater hope of coming to understand the general character of play theory, which is the ultimate objective here.

A Scale of Rhetorics

These seven play rhetorics can be illuminated by contrasting them, on the one hand, with rhetorics that are broader than they are, and on the other, with rhetorics that are narrower. Of the broader kind are those that derive from beliefs about religion, politics, social welfare, crime, and morality—that is, from all the matters that priests, politicians and salespersons constantly harangue folks about. These are the rhetorics that fill the airwaves of daily life, in churches, in schools, and in the community. People cannot live without them, even if they often can't stand some of them. They constitute the incessant discourse about who we are and how we should live. The group of rhetorics for the particular subject matter play are of the same broad kind, being about progress and power, but they are more limited in the present usage because they are applied only to the specific subject of play theories. The rhetorics of science are generally of a narrower and more explicit kind. Science, after all, has its own epistemological rhetorics of reliability, validity, and prediction. Scholarship in general has its required consistency, coherence, and authenticity. All of these scientific and scholarly tenets are also rhetorics, because they assume and propagate the view that there is a knowable world, or a knowable text, and then, acting as if that assumption is real (a hypothetical fiction), proceed to their methodological undertakings. As Pepper (1961) has shown, even philosophical scholars must make arbitrary distinctions about which part of the world they seek to study, some focusing on the structures or forms of reality, some on the causes of reality and behavior, others on the changing historical context in which these things occur, and yet others on the kinds of integration or organicism that they can discover. What is added here to any such "scientific" (play) rhetorics is that the subject-matter rhetorics (those seven listed above) may be able to suggest why the scientific rhetorics take the direction they do—and also suggest why that direction may often have limitations deriving not so much from the science or scholarship, but from the presuppositions of the value systems in which the science is embedded. Parenthetically, the present focus on such presuppositions is not meant to suggest that "objective" social science is without value, or that "objectivity" is not fruitful within the ideological frames being presented. My aim here is much more modest, it seeks only for the sources of ambiguity in play rhetoric.

In the past several decades the claims of scholarship or science for sheer objectivity have been frequently challenged. The limitations of the claims for scholarly literature's independence from propaganda are challenged by Burke in such works as *The Rhetoric of Motives* (1950) and *Language as Symbolic Action* (1966). The same orientation is made a criticism of general scientific objectivity by Kuhn's now famous *The Structure of Scientific Revolutions* (1970), in which he points out the role played by human motivation in the development of science, particularly in respect to the way in which accepted theories often are not displaced until a new generation of thinkers finds them irrelevant. Science is not as cumulative or as autonomously objective in the growth of its knowledge as has often been supposed. But the roots of the present enterprise can be found in the work of many other scholars as well, from Wittgenstein's emphasis on the meaning of language relying on its context of usage, for example, to Foucault's stricture that knowledge is always an exercise of power, never merely information. Those who create information are those who decide how others shall think about their lives. Leading play theorists who quite explicitly see themselves talking about the rhetorics of play in order to talk about play theory at all include Helen Schwartzman (1978), Margaret Duncan (1988), and Mihail Spariosu (1989).

Between the historically based subject-matter rhetorics that will be presented here (progress, power, and so on) and the most general scientific epistemological rhetorics, which involve, for example, the metaphysical assumptions underlying the expectancy of causal regularities in nature, a host of other disciplinary rhetorics also play their part in the amalgam that is social science. Elsewhere, for example, I have described rhetorics that are applied to childhood in modern life, with children variously being seen as: the child of god, the child as the future, the predictable child, the imaginary child, the child as consumer, and the gender androgynous child (Sutton-Smith, 1994c).

But the physical scientists are not immune to such rhetorics either, and there are disputes about how the public should interpret the personality of their science in the culture. These can be called questions about the ontological rhetorics of the scientists. They may be seen as "objective" or "cautious," but at times they are also seen as rebels, subversives, Frankensteins, relentless creatures of reason, conquerors of nature, empirical reductionists, mathematical formalists, artists, philosophers, secular saints, or irresponsible devils. And as Dyson (1995) shows, these kinds of rhetorics, when personal to the scientists, make an enormous difference in the direction of their inquiries. One might conclude that all scholars are creatures of their personal disposition, which may become a motivating rhetoric for them, and they are also, historically, inheritors of larger ideological or cultural patterns that affect their scholarship. They are the legatees as well of the rhetorics of disciplinary assumptions and disciplinary methodologies.

What needs most emphasis at this initial point is that rhetorical involvement at some or all of these levels is inescapable. Scholarly objectivity always exists within such contexts as broad cultural rhetorics (political, religious, moral), disciplinary rhetorics (sciences, humanities, arts), epistemological rhetorics (validity, reliability, causalism, formism), subject-matter rhetorics (in the present case, play rhetorics), general ontological rhetorics (objectivity, scientific caution), and personal rhetorics (idiosyncratic dispositions).

Within the subject of the present inquiry (play), the major emphasis is on the way in which the theories within this scholarly domain are underlain by the seven rhetorics outlined above. As William Kessen, a leading scholar of such reflexive self-consciousness in developmental psychology, states that we should

> recognize that, deeply carved into our professional intention is a desire to change the lives of our readers, to have them believe something that we believe. In grand nineteenth-century style, we

can call this the Unspoken Intention that is hidden by the wonderful devices all of us have learned to speak with the voice of certain authority . . . Our work is packed with our values, our intentions for our small part of the world: a great deal would be gained by a critical analysis and display of those intentions, [but] the governing principle for evidence in both psychology and history [is that] we do not seek proofs; we do not attempt demonstrations. We all want to tell plausible stories. (1993, p. 229)

Validating the Existence of the Seven Rhetorics

Though it is not difficult to assert in a general way that the science of play is underlain by these seven subject-matter narratives, or rhetorics, the assertion itself has fairly vague "scientific" or "scholarly" cogency without some criteria of coherence that can be used to affirm their presence. The criteria I use to frame the rhetorical contentions are as follows:

1. That the assumed seven rhetorics can be shown to have a clear basis in well-known cultural attitudes of a contemporary or historical kind. This historical context, although not dealt with in great detail here, is the most basic source of their cultural construction (Glassie, 1982).
2. That the rhetorics have their own specific groups of advocates, a necessary precondition if these phenomena are to be seen as not just narratives but also rhetorics of persuasion.
3. That each rhetoric applies primarily to a distinct kind of play or playfulness. If this is so, it suggests some kind of epistemological affinity between the rhetorics and their ludic subject matter. They are not accidentally correlated.
4. That each rhetoric applies primarily to distinct kinds of players.
5. That there is an affinity between the rhetoric and particular scholarly or scientific disciplines, and between particular play theories and play theorists.
6. That (following criteria 2 through 5), there is a "matching" interplay between the nature of the rhetorical assertions and the character of the forms of play to which they are applied. Thus a rhetoric of progress might find partial substantiation in the finding that

some kinds of skill during play can take "progressive" forms. In addition it may be possible to show that the rhetoric itself is often the way in which the play passes into the culture, because the play practice is thus justified ideologically. In this way, the two, play and rhetoric, have an impact on each other. The recommendation that the interplay between play and nonplay should be more carefully studied was made by the famous play theorist Erik Erikson in his book *Toys and Reasons* (1977). But this recommendation is also the constant beguilement of all those who study the interrelationships between play and nonplay to try to puzzle out how they reciprocally affect each other (Abrahams, 1977).

7. That the group that maintains the rhetoric benefits by the exercise of hegemony over the players, over their competitors, or over those who are excluded from the play. This postulate makes explicit why the present approach to play centers on the rhetorics of the theorists rather than, more simply, on the narratives they tell themselves. Rhetorics are narratives that have the intent to persuade because there is some kind of gain for those who are successful in their persuasion. Telling plausible stories would not be enough.

8. That the way in which the scholarly disciplines define the subject matter of play may or may not make sense in terms of the rhetorics that are being proposed in this work. This is open to investigation. Three kinds of play definitions will be considered where they are available:

(a) The definitions by players of their own *play experiences* and functions. What do the players reckon to be the character of and the reasons for their own participation? Obviously there is not much research to be referred to here, although there is a considerable amount of anecdotal opinion to be cited. It is useful to discover that there can be—and often is—very little relationship between the players' own play definitions and those of the theorists.

(b) The definitions by theorists of *intrinsic play functions*. These are definitions drawn from the research literature, or new ones arising out of the present analysis, that are supposed to account scientifically for the play's functioning by pointing to the players' game-related motives for playing.

(c) The definitions by the theorists of *extrinsic play functions*, which account for the forms of play in terms of functions they are supposed to serve in the larger culture.

It is with the two last types of definitions (b and c) that this study is preoccupied. It is quite possible, for example, for players to have one rhetoric while "experts" have another. But it is also possible for experts to use one rhetoric when talking about the players' responses and another rhetoric when discussing theoretically what they think is the underlying function of the forms of play. A description of the players' enjoyments, after all, need not be the same as an account of the supposed adaptive functions of those enjoyments. More important, finding the relationship between accounts of play in terms of intrinsic and extrinsic functions is yet another way of talking about the interplay of play and nonplay. There is promise here of some clarification of the causalities of play and life.

As a final point of each chapter, it will be necessary to return to the issue of play's ambiguity, with which this work begins. My aim is to establish to what extent ambiguity is an outcome of the seven rhetorics, or if it must instead be attributed to the character of play itself.

2

Rhetorics of Animal Progress

When I play with my cat, who knows if I am not a pastime to her more than she is to me?

Michel Eyquem de Montaigne

Let's get on with the monkey business.
after Stanley Hall

What seems most obvious about play, whether that of animals, children, or adults, is that it is a very exciting kind of activity that players carry on because they like doing so. It doesn't seem to have too much to do with anything else. Yet, as this work will attest, it is typically interpreted as having value not just for itself but because of other functions that it serves in individual development and group culture. For example, in the general literature about child development, most theories hold that play is some form of adaptation, or that it provides for some useful development. The main concern is to show that increases in the complexity of play skill—physical, mental, imaginative, or social—lead to increases in some parallel kind of human growth or adaptation. This subordination of intrinsic play functions to other extrinsic developmental functions occurs apparently because the theorists are primarily concerned with child socialization and maturity, and children's civilized progress in general. As a result, their broader sentiments about child development carry over into their attitudes toward play, which then become as much determined by the rhetoric of progress as by any empirical data about the causal value of play itself. The rhetoric of progress derives from the historical view, said to originate in the eighteenth century, that progress is inevitable, or at least achievable, in human society. Known as histori-cism, this view was once associated with the expectation that society would be able to progress with the same regularity as was the case in the physical sciences. Backed by the theory of evolution, it led to the general expectation that child development could also be seen as a form of progress and adaptation. Its current application to the inter-pretation of children's play is associated with its application to child development in general.*

The main tenet of the rhetoric of progress is that adulthood and childhood are quite separate, childhood being innocent, nonsexual, and dependent (Benedict, 1938). It is said that children's and adults' play are also quite different, that of children being open, or creative, and that of adults being closed, or recreative. The desire for children to make progress in development and schooling has led to play's being considered either a waste of time (the view of educational "conservatives") or a form of children's work (the belief of educa-tional "progressives"). The one view is that play is not usefully adap-tive, the other is that it is.

Animal Play

Most biologists have assumed that play has indeed had some construc-tive purpose in species and individual evolution, and their advocacy is itself a much grander conceptualization than any modern attempts to rationalize human play simply as growth or socialization. The question is, are the empirical data of biology what ultimately fuel the notions of progress through play, or do our twentieth-century psychological and educational notions of progress through play bias us in favor of this in-terpretation of the data? To those who are skeptical about the rele-vance of the study of animal play to that of human play—given that we cannot ask the animals any questions, and because they can hardly be said to have complex culture in the human sense—one can only indi-cate that the amount of scientific research on animal play far exceeds

*The rhetorics of childhood is now a developing field in child history and develop-mental psychology. Key references include: Ariés, 1962; Davis, 1965; DeLone 1979; Gillis, 1981; Luke, 1989; Megill, 1985; Wilson, 1980. My own prior writings on the rhetorics of childhood are Sutton-Smith, 1993a and 1994c, and were my source for thinking of play as bound by rhetoric.

that on human play, and therefore it at least merits our attention.

First, to illustrate what animal researchers have to say about animal play, I offer the following quotation from Robert Fagen, whose book *Animal Play Behavior* (1981), with its comprehensive descriptions and references and its ingenious theorization, is the bible in this field. Fagen writes in a more recent work: "play occurs in only a small minority of the Earth's million or more species. Animal play is easy to recognize. Specific movement qualities and signal patterns characterize the familiar play behavior of cats, dogs, and human children as well as the play of other animals. Mammals and birds, and perhaps a few fishes and reptiles are the only kinds of animals known to play" (1995, p. 24). He suggests that the immense diversity of animal play behavior can fit into five fuzzy categories, which he describes, in ascending order of complexity, as italicized below.

Fagen's first category: *isolated, brief jerky movements performed repeatedly without defense or counterattack by others: typical of rodents.* This description of Fagen's is not unlike that of the great genetic psychologist Piaget in his discussion of primary circular reactions in human infants, such as sucking—reactions first begun for adaptive reasons and subsequently repeated without any such concern. A baby, having sucked vigorously, may, as its hunger subsides, begin to push the nipple around, letting it go and gobbling it back. Thus what had just been an adaptive act is now separated, as a figure from its ground, and manipulated for whatever else it can be found to accomplish. The behavior is then repeated at great length, sometimes with an accompanying smile on the infant's lips. Whatever else is conveyed by such an observation, one does get the impression that these slightest of play acts are themselves preliminary signs of the greater versatility we expect from the larger cortex of the playing species. That is, an action, once embedded in a semireflexive concatenation of acts, is by some incongruity "disembedded" and reexamined in all its new context-relevant singularity. Any such "playful" act might not in itself rehearse a specific subsequent adaptive linkage, but it would make it apparent to implicit memory that such distinctions would be possible.

The danger of stating things in behavioral terms, however, is that this may underestimate the extent to which such separating of incongruous play acts is instigated by the already fantasizing brain. To suggest that an act is varied contextually may be to neglect the source of the impulse for such variation. Thus Sacks, quoting Rodolfo Llin'as and colleagues, says that when

> comparing the properties of the brain in waking and dreaming, [they] postulate a single fundamental mechanism for both, a ceaseless inner talking between cerebral cortex and thalamus, a ceaseless interplay of image and feeling, irrespective of whether there is sensory input or not. When there is sensory input, this interplay continues to generate brain states, those brain states we call fantasy, hallucination or dreams. Thus waking consciousness is dreaming, but dreaming constrained by external reality. (1995, p. 57)

This might mean that an infant or animal is "wired" to fantasize at all times, and the act of play is in the first place an extrusion of internal mental fantasy into the web of external constraints. The fantasy of mind that we do not control becomes the play behavior that we do control. It might be said that the serious, adaptive, externally controlled act (sucking) is taken over by constant fantasy when the controls are relaxed; once hunger has been satisfied through sucking, the sucking action offers an occasion for seeing what internal fantasy can do with otherwise neglected behavior. Again, the internal or passively received fantasy can manifest itself only in terms of the external and actively controlled play to which the child has access. Fantasy play that is rooted in the mind is, in these terms, actively converted into what is observed as playful behavior. This of course blurs the distinction between play as erupting into behavior from a source in fantasy, and play as triggered by some incongruity in the nature of the child's mundane processing. There are obvious cases of both, as when a toy falls over or a child daydreams, so perhaps some dimension of internal-external provocation will be necessary, ultimately, to handle the evocations of the ludic. If this is true, then the classic Western distinctions between so-called participant play and "passive" spectator play may not be as clear-cut as some moral evaluations would suppose. Or alternatively, perhaps each parallels major modes of human play as active or vicarious. A more important point may be that whatever instigates the heightened variability and laid-back responsiveness called play, its variability is in marked contrast to the incisive reflexlike actions that typically characterize the behavior of pre-ludic animals. Watch, for example, the nonplayful alligator move suddenly from motionless sleep to blinding reflexive speed with his snapping jaws when he is touched, say, by an errant turtle. Isolated brief jerky movement at this level might appear to be a buffer device against hasty decision making. Kenneth Burke's writings even imply that play might be the earliest form of a negative, prior to the existence of the negative in language (1966). Play, as a way of not doing whatever it represents, prevents error. It is a positive behavioral negative. It says no by saying yes. It is not a bite but it is a nip (Bateson, 1956). Whatever the case, there is certainly some implication of heightened variability and action delay for species that can substitute even highly brief, jerky, and isolated ludic acts for reflexive ones.

Fagen's second category: *noncontact solo play and the social play of moving bodies through space, running and jumping in a variety of patterns; characteristic of hoofed mammals, some rodents, and some birds.* Much of this running and jumping has about it a peculiar exaggeration and even beauty, as in "bouncing, bucking, rolling, running in circles, chasing one's tail if one has one, whirling, pirouetting, somersaulting, hanging upside down, and variations and combinations of these rotational locomotion movements" (Brown, 1995, p. 6). Separating these acts from their more usually exigent contexts allows them to take on a choreography unique to each species. Once the moving figure (say, leaping) is separated from its ground (of a real chase or escape), the peculiar bounding and prancing may be considered the most primeval form of "aesthetic stylization," if such a notion dare be used. But then, why not? It has to begin somewhere. Films of rhesus monkeys jumping one by one out of a tree and into the water, then rushing back up the tree for further jumps, which they execute in ever more idiosyncratically flagrant patterns, throwing their bodies first this way or that way as they hurtle through the air, certainly appear to reveal the character of ecstatic performances, even if the actions may not yet be thought to be taken with aesthetic intent (Brown, 1994, 1995). The animal ecstasies of stylization are theirs; calling it aesthetic is a human projection. But then, presumably, "aesthetic" performances precede aesthetic theories in evolution. This is an issue that I return to in Chapter 10, where I make a distinction between aesthetic and ordinary ludic performances. The word *ecstatic* is being used here for the heightened joy that players seem to get from their own successful play actions.

Fagen's third category: *social play, some with no contact, like chasing, and some with contact, like sparring and wrestling: characteristic of most primates and carnivores, many ungulates, pinnipeds, and marsupials, and some birds.* It is important to note here that fighting acts are simulated and exaggerated but fighting outcomes are inhibited. This may be a display of fighting, but it is also the opposite of fighting, seeing as it is carried on by those who are not enemies and who do not intend to harm each other, and always accompanied by the special faces and signals that different species use to convey that their intent is only to play. Playfighting as an analogy to real fighting seems more like displaying the meaning of fighting than rehearsing for real combat. It is more about meaning than about mauling. Thus Schwartzman, following the path pioneered by Bateson (1956), says that play "is a mode not a distinctive behavioral category . . . play is viewed as an attitude or frame that can be adopted towards anything . . . [it] occurs at a logical level different from that it qualifies . . . play is functional because it teaches about contexts; it teaches about frames not being at the same level as the acts they contain" (1978, p. 169). I include this important quotation here to draw attention to the metacommunicative or framing function of play, but not to agree with the statement that play is not also a distinctive behavioral category. I believe more expansively that play is both a kind of communication (a mode) and also a kind of action. In the pages that follow, I will discuss the distinctive behavior characteristics that Fagen says animal-play students agree on: repetition, reversal, fragmentation, exaggeration, inhibition, and unpredictability. My point is that any metacommunicative autonomy presupposes the fantasizing autonomy (or whatever passes for it) and intersubjectivity of the sharing animals' brains (Goncu, 1993). The message that "this is play" can be transmitted because the communicating players already know, to some extent internally, the behaviors that they are signaling about externally. Bringing these two, internal and external, together is much of what infant social play is about. The fact that only some of the kinds of action are present on a given occasion (say, exaggeration or fragmentation) need not detract from the sustaining view that there is indeed a family of action features that make up the meaning of play.

The fourth category: *complex social play, which involves games with objects and features of the landscape. This form of play is enacted by adult as well as young animals, whereas most play of the former kinds is enacted only by juveniles or by parents with their young; typical of social carnivores, primates, elephants, some whales, dolphins, and porpoises.* It is surprising to learn that research seems to indicate the animals Fagen lists here play games that we (but perhaps not they) would best describe as king on the mountain, tag, hide-and-seek, follow the leader, tug-of-war, and keep away. These group social behaviors are never only simulations of adaptive behavior; they are instead at times a reordering, a fragmentation, a disordering, or a total and unpredictable novelty. Such play makes it appear almost as if the animals at the highest level have the ability to enact a story or an allegory of, for example, chase and escape, as young children certainly do in games of this kind. The data surely suggest that even animal play at this level is a kind of culture. These higher animals show the basic features of culture, such as predictable, sequential, and consistent patterns of behavior with each other; social hierarchies; and shared understanding (as defined in Chapter 9). Obviously the relationships between such social culture and play culture are more complex than was imagined by Huizinga (1955).

Fagen's fifth and last category: *mother-infant games, such as peekaboo, as well as object construction and play with pebbles, sticks, flowers, feathers, and bones, and play with snow, water, and trees.* These are the beginnings of that object play for which humans especially like to pride themselves. Apparently playthings existed long before humans created their own toys. Different species have also been known to play and dance with each other (dogs and cats, dogs and bears, humans and animals); and some species have been heralded as producing champion players, such as polar bears, otters (weazels), parrots (macaws), birds (keas), and, in general, chimpanzees. Fagen summed all of this up in a speech he entitled "The Perilous Magic of Animal Play": "Simply stated," he said, "animal play is extraordinary."

It Is Not Proven That Animal Play Is Adaptive

In general those who have studied the remarkable realm of animal play have felt that it must be of some profound evolutionary significance. After all, the levels of the play's complexity are paralleled by increasing brain size. Surely there must be a connection between the one and the other, scholars aver. Nevertheless, numbers of those who have studied play in an evolutionary, biological, ethological, or comparative psychological perspective are skeptical about the state of our knowledge of the play-evolution relationship.

For example, in an outstanding symposium, Peter K. Smith (1982) presented his own analysis of the issue, and many scholars commented:

"The case of play . . . is still in its earliest stages of scientific analysis. Many hypotheses abound, but their empirical testing has just begun" (C. M. Berman; Smith, 1982, p. 157).

"Perusal of the detailed facts about animal play, and attendant speculations about its function, run the risk of confusing our understanding of human play rather than bringing light to the subject" (M. Csikszentmihalyi; ibid., p. 160).

"It would be difficult at the present time to demonstrate beyond any doubt that play is the relevant factor in eliciting brain and behavioural changes" (P. A. Ferchmin and V. A. Eterovic; ibid., p. 164).

"A mere correlation between what an animal does in play and in other activities constitutes a most dubious grounds for invoking [play] practice as a cause" (M. T. Ghiselin; ibid, p. 165).

"Play, therefore, may or may not have evolved and may or may not be adaptive . . . such a view . . . is not one which I favor" (M. Lewis; ibid., p. 166).

In more recent writing on the same subject, one finds the statement: "Of course, it remains very attractive to assume that the consequences of playful activities are adaptive in many ways, but there are no robust and credible demonstrations of that in either humans or animals" (Panksepp, 1993).

And finally, from the Smith symposium again, a statement by Robert Fagen, an advocate of play's biological significance: "[I emphasize] the tentative nature of all existing conclusions about the consequences of play" (Smith, 1982, p. 162).

One response to this uncertainty about the significance of play is to contend that it is due simply to the present early stage of serious and systematic play analysis in the field of animal behavior. Many of the hundreds of studies that have been done have a highly anecdotal or case study character, and they are usually confined to one or a few of the hundreds of possible species, therefore allowing for little cross-species generalization. What is true of one species is not necessarily true of another. At times one feels like a sixteenth-century homebody listening to the fanciful tales of discovery brought back from many foreign and strange lands. Nevertheless it is only fair to record that practically all of the commentators in Smith's 1982 analysis believe that, despite the nondefinitive state of the evidence, play must indeed serve adaptive functions. Skeptics can wave them all aside and suggest that this is nothing but the residual effects of historicism, or they can try to represent their propositions as well as the opposition has in the field of play research. The compromise I adopt here is to present the animal researchers' propositions as they might be viewed in terms of several of the rhetorics; thus they become statements about animal play as skill training (progress), playfighting (power), bonding (identity), flexibility (the imaginary), and emotional experience (the self). The categorization of the animal literature in parallel with the rhetorics is not quite as humorous as these headings might suggest. Either the parallel is drawn because there is an empirical relationship between animal play and human play, or the animal play theories are an anthropomorphic projection of the human rhetorics.

Animal Play as Skill Training

The notion that animal play is a kind of physical skill training has probably received the most acceptance in the literature. As Peter Smith says, "one postulates that animals incur the cost of energy expenditure in active physical play in order to get the future benefits of well exercised muscles and superior physical capacity" (1982, p. 142). The physical fitness, stamina, and skills resulting from play are said to have immediate energy and risk-taking costs but to give future benefits. Juveniles at play may attract predators and they may have accidents, but if they survive they will be in better shape because of the play. In fact most advocates of growth via play characterize play as the "safer" alternative when contrasted with real running after prey or running away from predators. It is suggested that the real alternatives are much more risky than the playful alternatives, even though the latter also can be dangerous.

Remembering that the empirical evidence is inconclusive, there are several further objections against this apparently sensible argument in favor of play as preparatory, growth-oriented behavior. First, the argument is largely metaphoric; that is, it is said that because the youthful locomotion looks something like the pursuit or escape activities of adults, it is, therefore, said to be the same thing or at least connected with it in some functional way. But on closer examination play is always explicitly not "the real thing." If it is to be safe, it must not be the real thing. How then can such unreality be a training for reality? In human terms, how many of us go to the theater or the cinema or watch cartoons primarily to gain information about useful real-life skills?

Second, characteristics of animal play seem inversive for rehearsal purposes. The distinctive play behavior characteristics most often suggested by theorists of animal play are, in order of frequency, repetitiveness, reordering or reversal of usual behavior sequences, fragmentation or incompleteness of typical behavior sequences, exaggeration of such characteristics, strong inhibitions of dangerous acts (such as biting), unpredictable or novel actions (based on Fagen, 1981, pp. 505–508). Most of these do not seem of much value for an orthodox training program. They seem opposite to the kind of behaviors usually supported by schoolteachers, except perhaps for teachers of improvisation in the arts. Even repetitiveness is not of the same kind as that required in learning. Repetitions that assist in learning cease as the learner habituates to the stimuli involved. In play, on the contrary, repetitions go on for the sake of the associated excitement and do not normally disappear with habituation. Play is not just repetitive, it is obsessive.

Third, the term *play* is typically used for much of what is done by immature organisms, when in fact their behavior is typically undifferentiated, so that it is difficult to tell, for example, when they are exploring, learning imitatively, learning by trial and error, practicing a real skill or a play skill, or, finally, playing. As the noted developmental theorist Heinz Werner once emphasized, the behavior of the young is often undifferentiated, labile, rigid, and syncretic. Our adult categories and definitions, which imply much more differentiation, stability, flexibility, and discreteness in our observations, can easily be misleading about such inchoate forms (Werner, 1957). It has been shown in research that adults and children can reliably agree that what they see as play is play, but this may have more to do with a cultural consensus than be a valid indicator of the verity of their observations. Connor (1991) has shown, for example, that whether adults see children's playfighting as pretense or as violence depends mainly on their own value predispositions. Men see more of it as pretense, women see more of it as aggression, nursery-school teachers see most all of it as aggression. Aggression, when ambiguous, is apparently in the eye of the beholder. And Panksepp has shown similar differences both with adults and children in the perception of whether rats are just playfighting or are really being aggressive (Panksepp, 1993). Even most children subsequently reviewing their own playroom behavior on videotape will call all of it play, when an examination of the tapes shows that what they are talking about involves the kind of variety mentioned above (Magee, 1987). Our observations of animals, because of our detachment from them, may indeed be less biased than cultural attitudes toward our own human "play," but they are probably just as inaccurate about distinctions between learning and play among the very young. These distinctions are often difficult to discern in the long, undifferentiated sequences of behavior that are typical of all immature organisms, not just human young.

Fourth, all of these arguments are normative. They all assume that we can treat each species as a whole, when it is not impossible that individuals of any group vary greatly in their playfulness. We know on the human side that this is true for musical, artistic, spatial, logical, numerical, kinesthetic, and literary skill (Gardner, 1983). It could be true as well for humor and play. There are also anecdotal accounts of variation within the same animal species, particularly those living in different contexts, that demonstrate great play differences (Brown, 1994). The evolutionary issue, and for humans the cultural evolutionary issue, would then become the usual one of seeking which conditions selected players (or musicians, or humorists) for survival and which did not. Perhaps the problem, with the research as it stands, is the averaging out of such individual differences because of the researchers' normative evolutionary preconceptions.

Animal Play as Playfighting

The term *power* is used in this book to stand for play's expression of conflict, including competitions for superior positions in some hierarchy—either of those who organize the play or those who are the players—or for personal control in solitary play, as in mastery and empowerment. In the animal play data, this forceful kind of play refers to fighting skills, also called playfighting or rough-and-tumble, and to predatory play and predator-avoidance play. Some feel that this kind of play is probably the most basic of all and is the beginning point for play in evolution—a fundamental process that underlies all the other kinds of play that ultimately develop from it (Aldis, 1975, p. 139; Panksepp, 1993, p. 150). At some spot in evolution, it is contended, those species that could fight without injuring each other triggered the beginning of an alternative to reflexive or instinctive reactions. This would be the world of possibility, the world where possibilities are acted out, or the world of the *enacted subjunctive,* as it will be called here. Playfighting is said to be about how to supercede the supposed law of the jungle to kill or be killed. There are lots of kinds of evidence from multiple species of the occurrence of playfighting. By and large it looks as if males do more of it than females, as might be expected, and sometimes there is very little difference from real fighting except that the biting is inhibited just before completion. But finally, as Peter Smith says, "The best direct test of the fighting skills hypothesis would be to show that high levels of play fighting in infancy are linked to better fighting skills as an adult. At present the evidence is not available" (1982, p. 144). Bekoff adds the point that even if playfighting is rehearsive for some species, for others it is not, because they learn these skills without playing. Even animals reared in isolation can show fighting skills without having played at them. Also, in some species males do the playfighting but females do the real fighting. Bekoff says that it is a mistake to apply just one function or one set of related functions to such a variable activity as play (Smith, 1982, p. 156). I would add that, while on one intellectual level this is a search for more evidence about the function of playfighting, on a rhetorical level it is also further evidence of the belief and value that power analyses have gained in Western scholarship for explaining matters of animal and human importance.

Animal Play as Bonding

The idea here is that those who play together when young will be bonded together, so that when mature they will function more effectively as a reproductive or predatory group; in effect, that those who play together will stay together. Unfortunately this thesis is even more lacking of support than the former. "Furthermore, the prediction that for most species the females (who do form the stable core of the group) should play in infancy more than males, is definitely not confirmed" (Smith, 1982, p. 145). Apparently the females do not need to play in order to experience bonding. Two subsidiary theses are that animals learn their social ranking, their hierarchy, through play, and that they also develop their communicative skills through play. But apparently social ranking is more likely to be learned through direct fighting. The theory that communication is learned through play also lacks direct evidence. Because establishing a status hierarchy involves exercising power, this aspect of social bonding has as much to do with power rhetorics as with bonding rhetorics. These two rhetorics have considerable commonality. Some like to suggest that the difference between the two, power versus bondings, or community, reflects a fundamental difference between the genders in their dominant social concern. Recent work on macaques, however, shows that it can also reflect a difference in personality. There are some monkeys (male and female) who get what they want (food and sex) through power, and others who get the same through gentleness and bonding (Angier, 1995).

Animal Play as Flexibility

In recent years the idea that play functions largely to yield innovative responses has been the most popular play explanation among many animal theorists. It is the preferred theory in Fagen's *Animal Play*

Behavior. In his response to Peter Smith's greater emphasis on skill training, Fagen says:

> The development of specific skills through play is apparently contradicted by field and laboratory data indicating that play follows rather than precedes mastery of these skills, and by the regular occurrence of play amongst skilled adults in many species. For these reasons I am more inclined than is Smith to believe that play was selected to develop complex social and generalized cognitive abilities including the potential to innovate and to maintain or enhance the flexibility of existing skills at the cost of their efficiency in particular contexts . . . Play generalizes skill by varying and recombining previously mastered behavioral routines in new contexts, freeing the animal from the unanticipated limitation of these routines. (Smith, 1982 p. 162)

This is like the earlier described Piagetian figure-ground decontextualization that occurs in the most elementary kinds of play. Perhaps when this occurs, play opens up these categories to thought, rather than leaving them embedded in instinct. However, opportunity rather than rehearsal is implied by this kind of analysis. And while it suggests more flexibility than instinct in play, it is not established that flexibility is play's main function. For even supposing that the most elemental forms of play do derive from such decontextualizations and ensuing metacommunications, how is it that things apparently so flexible can be put to the service of something as repetitive as play routines and games? On both the animal and the human level, the play phenomenon is for the greater part banal and repetitive. Little girls play a game called house for years on end, and little boys play a game called trucks, while mothers do crossword puzzles every morning for thirty years and fathers either play or watch baseball or golf every day, forever. Facetiously, but kindly, one might add that one of the most paradoxical things about animal play may be actually Robert Fagen himself, the great animal play inquirer, who while advancing his thesis adequately and sophisticatedly in his book, and in the Smith symposium of 1982, also concludes "that the case for the evolution of play as an immediate source of novel, innovative behavior in nonhumans was previously overstated by myself and others" (ibid., p. 475).

Animal Play as Emotional Experience

Michael Lewis says, in the Smith symposium, "The importance and meaning of play, at least for humans, would appear to be in its affective function; in a word, play is fun. In fact, I would like to argue that the chief function of play is its positive affective quality, a combination of fun and whimsy, which distinguishes this activity from all others, even other positive experiences such as eating or sexual behavior" (Smith, 1982, p. 166). Similarly Jaak Panksepp concludes a long piece on the evolutionary centrality of rough-and-tumble in rodents with the statement, "Perhaps excessive expectations have been generated concerning the long term functions of play. It is worth considering that the main adaptive function of play may be the generation of positive emotional states. In such states animals may be more willing and more likely to behave in flexible and creative ways" (1993, p. 177). Somewhat in agreement, Peter Smith suggests: "Rather than arguing that play behavior functions to modulate arousal level" (keeping it neither to high or too low, somewhere between anxiety and boredom, as Csikszentmihalyi might put it), "it is more realistic to argue that arousal level may be one part of the causal mechanism by which playful behavior is or is not facilitated" (1982, p. 176).

In her preschool child studies, for many years Greta Fein has maintained that more attention should be paid to these affective issues rather than to the reigning cognitive focus (Fein and Kinney, 1994). In a note to me, she writes: "I do not think play is about cognition and I don't think playing makes kids especially smarter. It most likely makes them happier . . . Little kids who do not play are usually very unhappy." Recollecting the zest with which the monkeys jump out of the trees, and babies play with nipples, it is not difficult to suggest that play is as much about zest as it is about flex(ibility). Perhaps the ability to playfully dissociate actions is wired into higher-order animals as well as all humans, and brings with it the motivation of being an exciting and regressive frontal lobe process (Sacks, 1995, p. 57). At the same time, the ability to consider adaptive possibilities is also innate and can proceed along a parallel path without play activities. Play's contribution in these terms is that it reinforces the zestfulness in organisms that have the capacity for anticipating and enacting possibilities. After all, seeing alternatives can be frightening as well as promising. Any organism that is to pursue the subjunctive life needs to be optimistic about what can be done with possibility (Fogel, Nwokah, and Karns, 1993). Perhaps what is being contemplated in this affective category is a discourse or rhetoric on play's intrinsic functions, whereas arguments in the earlier categories (skill, fighting, bonding) have to do with the extrinsic functions of play. Whatever their merit, however, these speculations take us beyond the issue of the progress rhetorics and animal play. In fact, they could be criticized as being just one more example of the very same thing.

Given the actual data, there is at present no better way to sum up this quest for the adaptational significance of animal play than with Robert Fagen's words, that "perhaps play will prove inexplicable within an adaptionist framework" (1981, p. 482). Given his vacillation, there is clearly a good case for giving the ideological rhetoric of progress priority over these ambiguous scientific findings as a historical influence. Most of the work quoted thus far has been from the Fagen 1981 study or the Smith 1982 symposium. In 1985 Paul Martin and T. M. Caro published a new survey, and both Smith and Fagen have cited and accepted the credibility of their findings. Martin and Caro concluded:

> There is currently no direct evidence that play has any detectable benefits, with the possible exception of some immediate effects on children's behavior. The most parsimonious explanation for this lack of evidence is that play does not in fact have any major benefits, but is instead a facilitative developmental determinant of minor importance. (p. 71)

They felt that the research supported this finding of play's minor importance and did not support the view that the true function of play has not yet been detected. Ten years later both Smith and Fagen, in consequence of Martin and Caro's survey and their own further work, have seriously modified their former adaptationist enthusiasm. After a series of human studies that seemed to negate the positive effects of play training on children's creativity and children's problem solving (studies to be referred to in more detail later), Smith writes:

> In so far as "play" could be considered a unitary behavioral phenomenon in retrospect, may be more of a mistake than I thought at the time. I argued that it could give safe practice for useful later skills in cases where such practice was either dangerous for young animals (for example, fighting and predatory behavior), or unlikely to occur

(for example, problem solving skills with objects, in children). At the time I wrote this, the experimental work on children's play had not been thoroughly criticized. (1995, p. 14–15)

But still Smith does not agree with Martin and Caro's conclusion, that play's function is of minor importance. He says he finds it implausible that play does not have an important function. It is just that its function has been overemphasized because of what he calls "the play ethos" and what is here called the rhetoric of progress. He says this ethos "has even distorted the direction of research for a while. Rather than providing simple answers, one has to consider issues such as whether play has benefits which can also be provided by other kinds of experiences: whether some minimum level or 'threshold' value of play is all that is needed; whether the value of playful experiences varies appreciably with culture and individual experience. I think these questions are still substantially unanswered" (p. 15).

Fagen (1995) has also modified his earlier positions, now saying very little about practice or bonding or flexibility and instead emphasizing play as a motivational attitude and a state of well-being (as in the rhetoric of the self), and in particular paying attention to the role of aesthetic factors in evolution. Play as aesthetic performance now comes into his field of focus, and he suggests parallels between animal games and human narratives. Fagen's shift from the rhetorics of progress and power to that of the self parallels shifts in the cultural esteem in which these discourses have been held throughout the past hundred years. All of this criticism opens up the way to ask: Is it not possible to think of the adaptive function of play as being quite intrinsic and independent of its usefulness for other more extrinsic forms of survival? Its adaptiveness then might center on what play does for a sense of well-being, as ecstatic play, rather than what play does as work or as adaptation. But still there is a problem, because that's precisely what the voguish rhetoric of the self would have us believe, that play is largely about our own feelings, not about any external consequences.

One cannot finish reading this chapter without noting the immense empirical as well as theoretical ambiguity that surrounds the study of play. With or without the progress rhetoric, no one is making great progress in demonstrating adaptation to be play's main function.

3

Rhetorics of Child Play

If the toy is a transitional object, your young sister gets it first.
after Mrs. Frech

Following naturally from the earlier, evolution-based, biological theories of the function of play, most psychological play scholarship in this century has focused on the developmental stages children go through in their play. The first historical step toward supposing that this is what the science of play should be about was the theory of recapitulation. According to this theory, a child's play proceeds through a series of increasingly complex and social stages as the child proceeds to maturity, and these stages are believed to parallel the evolution of the species. As Stanley Hall, the founder of child psychology in the United States, said: "In play every word and movement is instinct with heredity. Thus we rehearse the activities of our ancestors, back we know not how far, and repeat their life's work in summative and adumbrated ways . . . Thus stage by stage we enact their lives" (Ellis, 1973, p. 43).

This theory did not endure, given that the parallel drawn between children's development and that of the origin of the species, or even the origins of human culture, is tenuous at best and also varies markedly across cultures. Yet the recapitulation theory left a major unilinear mark on play psychology, in the idea that how children develop through the stages of play should be central to our knowledge of play. Most play studies in the first half of the century have been of the normative kind (Herron and Sutton-Smith, 1971). Even in the great original work of Piaget, *Play, Dreams and Imitation in Childhood* (1951), in which play is harnessed to cognitive development, development is laid before us primarily as a set of stages through which children must proceed both in cognition and in play. Despite its purported evolutionary origins, part of the attraction of this kind of research and formulation to psychologists, as scientists, is the promise of predictable regularities of a reliable kind. Developmental psychology has been focused on mapping the increasing complexity of the human organism; or, as some skeptics might say, on the increasing rationality of the human organism—which is to say, focused on progressive development. Despite the justifiable science involved, it is also possible to argue that, once again, the spur of the ideological progress rhetoric lies in the background. What play psychologists so often do is convert the maps of development toward maturity into recommendations for how to accelerate childrens' progress across those maps.

Furthermore, the relationship between play and development has come to be so taken for granted that it is invoked almost any time an investigator finds an analogy between a play process and some other developmental process. The progress rhetoric of play is very much also a rhetoric of developmental stages. I offer some typical contemporary examples of parallels between play and life that are taken to be true purely on the grounds of what one might call their "metaphoric validity." They may not be false, but we certainly cannot assume that they are automatically true. It is conceivable that play may instigate the processes mentioned here, or play may be an epiphenomenon of such processes; alternatively, the processes may operate in ways that are parallel to other growth processes but separate from them in function. In their own context, the following statements about play as a cause of growth are made to sound self-evident. In this chapter's skeptical context, they are merely presuppositions. Because the content here is invidious, references to the authors are not given. I have made many similar statements in the past myself.

> "The contents of the social world that surrounds a child, its moral norms and rules, are reflected in play. Accepting a role, a child complies to the rules and tries to act according to them . . . This improves his absorption of commonly accepted social standards and his formation of moral motivation and voluntary behavior as well as introducing the child into national and general spiritual values."

"Play being an original form of the child's practical reflection on reality substantially contributes to a child's development . . . Play as practical reflection (in action) on this or that essence of child experience is the mechanism of adoption, reproduction and transformation of intellectual, affective, social and moral experience by the child."

"Within that inner life, play is a mental process that builds upon and integrates many other processes in the developing child's mind—thinking, imagining, pretending, planning, wondering, doubting, remembering, guessing, hoping, experimenting, redoing and working through. The child at play, using these varied mental processes, integrates past experiences and current feelings and desires."

"Compensatory play can allow a child to handle emotions. If a parent has scolded a child, later in the day, that child can scold its doll, or stuffed animal."

"At first babies learn means-end relations through play when the stimuli are in the perceptual fields, as in operant conditioning, contingent learning and secondary circular reactions."

"As they learn to step in and out of the "playframe" in their symbolic play, children also enhance their metacognition—the ability to think about one's own cognitive processes."

"But all learnings must be rehearsed and a child rehearses what he or she has learned through play."

"Children are programmed to actively seek out information and play is the principle mechanism for doing so."

"I believe that play is the most ideally effective form of developmental aid because the child becomes familiar with the world, himself and his limits."

"Perhaps the most important, it is through play that a child develops imagination and curiosity."

Children's Play as Learning

After the Second World War it appeared increasingly possible that developmental science would shift from the plotting of developmental regularities in play to studies that would yield a more specific causal understanding of the role of play in child development. Empirical studies of the mother-infant relationship during the period from 1940 to 1960 repeatedly showed, for example, that the more stimulating the parents, the more precocious the children.

> While few of these investigations were at first directly concerned with the role of mother's play as a part of her infant stimulation, play variables were increasingly discovered to be significant. Even within behavioristic theoretical paradigms, mothers who responded contingently to the baby's initiative of coos and smiles were found to have the greatest reinforcing effects. There was recognition that if you wanted the baby's attention you had to respond to the baby by copying its behavior and then varying it in novel ways. To keep the baby's attention you had to become something of a playful mimic or fool. (Sutton-Smith, 1994c, p. 16)

Some of us figured it was time to advise parents on how to play with children (Sutton-Smith and Sutton-Smith, 1974) and how to become partners in play (Singer and Singer, 1977). Other parallel research heightened the belief that a causal understanding of children's play was possible:

Studies showing that infants in the crib practiced language while playing with sounds (Weir, 1962; Kuczaj, 1983; Nelson, 1989).

Studies indicating that the provision of appropriate toys in infancy correlates with advanced maturity measures in early childhood (Brown and Gottfried, 1985).

Studies of children's exploratory and play behavior that showed how both were increased by novel stimulation (Berlyne, 1960; Hutt, 1971).

Studies showing that prior play experience with materials subsequently heightened a child's ability to solve problems with those materials (Bruner, Jolly, and Sylva, 1976).

Studies showing relationships between playfulness and creative capacity (Sutton-Smith, 1967b, 1968; Lieberman, 1977; Dansky
1980a, 1980b).

Studies showing that more imaginative children were better behaved,
more expressive emotionally, more cooperative, and better at their
schoolwork (Singer, 1973; Singer and Singer, 1992).

Studies showing that increasing children's classroom-sponsored sociodramatic play or story dramatization also heightened the children's reading and storytelling competency (Smilansky, 1968;
Saltz, Dixon, and Johnson, 1977; Johnson, Christie, and Yawkey,
1987).

Studies showing that parents who play pretend games with children
have children who are more capable of pretend play with their
peers (Singer and Singer, 1992; Haight and Miller, 1993).

Studies indicating that when teachers or parents are more involved
with children's pretend play, there are positive increases in the
children's literacy, language, reading, and writing (Galda and
Pellegrini, 1985; Bloch and Pellegrini, 1989; Christie, 1991; Pellegrini and Galda, 1993; Goelman and Jacobs, 1994).

In all of this, higher forms of play, as judged by imaginative or verbal
complexity, are again and again correlated with higher forms of
school-related social or educational success (Howes, 1992).

Metanalysis of these multiple disparate studies, showing that play contributes to early development by enhancing adjustment and reducing language problems and socioemotional difficulties, with
variances ranging between 33 percent to 67 percent (Fisher, 1992).

The Terman longitudinal studies of people of advanced intelligence,
showing that those who are successful in life are those who have
participated in more extracurricular activities, including sports, in
school and throughout their life (Goleman, 1995).

Longitudinal research showing that the more interesting and
fulfilling lives are those in which playfulness was kept at the center
of things (Erikson, 1972; quoted by Bruner, Jolly, and Sylva, 1976,
p. 17). "The new work begins to show why play is the principle
business of childhood, the vehicle of improvisation and combination, the first carrier of rule systems through which a world of
cultural restraint is substituted for the operation of impulse"
(Bruner, Jolly, and Sylva, 1976, p. 20).

Ethnographies suggesting that children play in more complex ways in cultures where there are greater requirements for them to use complex social strategies as adults (Sutton-Smith, 1972b).

The early high point for these apparent congruences of play and development was a 1972 article by Jerome Bruner, "The Nature and Uses of Immaturity," as well as his 1976 book with Alison Jolly and Kathy Sylva, entitled: *Play: Its Role in Development and Evolution*. It has been easy to believe that there is validity to the finding that play is associated positively with learning and development, for it has long been known that the reverse also seems to be true; that is, that those who are mentally ill or poorly adjusted and cannot learn effectively also cannot play, or if they play, they tend to do so in highly rigid or obsessive ways (Gordon, 1993; Brown, 1995). Here human findings parallel animal research: animals, when confined and in stress, also do not play, and their recovery, in turn, is signaled by the return of play (Goodall, 1986). Furthermore, recent research has shown that children who are neglected or rejected by their peers, and thus have reduced play opportunities, tend to do less well in their subsequent social and school development (Asher and Coie, 1990; Hart, 1993). When such children are incorporated in repeated play-treatment sessions with play buddies who play at a higher level, their play and social incompetence can be positively modified (Fantuzzo et al., 1988, 1995).

Skepticism

In recent years, criticism of the view that play is the cause of positive developmental outcomes has increased. One view is that the increases in various scores following play training by teachers or others are due as much to the new relationship between the teachers and the children as it is to the play forms that are introduced. This has been called the *tutorial stimulation effect*. It is said that it is not the play alone that causes the upward change in the children's competencies; it is, rather, the new and special relationship with the tutor. Nevertheless, let it be said that these tutorial-play studies themselves seem to be of considerable value to education, even if they have so far failed to clarify the nature of the role of play in such educational processes.

It seems that play is seldom the only determinant of any of the important forms of learning that occur in young children. Even if it does function in any such a way, it is only one of multiple influences (Christie, 1991). Still, there is potential here for thinking of the rhetorics that direct adult attempts to view child play as progressive as being themselves the very phenomena that cause such transfers of skill from play to everyday reality. What may not transfer typically except by accident or luck may be facilitated by the intrusion of these progress-oriented rhetorics in the minds of the teachers. It is a cliché in learning theory that the transfer of skill from one mode or response to another generally occurs only if there is an active attempt to make it do so. This is an important point, and the phenomenon might be called the tutorial transfer effect, or the progress rhetoric transfer effect.

Skepticism also arises from the finding that the increases in a play group's skills result in part from inadequately matched control groups who not only get less play opportunity but also less teacher stimulation. When the control groups are adequate and both groups get the same verbal stimulation, whether about play or about skills, then the subject matter outcomes are similar. This is consistent with a generation of research on simulation games at the high school level in which it has been shown many times that those who learn through simulation techniques (play) do as well as those who learn from the regular textbook-oriented curriculum (Boocock, and Schild, 1968).

Much of the apparent increase in creativity and problem-solving capacity due to forms of "play training" may have been due to *experimenter effects* in which investigators, knowing the hypotheses, unwittingly favor scores for the experimental groups over the control groups. When some of these studies have been repeated with adequate controls in the scoring process, then differences have not been found (Simon and Smith, 1985; Smith, 1995).

These experiments seldom really involve "play" in any substantial sense; the children often are given just a few minutes of play in the experimental condition, which is hardly sufficient to result in any profound changes in behavior. This is less true of the lengthy sociodramatic play participations, and those studies, along with the adult tutorial stimulation, account for the strongest positive results in the Fisher meta-analysis (1992).

Skeptical reviews presenting these negative findings about play were to be found throughout the literature in the 1980s (for example, Rubin, 1980; Brainerd, 1982; Martin and Caro, 1985; Smith, 1982, 1984, 1986, 1995). Smith sums up his own views as follows:

> Indeed from at least the 1930's until the present day, the "play ethos" has been very influential in educational circles in Britain and North America if not elsewhere. This has held that "play is the child's work" (Isaacs, 1933) and that "play is essential for survival." This was a prevailing view, and I accepted it without question through the 1970's . . . Neither their critique [Martin and Caro's] of the animal work, nor mine of the work on children's play was intended to suggest that play has no function. I find this implausible. But we were both arguing that many previous researchers in the area had gone too far in assuming many functions for play, and in assuming that these functions were essential (the "play ethos"). (1995, p. 11)

The Interplay between Play Rhetoric and Play Activity

Although the progress rhetoric appears to serve adult needs rather than the needs of children, the phenomena of play and learning are not completely foreign to each other. There is a substantial amount of development going on when children are playing. As they get older, they play increasingly complex games and develop complexity in the social skills required to play. The evidence of play studies and game studies is that complexity in play is highly correlated with age. So given this correlation, it is an easy mistake to believe that the major purpose of play development is to contribute to other kinds of age-related development—social, emotional, and cognitive. All move along paths of increasing complexity. As I have shown, however, the evidence does not seem to support very clear causal relationships, although it would be surprising if they did not share and transfer skills back and forth.

In addition, because children are so highly motivated to play, those who work with children have used play to facilitate their own interventions, giving rise to another obscuring factor (Hellendorn, Van der Kooij, and Sutton-Smith, 1994). Therapists, hospital staffers, teachers, camp counselors, social workers, and recreation directors have often used play as a major technique for reinforcing, invigorating, or controlling children. In the case of therapists and hospital caregivers, play is said to be the best way in which they can communicate with children and the major way in which they seem to be able to assist them toward recovery. For teachers, the association of play and the curriculum seems to lead to general increases in motivation at school (Hartmann and Rollett, 1994). It was a cliché during my own early teaching career that joining in with the children's sports outdoors was a primary way to exercise discipline and control over them indoors. Which is to say that children's play is of considerable assistance to those who associate it with their own more academic or therapeutic goals for children, although as Christie shows, the process works better when there is a close association between the children's own play forms and the teachers' generalizations therefrom (1991). However, although play may be involved directly in education, as in, for example, the use of game forms to simulate geography, its more typical use seems to be as a reward, to give children enjoyment and motivation, which increase their willingness to pursue the other things that the adults require of them. Basically it becomes a reinforcement technique (Block and King, 1987).

Another factor, which receives less attention and also confuses the relationship between play and development, is the finding that children appear to develop play skills through play, which enable them to go on playing with other children, thus substantially increasing their happiness. Sometimes their play skills enable them to become so competent that they go on to play on representative teams; to travel to other towns, cities, and countries; and, on some occasions, to become professional players, in games from sports and gymnastics to chess. More generally, play skills become the basis of enduring friendships and social relationships and also offer a way of becoming involved with other children when shifting to new communities. Obviously this is also true for adults. Play is of direct value to those who are successful in their play.

Studies of playground play show that it is a very difficult social arena in which children sometimes succeed and sometimes fail at getting playmates, having successful playground experiences, and prospering playfully, as discussed above. Play development is not assured just because children are on the playground. There are bullies, and often conflicts and scapegoating, and while it looks like an arena for learning social adaptation, it is difficult to be sure how much outcomes are due to the social skills the children bring with them and how much they are due to the social skills that they acquire while there. There are multiple findings that some patterns of prior parental interaction, positive and negative, transfer to the playground. Patterns of positive attachment are correlated with positive playground relationships, and patterns of negative attachment correlate with dysfunctional playground relationships (Parke and Ladd, 1992; Hart, 1993). But it is unlikely that this tells the whole story, because developmental psychologists have always tended to focus more on parent-child socialization than they have on child-child socialization, and they have also given less attention to the many other buffers for development that might operate, such as neighborhood playmates, grandparents, churches, and gangs (Kupersmidt et al., 1995). It is probable that for many children much of the variance in how they get along with others actually results from playground experience. Children are so motivated to be accepted in play that they make sacrifices of egocentricity for membership in the group. In addition there are ethnographic playground accounts, such as those of Hughes (1983) and Beresin (1993), that reveal that a great variety of social subtleties—about group membership and group power —are being learned and exercised on the playgrounds. Girls in particular have been observed to be willing to assimilate younger girls, step by step, into their more difficult games, such as jump rope (Goodwin, 1990). Thus it is probable that many children do learn how to play on playgrounds and at other play places; it is hard to believe that such would not be the case. It also becomes probable that, with this background, they go on to increasingly successful play activities in their subsequent lives. It is probable as well, but certainly not proven, that their play successes transfer to their more general social and emotional competencies. If the rhetoric of progress has any winners, they are probably in this arena of generalized social competence; that is, those who become good social players improve in their general social skills. What is more certain is that successful play experience increases the potential for continued happy playing. But there still remains the issue of whether play need have a function apart from the joy of playing, the associated joy of living, the increases in enjoying one's own play skills, and the play interests and associations that naturally follow.

The final titillation, however, is Farver and colleagues' finding that when parents believe the rhetoric that children learn through their play and value play for its cognitive and educational benefits, they are more likely to join their children in their play activity. Fathers who believe in play's educational value are more likely to join their children in reading books, doing puzzles, and building with blocks. That this makes any difference in their subsequent school success is, however, less obvious (Farver, Kim, and Lee, 1995).

Returning to the point that what might be of greatest importance about play is the way in which persons develop within it, it is possible to sketch out a play scale of development, ranging from the most elementary to the most complex. The virtue of such a scale is the resulting recognition that play is itself a complex developmental form, and that the levels of play merit as much attention as the distinction between play and nonplay. The play-scale levels might be:

1. *The inability to play,* as in cases of mental illness or in highly stressful circumstances. What is remarkable is how some healthy individuals manage often to play in stressful circumstances (Eisen, 1988).
2. *Play as pathology,* as in cases of gambling addiction or in rigid forms of self-limiting repetitive behavior; as seen in pathological patients or in those with character defects who confine themselves, for example, to regressive or sadistic play forms (Brown, 1994; Slade and Wolf, 1994).
3. *Play as a form of security,* as is typical of what have been called "low players," persons who are anxious or aggressive in their expressive behavior and confine themselves to repetitive and minimally expressive forms of play (Fein and Kinney, 1994).
4. *Play as stereotypic.* Most play forms are highly stereotypic, from house play to crossword puzzles to team sports. These are the typical play forms of persons with average to complex playing capacity. Their games are culturally self-satisfying vehicles and increase the enjoyment in the lives of those who play them (Meckley, 1994).

5. *Playful forms of play.* These are the games of those who have a creative capacity for playing. Typically this is demonstrated by the variety and complexity of playful transformations of which the players are capable, and by their ability to convert their own playful characteristics into play scenarios for others. Because flexibility is the major characteristic of such play, play at this level has the greatest potential for transfer. The rhetorics of play as progress may apply most strongly to these relatively rare players, who are flexible enough to perceive the possibility of transfers. Such individual differences might explain why play sometimes seems to transfer and sometimes does not. In prior work, I have spoken of play as "adaptive potentiation," a "trickle-down" theory of play's occasional but not regular extrinsic adaptive value (Sutton-Smith, 1975a, 1975b). For example, the baseball pitcher might on rare occasions get to be an outstanding thrower of hand grenades. While this proposition seems to have some validity, the notion that some "high players" have the flexibility to see such connections suggests a way in which transfers from play to everyday behavior might come about.

Individual Differences

All of this adds up to the view that play is like most other psychological variables: individuals show great variation. Admittedly play, like language, is in the first place likely to be a universal human trait because it is one of the major forms of prelinguistic communication in animals. Beyond this, however, one notices marked differences between cultures in their kinds of play and in the amount of play (some cultures encourage play and some severely discourage it), and between individual players within any one culture. In recent years, for example, there has been considerable attention directed toward children who are especially playful (Lieberman, 1977), to children who are especially imaginative (Singer and Singer, 1992), and to the differences between children who play in dramatic ways and those who play in constructional ways (Wolf and Grollman, 1982). And we know, anecdotally at least, that there are considerable differences between physically skillful players and those who are intellectually skillful. Some games call on memory, some on strategy, some on acting. It would seem likely, therefore, that such individual play skills would be differentiated just as other human abilities are, as is indicated by individuals' different abilities in such areas as music, language, mathematics, spatial reasoning, logic, and kinesthesic and interpersonal skills (Gardner 1983). There are geniuses in these forms of skill just as there are geniuses in some distinct kinds of play (chess, poker, bridge, sports, crosswords).

What this means is that if play is a form of adaptation, it is one that is used by different human beings in different ways. The survival of the species may have been due to the distinctive contributions of individuals. It is possible that mutual support through differences in play as well as in other abilities was what contributed to such survival. Perhaps the poor results in determining play's functions in the preceding chapter and this one are due to the oversimplicity of the connections being made. If different individuals participate in different kinds and levels of play, and some individuals avoid operating in playful ways most of the time, then our ability to determine the meaning of the presence or absence of playful actions must be very limited. It may be that play is adaptive, but it may be that we do not have sufficiently complex paradigms to determine this. Alternatively it may be that I cannot escape the effects of the progress rhetoric any better than Fagen and Smith could.

The Old and the Young

If one still assumes that children's play is about general adaptation, growth, and development, despite the relatively negative results already presented, then what are the reasons for adult play? Erikson (1956), one of the few to even consider the matter, has suggested that while the child goes forward in his play, the adult goes sideways. This apparently means that children are growing up while they are playing and adults are not. Presumably adults have already grown up, so the supposed growth virtues of play are irrelevant. If play is a preparation for maturity (Groos, 1976), then what are the mature doing when they play? Are they preparing for death? Perhaps they are not preparing for anything.

In Florida, where I live, there are countless euphemistically labeled "executive" nine-hole golf courses for those erstwhile "executives" who are now too feeble to make it around an eighteen-hole course. About every eight minutes on these nine-hole courses, four aging persons, typically dressed in childlike leisure clothes, pass by at a crepuscular pace, accompanied by the periodic clacking of golf balls, which they hit several yards at a stroke. Approximately thirty of them pass by every hour—about three hundred per day—on a typical course in the high season. This prolonged and repetitive ritual, players marching every day in each other's footsteps, would seem to be more of a homily against death than any earnest of life to come. Round and round, day after day, week after week, year by year they go by in this ritual of "eternal return." What their play seems to be, besides just a way to get out of doors in a pleasant place with pleasant company to pass the time, is an assertion of the possibility of skill and persistence in the face of increasing evidence to the contrary. A ritual opposition to decay, perhaps, but hardly a preparation for life. Which is to say that a play theory that is only about progress and deals only with some small part of the population (children) could hardly claim to be an encompassing one. If it could be believed that elders do not play at all (as was often originally supposed both for animals and humans), then the rhetoric of progress would hold some cogency. It has indeed long been maintained that adult festivals, carnivals, sports, and parades are not play but merely entertainments or recreations. But this seems to be a disguise of decreasing credibility.

A play theory of any comprehensiveness must grasp this strange companionship of the very young and the very old, the first waiting to begin and the second to finish; one with dolls and trucks and the other with quilts and golf. And such a theory must account also for the invigorated play of soldiers waiting for battle, or the intensive play of Boccaccio's youthful fourteenth-century folk attempting to outlast the Black Plague. In all these cases play seems to have more to do with waiting than with preparing, more to do with boredom than with rehearsal, more to do with keeping up one's spirits than with depression.

Validations and Definitions

Finally, with respect to the scholarly authenticity of the claims presented in this chapter and the previous one that such a thing as a cultural progress rhetoric does in fact exist, the reader's attention is called:

to the historical antecedents of the progress rhetoric (the Enlightenment, the attitude known as historicism, and evolutionary theory)

to those who are its primary advocates, particularly teachers, preachers, commencement speakers, and in general the more affluent

to the play and games of children

to children as the players

to the attention paid to these players by play theorists from the psychological, biological, and educational disciplines

to the support for a match or interplay between child play theory and the progress rhetoric provided by the parallel growth that is cited in both domains, by the accidental or tutorially instigated transfers of skill and the transfers made by superior players, and perhaps by the trickling down of potentiating effects in the unpredictable future by ordinary players

to the hegemony of adults over children revealed in the way in which the theories provide rationalization for the adult control of children's play: to stimulate it, negate it, exclude it, or encourage limited forms of it

and, lastly, to the definitions of play that are used in the scholarly fields in which the rhetorics of play as progress are used.

The definitions of play given by child players themselves generally center on having fun, being outdoors, being with friends, choosing freely, not working, pretending, enacting, fantasy and drama, and playing games (King, 1979; Kaarby, 1986). There is little or no emphasis on the kind of growth that adults have in mind with their progress rhetoric. The children's rhetoric is by and large similar to that adopted by adults in the rhetorics of the self, which are about play as some kind of valued personal experience, so the children are probably echoing those modern public adult scripts. Mouritsen quotes the nine-year-old boy who, when his father asked if he really thought that play was good for child development, replied, "Does it matter as long as he can't help doing it?" (1996). In short we don't know why children play, even if they can't help doing it.

Among psychologist play theoreticians, definitions akin to the rhetorics of the self are also becoming popular. These are theories that say child play is a form of intrinsic motivation, attention to means rather than ends; it is organism dominated, noninstrumental, and free from externally imposed rules (Rubin, Fein, and Vandenberg, 1983). Somewhat similar are the definitions of play as existing for the generation of positive emotional states, to modulate arousal levels, and to effect metabolic restoration (Ellis, 1974). These definitions are not primarily concerned with the kinds of adaptation that are central to progress. There is not necessarily any contradiction between assuming that players play for intrinsic personal motivational reasons and that the effects of such play are useful for the extrinsics of other kinds of adaptation. Fagen's review of the play definitions of thirty-seven play authors shows much the same division between progress and self criteria (1981, pp. 500–504).

As indicated in Chapters 1 and 2, however, extrinsic academic, social, moral, physical, and cognitive play functions, with a progress-oriented thrust, have been the major focus of most child play scientists seeking to demonstrate that play is the practice of real-life adaptive skills for survival (the biological emphasis); that it can ensure feelings of mastery and competence through conflict resolution and compensatory activity (the psychogenic emphasis); and, more recently, that it can develop skills for cognition and education (the cognitive emphasis). More specifically it has been said that play recapitulates and is a catharsis for the past history of the species and culture (Hall, 1906); that play is an imitation of adult activities (Malinowski, 1944); that play is a preparation for the future (Groos, 1976); that it is a form of learning or socialization, and that it proceeds through a series of developmental stages and generates mastery and feelings of competence (Erikson, 1956; White, 1959); that it mirrors and consolidates the development of cognitive stages (Piaget, 1951); that it anticipates the development of cognition (Vygotsky, 1978); that it is an intermediary and transitional cathexis between developmental stages (Winnicott, 1971); that it has a complementary relationship to exploration (Berlyne, 1960; Hutt, Tyler, Hutt, and Christopherson, 1989; Görwitz and Wohlwill, 1987); that sociodramatic play is advantageous to education (Smilansky, 1968); and that there are parallels with animal behavior in play's preparatory, rough-and-tumble, bonding, flexible, and aesthetic functions (Fagen, 1981). While these various theories disagree about the specific kinds of development that are instigated by play, they all assume that play does indeed transfer to some other kinds of progress that are not in themselves forms of play. These extrinsic theories are the best demonstrations of the way in which the field of child play is dominated by the rhetoric of progress.

As a final note, it can be seen that the ambiguities in this part of the field of play owe much to the assumed parallel of forms between play's own skill development and other kinds of nonplay skill development. Analogies here are frequently passed off as causes. But ambiguities are also to be found in the dispute over functions, those that apply to children and those suitable for adults. As yet, the discontinuity between the generations has led to no marked clarification of their similarities or differences.

4

Rhetorics of Fate

Vicissitudes of fortune, which spares neither man nor the proudest of his works, which buries empires and cities in a common grave.
Edward Gibbon

Children are a lottery in the modern concept of progress.
after Frech

The ancient rhetorics of play, fate, power, identity, and frivolity are so called because they are of more ancient origin than the modern rhetorics, progress, the imaginary, and the self. The latter three can be traced to major historical concepts of the past two hundred years, those being the Enlightenment, romanticism, and individualism, while the ancient rhetorics have antecedents throughout history. But there are additional differences as well. The ancient rhetorics tend to be about groups rather than individuals. And in general, those who believe in one or more of the modern rhetorics of play tend to discount the ancient rhetorics as play forms. In part this is because the older rhetorics are less socialized, more crude, and less in synchrony with modern rational life, though this is somewhat more true of fate and frivolity than of power and identity. Nevertheless the violence of the power rhetorics and the carnivalesque quality of the rhetorics of identity are also often seen as beyond the pale of civilized credibility, as are the excesses of gambling and the travesties of folly. Additionally, these older forms of play are typically more obligatory than they are optional. They therefore offend the modern sensibility that play must be associated with voluntariness. The ancient rhetorics have more extrinsic motivation about them and imply that play can be coercive. The modern rhetorics state, contrarily, that play is an exercise of freedom. But to admit that play can be coercive is to deprive "freedom" of its legitimacy as a universal definition, so many moderns would prefer the alternative of denying that gambling and football and carnival are really play at all; they can be called addiction, violence, and orgy instead. There is also a deep reluctance to associate children with any of these ancient rhetorics. The point of view taken in this work, however, is that all of the rhetorics, whether modern or ancient, are based on or are simulacra of play forms, and all should be taken into account in any truly empirical examination of the character and functioning of play.

The first rhetoric of the ancient group, the rhetoric of fate, is the most pervasive of all play rhetorics but the least publicly ideologized in modern times. It is at the heart of the most ancient of religions (animism and mysticism) and is at the deepest level of even modern minds, because life and death are, after all, fateful, not rational and not escapable. This chapter deals with various forms of fate as play, such as the attributions that the gods are at play, that the universe is at play, that our brains are at play, and finally that we are creatures of the play of fortune and luck, as exemplified by games of chance. There is a sense in which the irrevocability of fate leaves no answers except the most desperate and universal of human answers, which is that one might perhaps escape by luck or its personified equivalent, God's favor. Luck is very much fate's last hope. It is the play of the last chance. It is the play of everyman. Though pitiful, it is the only recourse in the mortal situation, unless of course we really do rise by works rather than by grace. From a secular point of view, then, to be mortal is ultimately to be without hope, but in the game model of this predicament, there is a slight lottery like hope. The odds, though long, might occasionally be with us in the more confined worldly domain of chance. In this sense it is useful to think of games of chance not only as models of the irrevocability of fate but also as fate fantasied (though in Florida, as they say, the probability of winning the state lottery is the same as the chance of being hit by lightning three times—but then, as they also say, there is a lot of lightning in Florida).

Perhaps it can be said that the ones who lose at games of chance are at least playfully in control of the circumstances of their own losing. This is the definition of play—the illusion of mastery over life's circumstances—once offered by the great scholar of child play, Erik Erikson. In his words, the purpose of play is "to hallucinate ego mastery" (1956, p. 185). If such "illusory mastery" is indeed the spirit or motivation behind adults' play in games of chance, as it is an account of children's play, then it is surely a definition of play that escapes the limitations of the progress rhetoric. Play as an irrational act of gaining pleasure through one's own illusions is hardly consistent with the rationality of the rhetoric of progress. Of course if children and gamblers were put in a separate category of existence, then progressivists would not regard this reference to "illusion" as the ultimate definition of play. The discontinuity between adult and child play would be a discontinuity between rational adults and the collective group of irrational gamblers and nonrational children. Given the laws and prohibitions against gamblers and children throughout Western history, this negative collective category of children and gambling adults has actually existed, even though the groups are seldom theoretically linked in the present mordant way.

But calling the masteries of play in childhood or adulthood forms of hallucination or illusion is itself an epistemological discourse that implies something defective about them. This discourse implies that those who master their lives in more realistic ways are more mature or more adequate persons, and this may or may not be empirically true. Given that there is nothing more characteristic of human achievement than the creation of illusory cultural and theoretical worlds, as in music, dance, literature, and science, then children's and gamblers' full participation in such play worlds can be seen not as a defect, or as compensation for inadequacy, but rather as participation in a major central preoccupation of humankind. The modern computer-age habit of calling these "virtual worlds" rather than illusory worlds highlights this move toward a more positive, if narrower, epistemological attitude about their function. As we now see the creation of human meanings as central to human culture, we can give more primary appreciation to these manifestations in our artists, our children, and our gamblers (Hymes, 1974). We might borrow from Steiner the view that the issue is no longer whether there is superior reality versus inferior play, but whether the play is itself merely ordinary or a case of "brilliant virtuality" (1995). The rhetoric of fate is a real threat to the rhetoric of progress, because the concept of virtuality promises to put adults and children in the same ludic world.

The Play of the Gods

I move now to an array of examples in which play exemplifies not our own autonomy but our being controlled by some fate. The concept that play originates in the activities of the gods is well illustrated by O'Flaherty, who says, in her book *Dreams, Illusion and Other Realities* (1984), "This is a book about myths, dreams and illusion. It is about the ways in which they are alike, the ways in which they are different, and what each teaches us about reality. Transformations of one sort or another are the heart of myths" (p. 3). She goes on to show how, in Hindu mythology, the world is at play in the hands of the gods, and dreaming and playfulness are forms of reality treated as seriously as the so-called commonsense world. Play, like dreams, is not a secondary state of reality as it is with us but has primacy as a form of knowing. O'Flaherty says: "In India the realm of mental images is not on the defensive. Commonsense has a powerful lobby there, as it has with us, but it does not always have everything its own way. Reality has to share the burden of proof with unreality in India, and it is by no means a foregone conclusion that reality will win" (p. 304).

Handelman (1992) brings these ideas to bear on the issue of play when he says:

> In Indian cosmology, play is a top down idea. Passages to play and their premises are embedded at a high level of abstraction and generality. The qualities of play resonate and resound throughout the whole. But more than this, qualities of play are integral to the very operation of the cosmos. To be in play is to reproduce time and again the very premises that inform the existence of this kind of cosmos . . . Now in cosmologies where premises of play are not embedded at a high level and are not integral to the organization of the cosmos, as in Western society, the phenomenon of play seems to erupt from the bottom. By bottom up play I mean that play often is phrased in opposition to, or as a negation of, the order of things. This is the perception of play as unserious, illusory and ephemeral, but it is also the perception of play as subversive and resisting the order of things. (p. 12)

Schechner (1988), beginning with the same Hindu materials as O'Flaherty and extrapolating probably from his own iconoclastic career in theater direction, suggests that if we look more closely at Western play, particularly what he calls "dark play" and that I have called elsewhere "cruel play" (Sutton-Smith, 1982f) and the "masks of play" (Sutton-Smith and Kelly-Byrne, 1984), there are some strong similarities with the Indian tradition. He agrees that for moderns play has low status, whereas in Hindu metaphysics it is indeed the divine process of creation; and whereas for moderns play is framed as not real, for Hindus it is one of multiple realities, all transformable into each other. However, when he shifts this discourse from a concern with metaphysical and cultural forms to the more ontological or psychological plane, then it is possible to see modern parallels between our own play behavior, particularly in what he calls our dark play, and that of the Hindus. Thus while Handelman might wish to deny it, Schechner contends that playing is for us, as for the Hindus,

> a creative destabilizing action that frequently does not declare its existence, even less its intentions . . . Playing is a mood, an attitude, a force. It erupts or one falls into it. It may persist for a long time as specific games, rites, and artistic performances do—or it comes and goes suddenly—a wisecrack, an ironic glimpse of things, a bend or crack in behavior . . . [I]t's wrong to think of playing as the interruption of ordinary life. Consider instead playing as the underlying, always there, continuum of experience . . . Ordinary life is netted out of playing but play continually squeezes through even the smallest holes of the work net . . . work and other activities constantly feed on the underlying ground of playing, using the play mood for refreshment, energy, unusual ways of turning things around, insights, breaks, opening and especially looseness. (1988, pp. 16–18)

Here we have Schechner borrowing from his readings in Hindu metaphysics an interpretation of play as a highly transforming and powerful, often irrational experience, which he apparently presumes to be universal. In this he goes beyond the typical Western tradition of play interpretation, although there are some scholars who are attempting to do similar things within Western theology. They believe that the Christian God can be seen as a creative player (Berger, 1969; Miller, 1969; Moltmann, 1972; Nemoianu and Royal, 1992). But on closer analysis they seem to be talking about a fairly rational creator, whereas Schechner, like Nietzsche, has a fairly irrational and secular player in mind. In sum, while in part accepting Handelman's dichotomy of up and down, Schechner injects into the bottom-up Western psychological play attitude a more comprehensive and heteronomous theory of play's role than Handelman's cultural bottom-up implies.

On Schechner's behalf it might be added that dreams, daydreams, and illusions could be included as a part of his bottom-up view in Western thought, particularly as this seems to be the case neurologically, as it will be shown later. There is enough known about these oneiric phenomena to see that they have a kind of pervasiveness and automaticity of their own. They do seem to resist attempts to make the good things in life always a part of conscious control and choice. They constantly present us with other images of ourselves that seem to persist despite our desire to the contrary, so that even if we are usually reluctant to give dreams the ontological status of play, they do constantly permeate our thinking—and it is not certain that when this happens it is not itself a kind of play of mind. What makes interpretation more difficult is that what permeates minds day by day, "the underlying, always there, continuum of experience," is usually referred to as daydreaming, reverie, or rumination. Is play to be the name for all of these, as Schechner implies? Or is play to be only the more active next step that is taken willfully with these daydreams, to turn them into controlled fantasies or imaginings? There is truly a sense in which a mind plays its own recordings and has its own streams of consciousness, very little of which is actively under control. But human passivity in these respects contrasts with the active nature usually attributed to waking play and usually thought to be essential to most modern definitions of play. One can see how the passivity or receptivity of the Hindu in face of the metaphysical universe at play could mingle quite easily with the Hindu ontological sense of the individual mind at daydreaming play. Play could then be thought to be mainly a phenomenon to be experienced top down rather than actively manipulated bottom up. Typical Western definitions, by contrast, make the player a more entrepreneurial kind of being. And this allows Westerners to divide off the "daydream stuff" as a less credible part of the mind. But Schechner's alternative suggests that if the

Western concept of play, no matter how controlling, does rest on a bedrock of dreams, that would be a much more comprehensive bottom-up idea than most modern play theorists have in mind. A further advantage of Schechner's broad view might be that it could help account for the way in which players quickly become highly absorbed in their own play. The message "this is play" lets go a flood of internally instigated emotion and involvement. The continuity between such impelling automata and the more behavioral matters of play might well account for the ever present and sudden surge of ready engagement in virtual play experience.

Without confusing Schechner's ontological usage with the Hindu metaphysical usage, it can be proposed that the breadth of play he suggests for these secular nonmythic times provides a *broad play* rhetoric. In what follows, the modern broad play rhetoric will be presented as one that encompasses all the mind materials of dreams, daydreams, tropes, and active play forms. Contrarily the *narrow play* rhetoric will speak for the more limited rhetorics of progress, power, identity, and the self in this book. Briefly, these can be called the broad and narrow versions of play. In the broad version, everything is play that is clearly not of an immediate adaptive usefulness. In the narrow version, nothing is play unless contemporaneously so named. Most things, in this narrow version, are not play. Dreams are dreams, daydreams are daydreams, imagination is imagination (though it can become imaginative play), spectators are just spectators of someone else playing, and metaphors are simply figures of speech, unless we actually play with them. Children do many things that are not play, such as exploring, practicing, exercising, learning, imitating, problem solving, and all the art activities that are art, not play.

The Universe at Play

The broader definition, in which either the gods or our own brains influence us playfully beyond our control, has about it an externality not likely to be popular in modern everyday parlance. Of similar externality are those views of the universe that see it too as being at play. In the hard sciences the concept of play is constantly being applied as a metaphor or a metaphysic to handle the inconstancy, indeterminism, unpredictability, or chaos of basic physical processes throughout the universe. There is a daunting similarity between some of these views of the universe and some of the ways neurologists are beginning to talk about the brain. They are, universe and brain, both more or less beyond control, and all one can do is try to understand the rules by which they operate. Perhaps one of the fascinations of games of chance is that they mirror both physical nature and human nature more adequately than we want to believe.

I am grateful for Spariosu's assemblage of the play theories of the play-oriented Nobel Prize–winning physical scientists, and I quote here briefly from his extended accounts (1989). Jacques Monod contends that "life on earth is entirely a matter of chance . . . essentially unpredictable" (p. 217). Eigen and Winkler state that "everything that happens in our world resembles a vast game in which nothing is determined in advance but the rules, and only the rules are open to objective understanding . . . chance and necessity underlie all events. The history of play goes back to the beginnings of time . . . chance and rules are the elements of play. Once begun by the elementary particles, atoms, molecules, play is carried on by our brain cells. Man did not invent play. But it is 'play and only play that makes man complete'" (p. 224). Erwin Schrodinger goes considerably further when he sees science itself as belonging to the play sphere, not just driven by the logic of adaptation: "Play, art and science are the spheres of human activity where the action and aim are not rule determined by the aims imposed by the necessities of life" (p. 275). For Schrodinger, science is a rhetorical product of its age no less than all the other ideological rhetorics of the particular time and place. Werner Heisenberg takes a similar position on the comparability of art (and play) and science, as complementary modes of knowledge. The most playful of modern science philosophers, however, is Paul Feyerabend, who likens science to the play of infants with language: "It is a bricolage of experimentation . . . initial playful activity is an essential prerequisite of the final act of understanding . . . new scientific practice needs time to develop its conceptual tools and its empirical data by playing with them, that is, by constantly repeating and combining them until they become common usage or reality" (p. 295).

In his analysis Spariosu is able to show that even with this openness of science to the metaphor of play, the majority of the scientific philosophers are still dominated by a rational and progressive view of how science and art or play will proceed together. Like Kant and Schiller, they do not really allow for imagining as a subversive activity or allow themselves to be seriously attracted to an irrational view of the universe. Even Feyerabend, who comes closest to Nietzsche's view of the playful universe as a constant struggle between antagonistic powers, is still more moderate than Nietzsche. In his own pluralistic and idealistic notion of a postscientific world, Feyerabend suggests there can be balance, with different subcultural powers observing a certain amount of fair play in relation to each other.

The Neurological Player

These externalist and broad views of play have some parallel in modern neurological theory. In chapter 2, I quoted Sacks's speculation that the brain is engaged in a ceaseless inner talking that is like fantasy. In his view, playful states have a priority and an indeterminism of their own in our brain, not unlike the above-described views of the gods or the physical universe at play. Sacks's account also seems to provide a neurological basis for the broad views of play suggested by Schechner. For brevity's sake I will call my construction of his account the theory of *neural fabulation,* meaning that the brain is always creating some kind of ceaseless inner fiction, or is at play within itself.

A similar connotation for brain activity can be derived from Edelman's work, although he doesn't talk specifically about play. In *Bright Air, Brilliant Fire* (1992) he conceives of life in the brain as like life in the jungle: each response to external stimuli is a process of natural selection, with those cells that clone most adequately to that stimulus surviving, but most of them dying. The mind he envisages arising from this jungle is a correlator of myriad interactive neuronal loops and layers. It is a mind in which 80 percent of the action is inward, driven by the gene-based survivals of history as well as by the contingencies of its individualized memory and the existential moment. By correlating everything relevant in response to the urgencies of its own experience, it has the greatest chance of adequate circuits of responsivity. Thus it "dreams" ceaselessly along the correlated lines of its own experience and value. It is tempting to see this partly as another way of talking about neural fabulation. It is possible also to see this kind of correlator process as a model for informal play, for at best, within play's protean character, the player can pretend almost anything and connect almost anything with anything else. Such lability is one of play's most noted characteristics. Furthermore play seems usually to be driven by the novelties, excitements, or anxieties that are most urgent to the players. Put in these terms, play might imitate the fluidity and value-driven character of the mind's own internal processing, but with a transference to the agencies, agents, acts, and spatiotemporal scenes of the external world. Play is, as it were, a halfway house between the night and the day, the brain and the world. And as such it chatters to itself with the kind of unpredictable relevance and irrelevance that the dream life does, though aided somewhat by the rules and structures of the external world within which social, if not solitary, play is mostly cast. This *correlator brain model* is certainly a neat anthropomorphism for the theory of play as broad rather than narrow and passive as well as active. In this thesis those other voices in play may not be those of God, nor those of the external universe, but they are certainly the voices from within one's own head, though perhaps that is indeed the same thing.

Still, the analogy as stated here is quite fuzzy. The neurologist Damasio, in *Descartes' Error* (1994), provides a way to make the focus a little tighter. He points out that we, with our complex human brains, have a greater appreciation of external circumstances (accuracy), more refined responses (precision), and a better ability to predict the future through imagined scenarios than do lower animal life forms. In these areas, our brain's adaptability in the Edelman "jungle" drives it toward specific forms of learning. But as well as these adaptive forms of knowing, the human brain has the correlating capability that Edelman mentions, the ability to represent all relevant aspects of structure and function in basic and current detail (Damasio, ibid., p. 229). The question is why the correlator, which provides all this useful circuitry of an accurate, precise, and predictive nature, must also continue to fabulate its way through nighttime dreams and daytime fantasies. The answer I might offer, to complete this grand sketch of the neurological player, is that if the brain didn't keep itself labile, it might rigidify in terms of its prior specific adaptive successes. Sustaining its motivation for generality could be seen as the price of eternal alertness. The correlator must not rest, or it could be faulted by specialization. From this, if we are reckless, we might extrapolate that play, whether of the inner mind or outer behavior, becomes a self-rewarding process that keeps this holistic capacity in a state of alertness. Dreams exist to amuse the brain into continued labile alertness. Play exists to amuse the body to the same consummation of wholeness in a virtual world.* Both dreams and play, in these terms, exist primarily to provide motivation to sustain a holistic state of mind and body. What we see in everyday play, in these terms, is a worldly refraction of the motivation of a holistic brain. Play is the daytime refraction of the holistic brain. Though neither Edelman nor Damasio writes of play, they both provide the kind of neurological descriptions that prompt us to see a brain at play that is as universal as that kind of play envisaged for the gods, and for the physical universe. While it is true that none of these speculations and parallels is likely to last, the autonomy of the brain as a primal player seems likely to do so.

Dreams and Play

It would help such a neurological thesis, of course, if the parallel between dreams and play could be clearly established. But the intricacy of this research enterprise is baffling, and given the complexity and obscurity of both dream and play processes, there is only the hope of success at present. Still, the available parallels are positive. Obviously one is of the night and the other of the day. Obviously, too, the dream does not have to contend with the immediacies of waking, even though it does contend with the postscripts of waking. The dreamer, by and large, exercises no great power over dreaming, it being a largely automatic and irrevocable neural process; the player, however, has considerable control to start and stop, even he or she does not have too much control over the desired content. At the same time, the normal presence of dream and play is associated with general mental health, and their interruption is linked with dysfunction. They are both seen as recuperative, restitutive, and refructifying. Theories of dreams often parallel those for play, as in the claim that dreams are forms of memory consolidation, stress adaptation,

*The "body" here is the "body-mind" in Damasio's sense, as described in *Descartes' Error* (New York: Grosset-Putnam, 1994).

mood regulation, wish fulfillment, problem solving, and anticipation (Hunt, 1989). Similarly synesthesia is characteristic of the imagery in both, as discussed by Werner and Kaplan in their work *Symbol Formation* (1963). Both also seem to afford a unitary existential synthesis between person and reality that is less obvious in everyday circumstances. And both have been associated in a variety of empirical ways with measures of creativity, though the data here are still inconclusive. All of these positive items certainly add up at least to the view that it is not absurd to think there is a connection between the character of dreams and the character of play. The Singers sum it up in their book *The House of Make-Believe* (1992) when they write: "What little systematic data we have comparing the waking and sleeping thought streams suggests that if we subtract the on-task logical thought that characterizes waking thought and is infrequent during sleep, we find a continuity in structure and content" (p. 283). This commentary makes tenable the view that there is a connection between the passivity and involuntary character of dreams and the passivity and involuntariness of many kinds of play. The active forms of play rise, as it were, from this groundswell of incessant and relatively involuntary mental play. Dreams and play are perhaps as appetitive for the mind as are food and sex for the body.

Neonatal Ludicism

From another source of research also apparently close to the brain we gather that the characteristics of childhood immaturity may have a logic other than that of ignorance and incompetence. For example, Bjorklund and Green (1992) show that preschool children are innately unrealistically optimistic. They are not put off by failure. Until about the age of four years, they overestimate their own skill, and their own memory. Their optimism makes them persistent and keeps them continuing to learn despite their incompetence. Furthermore their very egocentricity, a negative in the Piagetian scheme of things, means that they learn better and remember more adequately things associated with their self-centered selves. If not for all their parallel monologues with other children, they might never discover that the others are present and require some consideration. Reversible thinking, it is argued, is ultimately assisted at this age by narcissistic involvement. Again, young children's lability and lack of differentiation make them hyperreactive to all salient stimuli; this may be one of the reasons for their remarkably speedy retention of all the languages in their environment, and perhaps it also accounts for their remarkably rapid acquisition of video-game skills, an area in which they typically outscore their elders.

It is possible to propose that these "neonatal" characteristics are not confined to the young but can be true at all age levels. Players need to be unrealistically optimistic, egocentrically motivated, and flexibly re-active (hyperreactive) to their play situation to be on top of it. Eighty-year-old golfers know very well that they can no longer reduce or even maintain their handicap; yet they go forth each day optimistically de-termined to perform better than the last time. Despite a lifetime of fail-ure, they persist, selectively and egocentrically, remembering their occasional victories; they are unrealistically optimistic. Beneath the etiquette of play there is also self-centered concern with personal vic-tory or personal fantasy. The thought that "we're number one" reigns in the hearts of all players and their supporters. "Look at me, look at me," says the four-year-old endlessly, as she jumps into the water or claims to be swimming. "Did you hear this one?" asks the old man at the bar, as he tells his latest or oldest fishing story. In addition, all social play requires extremely alert attention—to the context of play, the ac-tions, the equipment, the field, and the other players. The best players are magnificently reactive to novel stimulus opportunities, and their ecstasy may lie in the performance of unique ludic acts, whether in ball games, at the chess table, at poker, or in jumping out of trees.

So the peculiar association between play and growth in early child-hood, when it appears to assist maximal growth, in later years perhaps remains the possession of maturing persons who are still revived in everyday affairs by the optimism, egocentricity, and hyperreactivity with which they pursue their ludic activities. Looked at from the point of view of the player, who actively practices the fantasy of what is considered possible, the terms *enactive subunctivity* and *optimistic ludicism* appear very similar, although the former describes the acting out of possible play actions and the latter places these in the context of the roles of optimism, egocentricity, and lability in evolution. One might also say that the player of games of chance is an extreme case of one who refuses to believe that failure cannot be overcome.

The Player of Fate and Fortune

In the twentieth century the notions of progress and scientific rationality are so pervasive it is hard to realize that most humans, in prior eras and in most parts of the world still today, are more preoccupied with fate than they are with progress. The rhetoric of progress has a slim hold compared with the widespread rhetorics of fate and the exercises of divination, prayer, superstition, and gambling, through which attempts to influence fate are carried out.

In play, the ludic concern to receive the rewards of fate is exercised through the innumerable games of chance. As Roger Caillois puts it in his excellent account, *Man, Play and Games* (1961), these chance games are

> all games that are based on a decision independent of the player, an outcome over which he has no control, and in which winning is the result of fate rather than triumphing over an adversary. More properly destiny is the sole artisan of victory, and where there is rivalry what is meant is that the winner has been more favored by fortune than the loser. Perfect examples of this type are provided by the games of dice, roulette, heads or tails, baccarat, lotteries, etc. . . . [Chance] signifies and reveals the favor of destiny. The player is entirely passive: he does not deploy his resources, skill, muscles, intelligence. All he need do is await, in hope and trembling, the cast of the die . . . [Chance] negates work, patience, experience, qualifications . . . [it] grants the lucky player infinitely more than he could procure by a lifetime of labor, discipline, and fatigue. It seems an insolent and sovereign insult to merit. (p. 17)

> Recourse to chance helps people tolerate competition that is unfair or too rugged. At the same time it leaves hope in the dispossessed that free competition is still possible in the lowly stations of life. (p. 115)

There is a slight note of hysteria in this account, undoubtedly reflecting the generally negative attitude toward gamblers that has been a part of the past several centuries and that dominates most literature on games of chance or gambling. Now that so much gambling has been normalized, the participation of the masses is not quite so desperate as this account suggests, even if it is indeed a form of regressive taxation and accounts for an upsurge of addictives anonymous (Clotfelter and Cook, 1989). Furthermore, there is a great deal more insidious shrewdness, if not strategy, in many of these chance games than is always obvious on the surface. Caillois overemphasizes the passivity of the games. Still, given the omnipresence of progress rhetorics in modern life among the skillful and successful, it is not surprising that positive rhetorics for fate, fortune, chance, and gambling are found only in a minor key, despite the fact that more money is spent on these kinds of games than on all of the others combined. The estimate of $400 billion spent annually on such "playful" activities in the United States exceeds the combined total for all the other forms of play, as well as the defense budget. More people visit casinos than attend baseball games (Hirshey, 1994). In the United States, the older work-ethic rhetoric, which discounted gambling as a form of abnormality and often illegality, is gradually giving way to a consumer-oriented rhetoric in which legal forms of gambling are dubiously rationalized as harmless entertainment contributing money to the common welfare, as eliminating illegal gambling, and as stimulating city redevelopment (Abt et al., 1985). Current study seems to indicate that these claims are overly optimistic but are not without some validity in some locations (Peterson, 1995). However, even in this positive capitalistic vein, little attention is given to the value of games of chance in providing players with excitement and escape from everyday routine, as well as their being a way of enjoying the company of others in activities of circumscribed risk. While games of chance are being accepted into the ideology of the modern state, there is still reluctance to admit such games as a healthy form of play. The practice is said to be economically justified, but the pleasure of the players is seldom mentioned. In general there is no public play rhetoric for the play itself.

Something more needs to be said here about the conflict between modern religion and the rhetoric of fate. The historical and anthropological material show that they were once often tied together in ritual practice and festivals (Stallybrass and White, 1986). However, modern chance games and modern festivals have fallen away from religion and become secularized. Yet one can see that, along with all forms of play, they both still provide experiences of "otherness," "alterity," or "altered states of consciousness." And these or similar states of mind are as essential to religious ritual and prayer as they are to game involvement. In both cases one becomes "lost" in the experience and thus transcends everyday cares and concerns. It is worth considering that because the two (religion and play) are in modern times so separate, they are in effect rivals for the promotion of such altered states of consciousness. Which means they are rivals for the positive qualities that such alterity provides. One can say of both religion and play that they make life worth living and make everyday activities meaningful, because of the transcendence that they propose, one eternal and one mundane. Perhaps the unwillingness to attribute such experiential transcendence to games of fate exists not just because games of fate are heretical to the work ethic but because, through sharing transcendence with religion, they are actually rivals for its value. Believers are willing to acknowledge that religion has made their lives meaningful, but players are hesitant to say the same of their games, even though their endless obsession with those games suggests that this is indeed the case. This confines play to a secondary epistemological status. Players seldom say that if it weren't for their play their life would be meaningless. But this downgrading of play is a habit of Western self-conception rather than a necessary truth. One may suppose that with the development of the rhetoric of "optimal experience" (the rhetoric of the self), secular civilization may be gradually transforming itself to the point that it can indeed admit that play is as fundamental to life as are survival and religion. *The Feast of Fools* by Harvey Cox (1969) harbors just such an aspiration.

Because Abt and colleagues (1985) have found that the majority of players gamble moderately and with positive results for family life and pleasure, this strongly suggests that the copious psychological literature that focuses on only the pathological gambler is misleading as an account of the meaning of these kinds of play to ordinary people. Furthermore the puritanical unwillingness to entertain the idea that games of chance and gambling are indeed almost universal and normal forms of human play is part and parcel of a progress-oriented need to see play narrowly, as active and intrinsically motivated. The normality of such chance play actually suggests that it is quite possible for play to be both extrinsically motivated by anticipated rewards and relatively passive, as the players contribute very little to the outcome in some forms (lotteries, bingo, roulette). It is also possible for play to be much more active in other chance forms, such as various card games, particularly poker, which is a mixture of both chance and strategy. Furthermore both kinds of chance, active and reactive, are exciting forms of active fantasy as well as a direct experience of risk taking.

In sum, one can argue that chance play finds its motive in the excited arousal that it brings, regardless of whether this is personally activated, as in physical skill and strategy games, or impersonally activated, as in games of chance. What this might well also imply is that games of chance are a good metaphor for the other kinds of phenomena discussed in this chapter. These phenomena also picture the events and outcomes of play as originating outside the player, as when the gods are at play, the physical universe is at play, or the brain itself is (constantly) at play. Which is to say that luck can become a metaphor for fate (Rescher, 1995). Given that gambling phenomena are the original source of probability theory, which is the statistical method for analyzing the indeterminacy of most worldly things, it is as reasonable to see gambling as a metaphor for life as it is to count progress as such a metaphor (Gigerenzer et al., 1989). In this chapter, I am attempting to move toward a more cogent rhetoric for the kind of chance play events described, because, unlike in the other chapters, there is as yet no overall theory or rhetoric that adequately illustrates the breadth of the varied indeterminist and externalist matters involved.

Validations and Definitions

Several points might serve as validation for such a rhetoric of fate. First, the historical origins of the rhetoric of fate lie in our primitive desire to control the circumstances of life through magic and prayer. There is a broad and ancient history of cultural attempts to exercise such control through divination and magic and luck. Chance and gambling continue to carry on the spirit of these earlier forms of religiosity, but their contribution to modern well-being is still not as much acknowledged as the obsession with them suggests might be the case.

Advocates of a rhetoric of fate are those who own the gambling casinos and control sites of gambling, and they are churchmen and statesmen who see gambling as a way of raising money for their own charities and political institutions. The allegiance of the masses to these games is largely expressed with the rhetoric of their feet and their money as they frequent betting parlors, lottery windows, and, increasingly, casinos.

The play forms include games of chance, as well as betting on sports and any other events of uncertain outcome. There are multiple forms: slot machines, table games, pari-mutuel betting, horse racing, off-track betting, greyhound racing, jai alai, card games, bingo, legal bookmaking. And then there are the different games themselves: black jack, craps, roulette, baccarat, *Wheel of Fortune,* keno, pai gow, poker, and panguingui to mention a very small sample.

The players are players and gamblers who participate at levels from the simple (bingo) to the more complex (poker). But as Abt and colleagues (1985) point out, there are many kinds of players. They can be casual, occasional, risk-taking, professional, habitual, serious, obsessive, or compulsive, and each type of player has a different kind of play history and level of participation. All except the compulsive are more or less in control of their lives. The science behind the rhetoric of fate, the science that the players use, is the mathematics of probability theory.

Fate, with its emphasis on luck rather than talent, is the antithesis to the rhetoric of progress. As such it has been, and often is, an anathema to those who see life as manageable only in some rational or religious way. In an attempt to keep games of chance out of their lives, and out of their children's lives, the bourgeois have typically banned the games and any rhetorics speaking in their favor. The rhetoric of gambling has been a solidly negative rhetoric of avoidance for the past several hundred years in the West. At this present time, however, there is some moderation of the negative rhetoric. The virtues of state lotteries and selected casinos as sources of income to be used in charitable ways have become positive rhetorics, although these are now being counterbalanced by negative rhetorics that argue that new groups of low-income players are ruining themselves and their families through gambling addiction, and that political institutions gain little of value from these tax bases.

Obviously hegemony is disputed between those who control gambling and make money out of it, those who are abused by it, and those who seek to get rid of it or take over control. In a strong sense, there are two cultures that exist alongside each other and largely avoid each other in everyday life: one that lives for the control of fate through gambling and luck or through organizing these games for others, and the other that believes in the rational control of circumstances and in the work ethic. Both play different games and fight against each other's definitions of play, but—surprisingly enough—both advocacies find the games they pursue to be an exercise in optimism.

Given the generally negative public attitude toward games of chance and gambling, there are few treatises on the normal definitions for such games, though there is a host of theories on addiction. Game players and gamblers usually talk of the excitement of the games, of their fantasies of winning, or of getting out of the house and having the good company and conversation of the other players. Some lottery players say that, despite the fact that they know they will lose, they so enjoy the fantasy of winning, and dreaming of what they will do with their winnings, that it is well worth the price of the lottery ticket. One such gambler said that he had gotten more imaginative satisfaction out of his lottery tickets over the years than out of anything else in his life. Though he still hasn't ever had a winning ticket, he doesn't care. It is always the case that he might get one, and in the meantime he can continue to dream of purchasing boats and traveling the world. Some players speak also of the excitement generated by the settings of casinos and racetracks, both of which give the game situations a carnival atmosphere. A modern Las Vegas or Atlantic City casino is redolent with implied reward value. The mirrors, the thousands of busy players, the restaurants, the lights, the hostesses—all imply that one is in a zone of high excitement, not unlike being at a state fair, a carnival parade, or in a New Year's Eve crowd. In general, current data suggest that mild gambling and gaming are healthy recreative activities for the masses who pursue them (Halliday and Fuller, 1974).

There is an enormous body of psychoanalytic writing about gambling as a reflection of internal conflict of various kinds, with the theorists differing in whether they focus on sex, anality, masochism, and so on as the key terms for their analysis. In all of the theories the player is presumably driven to gambling activities by such internal conflict. In one example, attention is focused on inconsistently rewarding and punishing parents to explain gamblers' continued faith or lack of faith in their own gambling prospects. As Bergler puts it, games of chance are for losers, who know they are losers, and thus in a sense they have both the excitement of possibly winning and, more important, a way of gaining mastery over losing. Gamblers play in an attempt to be in control of their own losing. They are *psychic masochists*, says Bergler (1957). Unfortunately these theories cover the compulsive gamblers but none of the other categories of chance player mentioned above. A more rationalist theory of intrinsic motivation is the view that gambling is one of the few ways of risking something of personal value without the severely negative consequences that occur when you take real risks physically, emotionally, or socially. This is what makes it a play form, it is said, the fact that one can indeed take risks without disastrous consequences (Jones, 1973).

There are multiple opinions about the values of chance and gambling for society (Halliday and Fuller, 1974). There is the sociological rhetoric that gambling exists almost universally as a way for societies to give promise to those who are its failures. From potlatch to games of chance, it is said, there has to be some way in which fate can overturn the rich and lift the poor. In North American Indian potlatch ceremonies, often the wealthiest member of the tribe gave his possessions away, thus attaining the highest spiritual prestige. In modern games of chance, the reversals of fortune are less certain, but this is said to be the rationale behind the irrationality of the game. That is, that there is an egalitarian value to games of chance, because personal attributes count for nothing, and without these opportunities the poor might be more given to rebellion.

There is also the more cognitive psychological rhetoric that games of chance are models of the stock market and are a recreative form of the same values found in that vital economic activity. Games give clarity to these motives and activities in a way in which the confusion of everyday life cannot (Caillois, 1961). Thus much of human success requires making decisions in the face of uncertainty and having the courage to do so. Gambling, in these terms, is a model of courage and optimism. While it is not in itself typically a form of success, it is nevertheless a model of the belief that life should involve risk taking. At the same time, the progress-oriented opponents of these games would argue that they are only a perversion of play, that the games are controlled by external rewards that are real, and because these dominate the games, they are not a form of play. But, as noted, that criticism requires that play must be always only intrinsically rewarding, and this clearly need not be the case.

There is a metaphysical rhetoric that chance has religious not economic origins. What began as trial by ordeal, such as walking on hot coals to prove oneself innocent or drawing lots or other forms of testing, is said to be displaced into games of chance. According to this rhetoric, gambling is the poor man's religion; it is secularized divination. The virtue of this argument, if it has merit, is that it might help to explain the widespread hold that gaming has throughout the world. It is hard for modern civilization to accept that, even in today's world, chance games gain more attention (in monetary terms) than any other forms of play. This suggests that games of chance and gambling are so widespread because they are basically a kind of religious effort to deal with fate, a kind of existential optimism.

Returning momentarily to the nature of the progress rhetoric, and speaking quite speculatively, perhaps the paradox in which children are said to play and adults not to play has something to do with the contrast between the progress rhetoric and the rhetoric of fate. It could be argued, for example, that the emergence of childhood and the ideological desire for children to progress and to guarantee the future is more of a mythological hope than a product of reason. That is, the fate of children has behind it the kind of attitude of hopefulness that once was admitted only of religion. In their way, it might be said, children guarantee the future beyond our own mortality, just as do the gods. We pray to the gods and we school the children, different agencies for a common attempt to reckon with our own mortality. If there is any truth to this speculation, it might explain why we so restrict children's behavior and only favor it if it guarantees their own progressive development. They are not supposed to play for immortal solace, as we do, they are supposed, like Alice in Wonderland, to conduct their divinely sexless, affectless, rational pursuit of development through play. If there is any sense to this speculation, then the rhetoric of progress would be just a special case of the rhetorics of fate, and the progress of children would be another name for the way we use childhood as a lottery, to guarantee ourselves a brief immortality through their continuance.

The massive amounts of money spent on games of chance make them arguably the most important form of play in the modern world. They provide an underpinning of mass irrationality within our otherwise rationally structured urban societies. And yet, unlike all other forms of play, games of chance can perhaps be taken to give a fairer metaphysical representation of the actual chaos of both nature and humanity. Rhetorics of chance, or fate, speak more broadly to our immortal apprehensions, just as the progress rhetoric speaks more narrowly to our mortal aspirations. More important, games of chance show that it is possible for play to be largely passive, not involving much activity even when players take risks. They are also largely controlled by external rewards and involve an intermixture of the irreal (dice, roulette wheels, cards) and the real (money). The games are not only for the games' sake, they have external consequences; they are for money. Play and life interpenetrate here more completely than with any other games, and so these games deny the other definitions of play to be found in the majority of modern texts on the subject, where the player is supposed to be unconcerned with matters outside of the game, concerned only with means, not ends; where the play is supposed to be dominated by the player, who is active in decision making, and where there is freedom from externally imposed rules. Games of chance negate the supposed universality of that ever present, very modern philosophy of ludic voluntarism.

Finally, games of chance make it clearer than does the progress rhetoric that ambiguity lies in the character of play as well as in the advocacies of rhetoric. If play is top down or bottom up (Handelman), transformationally labile (Schechner), illusion (Erikson), virtual (Turkle), and dreamlike (Singer), and if the brain is at play as a neural fabulator (Sacks and Edelman), then the sources of ambiguity are manifold. All of these baffling possibilities suggest why there is an enmity between this and the prior rhetoric of progressive rationality. One might say that the rhetorics of progress and of fate are rivals for the human soul.

5

Rhetorics of Power

Play up! play up! and play the game!
Sir Henry Newbolt

The prior chapters have encountered play under the banners of progress and fatalism. This chapter, by contrast, and with as much willfulness as the others, presents the theories that the major form of human play is that of contest and that contests have a civilizing influence (Huizinga, 1955), and that play expressions can be viewed as either uncivilized, irrational expressions of power or as civilized and rational ones (Spariosu, 1989). In addition, there are the theories that play's cultural function is to mediate social conflict (Turner, 1969); that major social forms of play are introduced and manipulated for their own benefit by the rulers of society (Mac-Aloon, 1981; Azoy, 1982; Aercke, 1994); that the subordinate classes sometimes invert these play forms to express their own hidden rhetorics of resistance or subversion (Babcock, 1978; Gruneau, 1983; Scott, 1990; McMahon and Sutton-Smith, 1995); and that social play can be used even as a text to "interpret" the power relationships within the culture (Geertz, 1973). Most of these works about play as power refer to either one or both of the two most important forms of contest in society: those of physical skill and those of intellectual strategy. While they have contest in common, they are otherwise very different.

There is also a body of psychological literature about play as more or less a form of individual power expression. This includes the most primordial of modern play theories, Schiller's contention in the eighteenth century that play is due to the overflow of surplus energy (Schiller, 1965, p. 133), and instinct theories, which say that play is an expression of inborn and primitive forces (McDougall, 1923). It would certainly include aggression catharsis theories such as that expressed by Menninger (1942), and it might include Freud's emphases on abreaction and wish fulfillment, which he sometimes describes very much as if they are expressions of compensatory power (1959). However, as Freud is the genius who does more than anyone else to convert Western thinkers from cultural and genetic explanations for personal behavior to intrapsychic explanations, he primarily merits recognition as the father of the rhetoric of the self, where play explanations are located in the individual rather than in the collective society. He cannot be held accountable for the origin-of-power theories of play, which in historical terms far preceded him.

This chapter is about adult play. It takes for granted that sports, festivals, and contests are indeed matters of play and that the play concept is not to be applied only to children. Considerations of play and power come under various names, such as warfare, hegemony, conflict, competition, glory, manliness, contest, and resistance. Some of these are quite ancient terms historically, preceding the modern rhetorics of progress, the imaginary, and the self. The ancient power and identity rhetorics are also collective concepts, whereas the modern rhetorics generally focus on individuals. In modern times, however, the concept of power has also been applied in play theory to solitary play: the child plays because he enjoys the power of being a cause, or because he doesn't have power and in play is seeking empowerment as a kind of compensation or wish fulfillment. On the social play level, the general idea of the power rhetoric is that play or games or sports or athletics that have to do with some kind of contest and reflect a struggle for superiority between two groups (two people, two communities, two tribes, two social classes, two ethnic groups, two or more nations) exist because they give some kind of representation or expression to the existing real conflict between these groups. Whichever side wins the game or contest is said to bring glory to its own group, bonding the members together through their common contestive identity. Furthermore the two groups typically have in common their enthusiasm for this kind of contest, which may thus unite rather than divide them.

Those who study what is called the *agon motif*, however, typically associate contestive games with warfare and see these games originally as a means of socialization for warfare, not unlike what rough-and-tumble is supposed to do in preparing animals for fighting (Sipes, 1973; Chick, Loy, and Miracle, 1994; Loy and Hesketh, 1995). As I have shown, the animal evidence is not very convincing, and the human evidence does not appear to be either. Warlike cultures have warlike games, but here games are as likely to be expressive correlates as causal linkages. It is often difficult to decide whether the central theme of this kind of conflict play is superiority and conquest or the vindication of community identity. These are typically related themes, as, for example, in Victor Turner's view (1969) that festivals are both a way in which intracommunity conflict is mediated and also a successful way in which a greater sense of community, or "communitas," is engendered. Nevertheless there are some distinctive examples in which the two, power and identity, are relatively separable, as, for example, in most individualistic sports, in which power is said to prevail, in contrast with the new games movement (Fluegelman, 1976; De Koven, 1978) and some feminist writings in which games of cooperative identity are said to prevail (Oriard, 1991). The rhetoric of power and the rhetoric of traditional community identity are treated separately here and in Chapter 6 because, despite their linkages, they do seem to express quite different and often opposed ideologies.

Before proceeding further, however, I must stress that the terms of the power rhetorics, as in the case of the progress rhetorics, may have little to do with what the playing means to the players. Whether or not the players discuss their own contests in terms of these rhetorics, they must deal with the contests in terms of the actions that are specific to the play itself. The contests have to do with balls and bats, movements and strategies, and players spend years practicing them; in general they continue their games because they get immense satisfaction from specific moves in specific contests on both micro and macro levels: the momentary hitting of the ball as well as the larger winning of the game. This is similar to saying that the young child playing with building blocks is preoccupied with how the blocks go together but not concerned with educators' progress rhetorics about the role of block building in learning spatial relationships. Of course, adults in contest play may have in mind some of the larger ideological rhetorics under discussion here, but that is an imposition not typically required by the game playing itself. The rhetoric and the play are never identical. It has been said, for example, that it is easier for us to learn the games of another group than to learn their language; a naive understanding of play in animals and humans seems to be fairly immediate (Keesing, 1960).

Having said this, it must be admitted that in some cultures there may well be a greater overlap between the character of the moves in the game and the character of rhetorics about the game than is generally true in the modern case. "In Japanese Sumo wrestling, for example, which is the national sport of Japan, the wrestling is regarded as more than a sport; it is seen as an epitome of Japanese honor and the national ethos" (WuDunn, 1996). Sumo wrestling has spiritual ties to Shinto, the traditional Japanese religion, and Japanese emperors over the centuries have had a special attachment to it, sometimes being selected to rule through the contest itself. It is likely that the identification of rhetoric and action was higher like this in much earlier human culture. The connection of Americans with Superbowls and the World Series still carries a strong remnant of the connection between the requirements of the game and the character requirements for the players. Similarly one might ask two Olympic runners how much of their thought while racing is given to the moves within the race, how much to the gold medals that might follow it, and how much to the glory of the country they represent. It would seem that, during the race, the race itself provides all the meaning they need. But it must also be said that the notion that play has such independent meaning of its own, beyond the larger religious, warrior, or nationalistic rhetorics usually attributed to it, is a modern concept, in line with the kinds of rhetorics represented by those of the imaginary and the self. One might suppose that among the very young, the meaning of solitary play lies more in the idiosyncratic play actions themselves, but that with the acquisition of language more communal meanings (such as gender) begin to play a part: "This is for boys"; "this is for girls." During childhood, players hear peer, family, school, and commercial communications, and in addition to their enjoyment of the play itself, these become a part of their play at some of many possible levels. Presumably the more homogeneous the community, the earlier dominating rhetorics will penetrate the actual play. Later (with the rhetoric of frivolity) it will be claimed that this penetration is more true of homogeneous traditional communities. All of which is to say that the play and the game are played partly for their own sake and partly for the values attributed to them within the ideologies that are their context. The more naive the players, the greater the possibility that they are playing for their own sake. However, the social hierarchies of the sibling, peer, or family play group soon bring important hierarchical power considerations to the acts of power that are displayed.

Rational versus Irrational Power Forms

The two scholars of play theory who have dealt most directly with the rhetorics of conflict and power in play are Johan Huizinga and Mihail Spariosu, the first a historian and the second a classicist. Huizinga is the most influential of all historical scholars of play, probably in part because of his positive evocation of this machismo rhetoric of play as conflict. In *Homo Ludens: A Study of the Play Element in Culture,* first published in 1949, he suggests the highly novel notion that the major contestive and festival forms of play are a form of civilization. His claim is particularly remarkable in terms of the long-standing puritanical rhetoric that holds play to be useless, even dangerous, to Christian culture. In a sense both the rhetoric of progress and his particular rhetoric of power share this inversion of that earlier Christian rhetoric. Huizinga's position is that there is a morphological parallelism between playful contests and the actual contestive conduct of politics, the law, scholarship, and the arts. The forms of culture arise, he says, in such playful antitheses. From sports to crossword puzzles, people who are pitted against each other or who pit themselves against any obstacle in a way that requires skill can be at play or at work. Out of their desire to win or succeed, and the honor of so doing, they lift higher the aspirational levels of human society, even if their contests are to the death. From contest (power) comes the development of the social hierarchies (identity) around which the society constructs its values. "The point is for us that all these contests, even when fantastically depicted (in legend and story) as mortal and titanic combats with all their peculiarities still belong to the domain of play" (1955, p. 55).

The playful contests themselves, Huizinga says, are in earlier societies woven into the mythical ritual patterns of the culture as a means to affect and determine the ripening of the crops, the smooth running of the season, and the prosperity of the whole year. "Every victory represents, that is, realizes for the victor, the triumph of the good powers over the bad, and at the same time the salvation of the group that effects it" (p. 56). "From the life of childhood right up to the highest achievements of civilization one of the strongest incentives to perfection, both individual and social, is the desire to be praised and honored for one's excellence . . . Competition serves to give proof of superiority. This is particularly true of archaic society" (p. 63).

Huizinga includes not only physical contests but also slanging matches, debates, boasts, gift giving (potlatches), parading of wealth, drinking contests, abusing and deriding adversaries, beauty contests, singing, riddling, keeping awake. All of these and many other playful contests are the forms through which civilization rises and develops. As time passes, he says, they are unfortunately smothered and lost, becoming not civilization's foundation but merely secondary, as play. Only in archaic times is culture truly inspissated with the playful use of contestive forms. Huizinga is extremely pessimistic about modern professional forms of play, because they have been appropriated for the enrichment of the owners rather than existing as a display of virtue by the people.

There are many critics of Huizinga's excellent history. They wonder about all the forms of cooperative, solitary, or mental play that are not always based on contest and which he does not consider. They also argue that he has idealized certain kinds of contestive play in ritual contexts without admitting that most modern kinds of play are in different ways equally serious and equally playful, even if there is often more differentiation of the two forms, play and work. They also suspect that his contestive forms "in the play of culture" are abstract structural forms or "platonic universals" rather than something arrived at by the empirical examination of the historical record (Anchor, 1978; Gruneau, 1983; Duncan, 1988; Loy, 1995). Huizinga's thesis is also a particularly agonistic and machismo view of play history. His definition of play primarily as contest reflects the widespread male rhetoric that favors the exaltation of combative power instead of speaking comprehensively about play itself. Combat may be widespread but it is hardly a universal truth about all play forms.

More typically in Western culture, where play has been thought of as trivial or secondary, contests have been seen as a relatively nonserious expression of the general character of the people who play them. There are other theorists, however, who, though they have not given contests quite the formative and originative place in culture that Huizinga does, have at least given them the milder merit of being a catharsis or displacement of real conflict into the less harmful arena of play. This has been a common point of view in much of psychology and anthropology, although it has never had very strong research support. That may well be a function of the difficulty of adequately operationalizing the concept of catharsis for research purposes. It has also been said that this displacement of aggression into play permits the development of community among, and even between, groups of opposing players. Turner suggests that as societies are always suffering from internal and external conflict, they must find ways of mediating the problems that arise from such conflicts. They use war, they use law, they emigrate, they immigrate, and they also use forms of play as ways of taking the murder out of their conflicts while at the same expressing them (Turner, 1969). Not surprisingly, an even stronger idealization of the value of contests is to be found in those (progress rhetoric) works on children and adolescents that view sports as a socialization into the values of the larger society "based on the premise that sport is an integral aspect of society and culture that frequently and significantly affects individuals and groups . . . similar to the family" (McPherson, Curtis, and Loy, 1989, p. xii).

Other thinkers put forward a contrasting and more cynical view of the contestive nature of much play. The most striking is Mihail Spariosu, who, in his brilliant work *Dionysus Reborn* (1989), contends that there has always been disagreement among Western philosophers over whether play is basically an orderly and rule-governed affair, as Huizinga supposes, or a chaotic, violent, and indeterminate interaction of forces. Spariosu says, "I relate my history of the play concept to a history of the Western mentality as a whole, suggesting that this mentality has always fluctuated between various rational and prerational sets of values" (1989, p. ix). His work is an analysis of play in the light of the two power rhetorics that, as he contends, have prevailed throughout the ages. According to Spariosu, on the one hand there are the *orderly* rule-bound games of strategy and physical skill. There are children supposedly learning from their play in school and from their toys. There is play held up as a transcendental state of being or "flow," and there is the orderly play of girls in their folk games. All of this puts play in the category of order and civilization, as Huizinga does. But on the other hand there is also the play of *disorder:* games of chance, of symbolic inversion, of carnival, of "deep play," as well as the "games people play," "war toys," playfighting, play therapy, the thermonuclear war games of the military, "the gamesman," play as paradox, and the "masks of play," to mention a number of titles from the scholarship about play, all of which betoken some kind of disorder or chaos. Spariosu's own rhetoric is that while most Western philosophers have sought to rationalize play, to give it an orderly meaning as a contribution to society, as is done for children by declaring play a form of "progress," there is another modern approach that heralds play's basic indeterminism, chaos or irrationality (much of which has been described in Chapter 4). However, the philosophical evidence he cites in favor of the irrational play rhetoric seems relatively minor. For good or ill, as he demonstrates cogently, rationalistic thought seems to have dominated most Western thinking about play.

Part of the problem with this particular controversy over the kind of power reflected in play is that it is not always clear whether the theorist is talking metaphysically, about views of the world as orderly or chaotic, or empirically, about real games and festivals as orderly or chaotic. Obviously games and festivals are usually more orderly than chaotic or they could not take place on schedule. And if they are orderly, then they can hardly be totally irrational, as even a game of chance is not, with its organized arrangement of lotteries and casinos, and its many games, such as poker and bridge, in which strategy also plays a part. At the same time, it may often be the case that an author is using the term *irrational play* only as a metaphor, and thus is free to pick out this or that aspect for his own metaphoric and metaphysical purposes. Still it is true that, as Spariosu says, there are two conflicting rhetorics about the play: one that says it is positive, as a mode of cultural origination, humanization, catharsis, or socialization, and another that says it is a site for power seeking, domination, and hegemony, or disorder, inversion, and resistance. In short, playful contests as pictured in interpretive thought are a Rorschach, a projective screen, for scholars' ideological preferences. Play, which we have already found to be labile for rhetorical interpretations (such as progress), is equally a fulcrum for rhetorical conflict about play as conflict.

The rhetoric of play as rational power is also manifest in *game theory*, which is an attempt to use games of strategy, such as chess, to work out the systematics for anticipating an opponent's moves (Von Neumann and Morgenstern, 1944; Schelling, 1960; Rapoport, 1960), or, alternatively, to use the game models to develop processes for conflict reduction between warring groups (Tedeschi, Schlenker, and Bonoma, 1973). In one erstwhile scenario, rational Russians and rational Americans go about planning strategies for their zero-sum games, each group hoping to maximize its own gains at the expense of its opponent's. An empirical cross-cultural extension of the notion that games are models of rational power is found in the work of Roberts and collaborators, who assessed the child rearing, ecological, technological, and other correlates of the games of strategy, physical skill, and chance in several hundred societies available for analysis in the Human Relations Area Files. They were able to show that games are systematically related to culture in various statistically quantifiable ways and are not merely happenstance expressions. They proposed a theory about the way in which certain patterns of child rearing induce interest in games, which lead to forms of learning that are culturally useful. According to the conflict enculturation theory of games, children learn how to exercise power over others by cunning, physical skill, or spirituality. The results of their work are recorded in multiple publications (Roberts, Arth, and Bush, 1959; Roberts and Sutton-Smith, 1962; Roberts, Sutton-Smith, and Kendon, 1963; Roberts, Hoffman, and Sutton-Smith, 1965; Roberts, Thompson, and Sutton-Smith, 1966; Sutton-Smith and Roberts, 1963, 1964; Sutton-Smith et al., 1967; Sutton-Smith 1970a, 1972b, 1973a, 1973b, 1973c, 1973d, 1974a, 1974b, 1974g; Textor, 1967; Roberts and Barry, 1976; Chick 1994). As with most of the other progress rhetoric literature, the correlational character of these power findings makes the meaning of the empirical relationships discovered quite uncertain. Empirical discrepancies (Townshend, 1978), and the widespread and easy diffusion of all kinds of games in modern life strongly suggest that additional principles may be required to understand the way in which games as models come into being (Guttman, 1994), although the patterns of power discussed by Roberts and colleagues are also a part of the ludic variance within cultural history.

The use of the metaphor of games as a conflict-managing device has spread in modern society beyond these original applications. It is now applied to the marketplace, where the "gamesman" is imagined to be the coolest, least ethical, and most single-minded user of powerful winning strategies (Maccoby, 1976). It is also applied to therapy situations, as in Eric Berne's popular book *The Games People Play* (1964), which is about sinister, largely unconscious manipulations carried out by individuals supposedly joined by marriage or business but actually implicitly engaged in a hostile relationship. The same cynical but mellifluous use of the game metaphor is also reflected in political usage: Nixon talked about our "game plan" in Cambodia, thus reducing the horror of bombing that country. Clifford Geertz gives the award for disseminating the metaphor of games into the everyday sociology of American society to the famous sociologist Erving Goffman, about whom he writes, "The image of society that emerges from Goffman and from that of the swarm of scholars who in one way or another follow or depend on him, is of an unbroken stream of gambits, ploys, artifices, bluffs, disguises, conspiracies and outright impostures as individuals and coalitions of individuals struggle, sometimes cleverly, more often comically, to play enigmatical games whose structure is clear but whose point is not" (Geertz, 1983, p. 170; see also Sutton-Smith, 1987a).

On behalf of game theory, I must stress that it has also been idealized as a route to answering to the problems of education, administration, and politics, and it is said to bring to them a vitality not present in the usual forms of conflict resolution. As Abt says in his work *Serious Games:*

> Reduced to its formal essence, a game is an activity among two or more independent decision makers seeking to achieve their objectives in a limiting context . . . the emotional creative, dramatic

component of the game is made up of a curious combination of optimistic belief in the luck of "another chance" and a pessimistic respect for the odds, the chanciness of it all. It is basically an existential view of man's acting, despite uncertainty, to achieve conflicting goals that end up mattering less than the action itself . . . It is also . . . [romantic] . . . in its view of life as conflict, with others, with nature, with the self, but always unresolved oppositions, uncertainties, overcoming of obstacles. And it offers a kind of spiritual conquest of all evils by incorporating them into stimulaing adversary roles that are as necessary to the good as the black is to the red—something the religion game developed long ago. (1971, p. 6)

There has also been much such advocacy of game playing as a useful form of education for adolescents (Coleman, 1961).

Finally, play as a rhetoric of power and conflict can hardly be discussed without introducing *psychoanalysis* and its perennial concern with psychological conflict and therapy. Unlike all of the above rhetorical scenarios, this is one primarily about internal personal conflict (rather than external social conflict), and the play interpretation is a part of Freud's immense historical role in turning human concerns about reality away from the political to the personal level. While the inner conflicts he describes—supposedly between id and super ego, precariously balanced by the ego—are often irrational from a public point of view, that irrationality can, according to the doctrine, be rationalized by the play therapists who use play itself as both a diagnostic screen and a cure; the child works through the conflicts in play, giving himself the illusion of greater ego mastery and, with the help of a therapist, a greater understanding and control of himself. Whatever the merits of this view as science or therapy, both much disputed, it has certainly contributed to the "personalization" of politics and the conversion of television talk shows, court cases, and political elections into the kind of events that used to be found only in group psychotherapy sessions. According to some, ours has become a psychological society focused on personal conflicts (Gross, 1978; Reiff, 1966). If that is the case, play techniques of the individual and the group kind, as well as those of the mass kind (sports, festivals), have achieved an ideological rationalization that places them at the center of the conflicts in modern society.

There is a paradox in interpreting Freudian theory as a power theory, however, because although directly concerned with conflicts on an intrapersonal level, it seeks to use play mediation of those conflicts to reduce conflict on the social level. Play not only assuages personal conflict, it can also increase social adjustment. This can be thought of as a Foucaultian use of clinical play therapy to improve the socialization of maladjusted persons (1976). The theory discusses the power of the play, when it is perhaps the power of the therapist that is primary. But still, if the therapy works, it is again a nice example of the way in which the merits of play are transferred to the necessities of adjustment, through the play's being embedded in the power rhetorics of the theorist. From all of this it can be concluded that the power rhetorics, no less than the progress rhetorics, are forms of propaganda forever "playing" about the ecstatic competitive ludic forms within the culture, forever displaying the fantasies, anxieties, and urges of those who are actually powerful about what the play culture should mean and how its members should behave. Such a power ideology is parasitic on play just as it is on sex or art, other forms of ecstatic culture that similarly threaten to distract its members from the purposes of those who govern it. On these grounds play rhetorics, whether ideological or scientific, appear to be largely special cases of cultural hegemony.

The Machismo Immortality of Play

Games and play have often been associated with religious ceremonies such as funerals and fertility rites. Although the two, religion and play, are contrasted in Western society as sacred versus profane, in many societies some forms of contestive and festive play have been received as sacred and as obligatory on ceremonial occasions. And in some mythologies, as noted in Chapter 4, it is the gods at play who determine events in the universe. Even in modern society, in the past one hundred years, there has been a constant association made between games, sports, and moral development. It is possible to speculate that the primordial association of the two, play and religion, is due to the power of alterity, or otherness, that they both share. They both take participants beyond their present circumstances, one through prayer, meditation, song, or rapturous transport, the other through ecstatic play in the game. In both there is the experience of being possessed by something other and greater than the self. Similarly, as immortality is often the focus of religion, so superior sports figures may be mythologized as "immortals" in popular discourse. Religion and sport are ways of going beyond the restrictions of everyday life. In both, the participants may surpass themselves and gain a new sense of empowerment. What is a potential and yet unlimited promise in religion is an actual but temporary gift in play. Both offer the sense that the limitations of life can be transcended. When Native Americans once played lacrosse so hard, to speed the soul of a dead man on its proper path, the two genres, religion and play, coalesced (Salter, 1977). All of which suggests that, together with the various meanings of power discussed in this chapter—the power of the players over each other or over their opponents, the power of the organizers and owners over the players and their audience—there is also the issue of divine power and its role in play's empowerment. This is most obviously expressed in modern times when the boxer, for example, having pounded his opponent into the canvas, momentarily sinks to his knees in the corner, crosses himself, and gives thanks to God for his participation in the victory. The rhetoric of divine power is used to rationalize a direct manifestation of athletic power. Unlike with the progress rhetoric discussed in the prior chapters, however, where various claims on behalf of the way play contributes to orthodox school progress seem to gain little empirical support, despite some educators' support, in this case the adult male population believes so strongly in the virtues of the conflict validity of sports that they attribute a deific masculine resonance to all of those who play such sports. Progress play rhetoric may not credibly make a scholar, but power play rhetoric appears to constantly and successfully rationalize the warrior.

Validations and Definitions

The power rhetoric has ancient connections with the rhetorics of warfare and social hegemony. Its advocates vary from warmongers to football coaches. Its form is that of contest and sport. Its players are athletes or gladiators. The relevant disciplines tend to be mathematics (game theory) and the sociologies and histories of sports and power. The relationship of play to life and life to play, understood by the public, gives these games more grandeur than any other, as indicated by the playing of national anthems at sports and athletic events. These are the forms of play with the greatest public prestige in the modern world. They are the hegemonic forms of play in which the hegemony is typically that of the politically powerful over the less powerful, of the owners over the team. It is also, even more pervasively, the hegemony of men over women. Until recently in Western society, and most other societies, women seldom had a place in these kinds of play. They were condemned to the presumed frivolity of their own lesser play forms.

Defining these forms of play is complex. Most of the interpretations provided in the case of the rhetorics of progress also apply here: pleasure, escape, tension release, and displays of skill, none of which need have much to do with power. The players say they are involved in these sports for the joy of winning, for personal prestige, out of rivalry with competitors, and to develop "manly" skills. These are power-relevant variables. However, there is no limit to the ingenious possible explanations of play, as was evident in interviews conducted by Michael Dibb in his five-episode BBC television program *The Fields of Play* (1982).* In program four, "Playing Ball," Dibb interviews a number of ball game experts who have quite different things to say about the character of their games. An expert on juggling, for example, says that the extraordinary dexterity involved in juggling balls distracts the imagination and draws breathless admiration. "To do what appears as an impossibility and to do it with all the ease, the grace, the carelessness imaginable, is a skill surmounting difficulty and beauty, triumphing over skill . . . One of the interesting things about ball games," he continues, "is the way in which they do make space articulate. You are aware of space in a totally different way."

In the same television program, a pinball machine inventor says, by contrast, "Pinball is a kind of microcosm of American capitalism . . . it's a parody . . . of the capitalistic nature of the game in which everything is based on a 'win' situation." Since the fifties and science

---

The Fields of Play was a five-part television series produced and directed by Michael Dibb for the BBC. It was broadcast weekly, beginning March 18, 1982. I served as a consultant for the entire program and was the central commentator in episode one, "The Meaning of Play."

fiction movies, he opines, the man versus machine aspect has become a predominant factor. Switching to yet another kind of ball game, a tennis player on this program says, "I think women's tennis is a ballet type of game. It's got beautiful movements and I think there is nothing else that combines that beauty of movement with the tremendously graceful spirit. But it really is also an assassin's game: if one person has won, the other one is dead. There is no compromise. I become quite aggressive on court. I get a thrill out of hitting a winner." In the same vein, an American football professional says, "Football is not fun and games. It is an expression of the darker side of the individual. It is not, 'Let's go out and have a good time.' It's, 'Let's go out and beat the other team, let's pound them into submission, let's intimidate them and show that we are better than they are' . . . As it gets down to game time, the personality changes, the darker side, this different person comes out. But the game itself, the physically doing it and the physically being involved and being challenged and being put to the test, that fear of failure, I enjoy it, or though I don't enjoy it, at least it provides something for me."

About another type of contest, games of strategy (program five), David Spanier, author of *Total Poker,* says: "You've got to be aggressive, you have got to be cunning, you have got to be ruthless. At the same time, you have to give the impression of being a jolly good fellow that people want to have in their game. But it's not a matter of the cards so much as your feel for the other people around the table, the man you are playing against. You have to judge him, to see what he is doing. I suppose the key to it all is to have the kind of control and detachment which can analyze all these things and can control your own emotions. At the same time, really get in there and bet."

The comments made on this BBC television program provide just the slightest glimpse of the multiplicity of reasons why people play games and sports. While there are echoes of power rhetorics here, in both sport and strategy games, the specifics of particular forms of play, the actions and the objects, are also a primary source of values that players attribute to their play. What seems most intrinsically motivating to players are the intrinsic elements of the play processes themselves; they are attractive, exciting, and at times even beautiful to the ordinary participants.

The theorists generally give intrinsic motivational explanations more general grounds. Innumerable examples from sports theory specialists may be offered. This from Kenyon (1978) is representative: he says that the physical activity of sports and athletics is intrinsically motivating because it is a social experience, creates health and fitness, is a pursuit of vertigo, is aesthetic, is cathartic, and is ascetic. The social element, he says, refers to the sports' providing means for meeting other people and perpetuating existing relationships. Health and fitness follow the practice of the activity itself, and the same forms often potentiate feelings of beauty. By the pursuit of vertigo, he means that the physical experience provides risks with elements of thrill that arise through the media of speed, acceleration, sudden change in direction, and exposure to dangerous situations, with the participant usually remaining in control. Catharsis follows, he says, because the physical activity is perceived to provide, through some vicarious means, a release of tension precipitated by frustration. The ascetic character of sport refers to the long, often painful training involved and the stiff competition, both of which demand a deferment of gratification. This connotational mélange entails much that is intrinsically satisfying about sports, as well as implying much that requires considerable self-denial, which is resonant of the rhetorics of power.

In 1989 Kenyon's colleagues McPherson, Curtis, and Loy offered a somewhat revised accounting of sport as a form of intrinsic communication. They conceded that the competitiveness of sport would typically be extrinsically motivated by prestige, prizes, and money, but added that, following Goffman (1961a), sport has two major intrinsic elements, those of uncertain outcome and sanctioned display. These are the two elements that make it fun. The uncertainty provokes suspense and excitement. The sanctioned display allows for demonstrations of physical prowess, dexterity, strength, knowledge, intelligence, courage, and self-control (p. 17).

John M. Roberts, an expert on strategy games, offers a somewhat more mundane explanation in *The Fields of Play:*

> The game in my view is an "aspirin" for headaches developed in living in stratified societies. You simply cross-culturally don't find games of strategy existing in the absence of social hierarchy . . . and

now that we have the most complex society of all, one has a proliferation of games of strategy. There are games about tax evasion,
games about monopoly, about socialism, capitalism, and war. All
these elements of life with a highly strategic component in them
seem to be giving rise to play forms of the same thing . . . And that
suggests that a lot of people, despite the current conditions, are
developing headaches which are assuaged by these games. (Dibb,
1982, program five)

What must not be forgotten in these various accounts of contest is
that there are legitimate power interests intrinsic to the contest. The
application of force, skill, and leadership in actions and strategies
within the game are intrinsic power concerns. One would also suppose that the power politics of the contests and games themselves
(who gets to be leader, who gets the lowest roles, who gets elimi-
nated) are also intrinsic power concerns. Which is to say, power is an
essential ludic concept in these games, contests, and sports, and it will
continue to be, regardless of any rhetorics that are added to it. Where
interpreters go wrong at this level is in discounting the importance
of all the other kinds of play to be found in the other rhetorics
outlined in this book. Here the assertion of contest as the key form
of play is pure rhetoric.

But the greatest attention in scholarship on sports and contests has
been to the extrinsic functions performed by these play forms, such
as their being a preparation for war training, a patriotic duty, a test
of manliness, and so forth (Loy and Hesketh, 1995). This is, of
course, where the power rhetoric of play has its strongest representation as play theory. Play is exalted as a sanctification of power or
derided for its violence and the Machiavellianism with which it is
associated. The price for the rhetoric of power's having priority in the
world is the suspicions that it evokes in those who do not see it as fit
to be so honored. Finally, ambiguity surely exists between the joy that
contestive action evokes and the rhetorics of their ideological manipulation. But the contests themselves, as strategic ploys, also foster
the tactics of ambiguity as part of their modes of success.

6

Rhetorics of Identity

Folklore is said to be the study of artistic communication in small groups. But folk festivals can be better defined as the study of grotesque misrepresentation in groups of any size.

after Frech

The rhetorics of identity focus on the use of play forms as forms of bonding, including the exhibition and validation or parody of membership and traditions in a community. This expression is most often found in parades, celebrations, carnivals, and the use of play as a sanction for community. But it holds true as well for parochial, familial, or lovers' social playfulness and togetherness. Typically communities demonstrate both their power and their identity through sporting success or festival occasions. Most of the proponents of identity rhetorics, however, are talking about play as a form of bonding (Betcher, 1987), family interdependence (Greenfield and Cocking, 1994), cooperation (De Koven 1978), or *communitas* (Turner, 1969). In general these power and identity scholars do not present explicit play theories; rather they use examples of play to interpret the societies in which they are found or to interpret the findings of prior interpreters (Stewart, 1991). Following Geertz (but ultimately following Freud) communal play is typically treated as diagnostic material for cultural interpretation.

It is difficult to distinguish the rhetoric of power from the rhetoric of identity. The purpose of most conflicts, contests, and expressions of power is to prove the superiority of one's own identity, community, and traditions. In a general way, however, sports and contests are rhetorized as expressions of competitive power, while parades and celebrations and other mass spectacles are rhetorized as expressing traditional identity and community. James Fernandez has placed such issues of play at the heart of his theorizing. In his *Persuasions and Performances: The Play of Tropes in Culture* (1986), he says explicitly that such ludic performances are arranged to persuade ourselves (and others) to adopt the communal view of ourselves that we prefer. They are metaphoric representations of our own identity in grand terms. Fernandez, an anthropologist, appears to adopt the psychological view that we humans are argumentative beings, riven with uncertainty, and we need to set up these figurative realms (parades and the like) to persuade ourselves that we belong together. In his work *Beyond Metaphor: The Theory of Tropes in Anthropology* (1991), however, it is clear that he means this to be a collective cultural practice, not just a psychological disposition. Thus by performing mutually before each other in these play events, and by inventing them in the first case, we humanize ourselves and soften the contradictions that might otherwise spell disaster. The irony of celebrating our contestive and disorderly natures is, apparently, that we transcend them in these figurative ways. So what we have in Fernandez's account is a rhetoric about the transcendent and integrative character of group play as itself an "enactive rhetoric" that persuades us of the worth of belonging together. While it is becoming typical in scholarship these days to think of the communal identity of a playing group, or a folk group, as a product of such social imagining or invention, this was not always the case (Noyes, 1995). Group identity was said to be a matter of tradition or ethnos, race or nation. But whatever the rationalization, what is constant from earlier times to the present is this same rhetoric on the key nature of communal identity in the life of the folk, whoever they may be. Whatever the play value of festivals may actually be, or the power of the community may actually be, the rhetoric of identity through festivals has been with us in some form or other since the beginning of academic folklore (Stewart, 1991). One must remember, however, as Noyes says, that "a festival declared by all to be a celebration of unity is in fact animated by vigorous factionalism" (1995, p. 449).

The rhetoric of Fernandez is a very positive rhetoric about play, like that of Huizinga. Both find an ultimate social good in the playful contests and parades of humankind, though Fernandez focuses on communal ecstasies while Huizinga focuses on agonistic ones. In both cases the theoretical rhetorics subsume play. Fernandez and Huizinga make play subserve their own interpretive concerns with cultural integration or civilization. It is hard to believe, however, that for the players in these contests and parades, any such conflation of community or civilizing rhetoric and actual community play would be quite so complete. One supposes that with military parades the marchers and bands have some jingoistic community rhetoric close to their consciousness, but that with festivals and celebrations, such traditional rhetorical matters are most likely in the background, and the ecstacies of dress, dance, music, and song are in the foreground. There are some communal forms that model or mimic more orthodox rhetorical intent (parades) and others that mock and model more unorthodox rhetorical intent (festivals). In these identity rhetorics, it is not their formal character that makes play important; it is, rather, that, whether in the form of parade or celebration, play is a metaphoric sphere that can conjoin what is otherwise apart and divide what is otherwise together, and in a malleable way use these pretended identities to create a feeling of belonging. Fernandez says that metaphor, irony, and the panoply of tropes are all terms for that flexible medium of meaning out of which play can build a humanity for members. His is an amazing idealization of play, particularly as participants and their spectators are sometimes inclined to escalate these events into riots or factionalism or, alternatively, to use them as opportunities for their own bacchanalian enjoyments.

In this chapter I will consider some of the interactions of the desire to use play to express the rhetorics of power and traditional identity, as these have worked out in practical examples in world affairs. Though there are multiple historical examples (Endrei and Zolnay, 1988), Kristiaan P. Aercke's *Gods of Play: Baroque Festive Performances as Rhetorical Discourse* (1995) will suffice for primary illustration. The absolutist political courts in Rome, Madrid, Paris, Versailles, and Vienna between 1631 and 1668 constantly used splendid festive, musical, and dramatic performances to persuade their own followers of their political ascendance, even if, as in many cases, they were brought to the verge of bankruptcy by their playful, potlatch-like excesses. These performances were not just frivolous entertainments for the courtly class; they were serious activities meant to serve the nation's controlling institution, the absolute monarchy, and to enhance that identity. "These performances served specific social functions within the community of each court that hosted them, as well as, in a larger perspective, within the organized political competition of the Continent" (p. 2). The baroque spirit of play "materialized in total works of art: in the splendid festive performances in which all the arts, crafts, and ideas of the age were combined to celebrate and memorialize specific events" having to do, for example, with dynastic marriages or lineage (p. 3). "These 'do not seem' forms of trivial play," Aerke writes, "but rather very much like serious, even mythic, types of play, something like the 'unified play' concept that has been posited as existing from primeval times in the Western consciousness . . . They sought to persuade all and sundry by art and artifice, by game and celebrations, that the kings were not just like others but represented a divine linkage beyond nature." (p. 8).

A great deal of modern academic thinking about adult collective play follows this path of discovering who is, after all, controlling the situation and what they are getting out of it. Looking beyond the simple enactive, fortunistic, strategic, skillful, or erotic pleasures of the participants in their play, there is the prevailing bias that what is really important is to know who is organizing the festival, either for their own imperial identity or for commercial gain. In *Games and Empire* (1994), Guttman reviews the various theories for the way in which the political, economic, or cultural powers of the great nations are said to have caused the weaker powers dependent on them to adopt their sports forms. These theories speak to a cultural imperialism or cultural hegemony over the international play scene that has led, some say, to the destruction of authentic native cultural forms in the Third World countries over the past one hundred years. Much of the writing in an excellent set of essays on festivals entitled *Time out of Time* (Falassi, 1967) also follows this line of thought. The authors examined festivals from within a rhetoric of the importance of the powers who control them. But as I shall show, and as Guttman makes abundantly clear, the relations between the powers that be and the community of game players is highly complex and highly varied across time and place.

In modern times the Olympics present the easiest and best-known case study of the way in which ordinary explanations of the sports phenomena themselves can be overwhelmed by rhetorical views, in this case, of the Olympics. From the modern beginnings of the Olympic games at the turn of the nineteenth century, some argued that the international games would bring nations together (as Fernandez might claim), and others (more conservatively) said the sporting contests would merely stir up preexisting rivalries and lead to even greater conflict. Supporting the latter view, in 1896 the Greeks became intoxicated with their prowess in the first modern Olympic games. The victories intensified their patriotic enthusiasm and sense of the divine destiny to the point that Greece declared war on its rival Turkey and lost disastrously in the thirty-day conflict that ensued (MacAloon, 1981). This is wonderful and not exceptional case of a fantasy of identity, inflated by sports rhetoric, leading to gross miscalculation in the real world.

The pompous use of the games in Germany in 1936 by the Nazis, and the boycotts of the games by the Soviets and the Americans in later years, may be taken as further demonstrations of the power of the Olympics, which can be made into an event that is more than just games, and can indeed become war by another means. At the same time, as MacAloon contends, the games may be the most dramatic twentieth-century celebration of world community and the historical process—a process developed in other ways through international trade, travel, television, and United Nations politics. Perhaps some would claim that the Olympics' playful symbolization of communal unity preceded all others and was a first fantasy embodiment of international unity. However, the connection between contemporary play and future reality is always tenuous at best, even though the contemporary play seems of vital importance to the participants at the time. Still, the important "evidence" here is that people, no less than scholars, thought the games had this or that practical value and explained the games in these terms.

In a way, the identity rhetoric of play is again like Erikson's "interplay." Having, shall we say, stopped war, and having begun the games, then the fantasy of cooperation is floated; add to this some peace rhetoric about the games, and this alternative to war, which was merely play, may develop into a real international peace symbol. The Greek example is a marvelous illustration of how, with the reverse rhetoric, the games can also lead to war.

The Formation of Communal Identity through Contestive Play

On a practical level, on smaller scale than the Olympics, the same kind of rhetorical identity-forming activity is endlessly carried out in the form of playful contests between national and local groups. In general the view seems to be that the more powerful group induces the subordinate group by persuasion or example to play the hegemonial group's games, under the presumption of their moral superiority—although it can also be argued that the subordinate group finds in the games a fantasy of the powers possessed by those who dominate them. The value for the hegemonial group is that playing the games can become a kind of persuasion to believe in the general ideology surrounding them. The history of play in the twentieth century is largely the history of colonial or subordinated peoples shedding their own folklife for imitations of the play identity of their conquerors. Thus local folk games have gradually given way to international sports, including those modeled by the Olympics, and this has occurred even at the childhood level. In New Zealand, for example, the nineteenth-century missionaries and schoolteachers exercised their "Christian" influence in part by deprecating games that were not congruent with their own; the native Maori children ultimately continued to play only their own games that had parallels with those of the Europeans, such as jacks or knucklebones, kites, tops, hand and string games, not those that were fundamentally different from the *pakeha* (white man) games. The Europeans argued that the parallel Maori games signified parallel humanity, whereas nonparallel games were heathen forms (Sutton-Smith, 1951).

Unfortunately we lack a general history of the multiple rhetorics that dominant powers have used to demonstrate that their sports are morally superior. One that is much written about, however, is that which derived from the British moralization of cricket and rugby football as they were introduced in schools for the privileged in midnineteenth-century England. Those once traditional folk games were developed into more codified public forms partly as a means of disciplining the new class of boys. They were advanced with the rhetoric that their forms of conflict provided the essential moral training ground for the gentlemen of the future. The moralization of these games is said to have made the schools more salable to the rising middle classes. The rhetorics involved are implied by such titles as E. Dunning and K. Sheard's *Barbarians, Gentlemen, and Players* (1979) and J. A. Mangan's *The Games Ethic and Imperialism* (1986).

The successful twentieth-century selling of the rhetoric that international contests, including the Olympics, should be restricted to amateurs, who played the game for the game's sake, seems to have derived from this same British rhetoric of the morally enhancing effect of sports. This "amateurism" theory, which naturally favored the "gentlemen" who could afford such leisure, even led to what have turned out to be spurious historical accounts of the amateurism of the players in the original Greek Olympics of 600 B.C. The earlier, romantically idealized Greek players, it now seems, were no better and no worse than today's professionals. Most played for glory and also for tangible rewards (Young, 1984). Here is a rhetoric idealizing certain kinds of play as morally superior that was itself the manifest form of an underlying social class rhetoric about the superiority of those who are wealthy. Those who play games for the games' sake have to be able to afford the time so to do. The paradox is that, in this century, the same rhetoric has been applied to the play of children, who, being increasingly disentangled from the work of their parents, have become small aristocrats of conspicuous leisure consumption. This later argument, however, belongs to the sixth rhetoric about play as a modern consumer value, where once again many affluent people pursue what they imagine to be superior kinds of play forms.

The selling of sports, however, although it often resulted in the acquisition of the *direct ludic identity* of the imperial sports teams, also led the colonials or Third World people to adopt the rhetoric of game superiority (called winning) that went with playing those sports; in the long run they sometimes successfully contested their overlords for that same glory. It is another paradox that the British imperial powers should use contestive games to sell their own rhetoric identity of moral gentlemanliness when they were also, less wittingly, selling the game notion of legitimate opposition. There are a number of cases where the rhetoric of superiority through *contestive ludic identity* by the subordinates seems to have contributed mightily to the increase of the rhetorics of "nationalism" in the countries that successfully engaged their masters in these games and beat them. Rugby in New Zealand, South Africa, and Wales has been written about in these ways; cricket in Australia, the West Indies, and Pakistan; hockey in India; soccer in South America. One of the best recorded accounts of the way in which this inversion has occurred is *Beyond a Boundary* (1963), the autobiography of C. L. James, in which he relates how the local Trinidadians gradually penetrated the game of cricket, first serving as groundsmen, then gradually moving to take fielding positions, and from there advancing to become bowlers, batsmen, and, finally, team captains. Even more remarkable, some of them became politicians in their own country when it moved to independence. Those who are successful in the sports through which people seek to identify themselves also sometimes increase their own political and economic potential. The rhetoric of play's glory, when applied to great players, is believed to generalize to other kinds of leadership, and in some cases the particular sports figures are able to match the required political or economic expectations. The important point is that no one would have such expectations in the first place if games were indeed played only for the games' sake. The paradox is that this rhetoric of play was advanced by those using the advocacy of amateur games to demonstrate their own superiority. The games were for *their* sake, not for the games' sake, and in a select few cases, as mentioned, they also became games for the vindication of the powerless.

Perhaps it can be said that whenever one is taught and beaten at games by another group—whoever they are, masters, aliens, foreigners, adults, gangs, or the opposite sex—one's own group frequently develops a desire to contest that superiority on the same playing field. This opposition is a public transcript widely shared by the world's underdogs and indeed is a breach in the hegemony of the dominant groups, even though the playing of the same games is itself consistent with such hegemony (Scott, 1990). Many authors have seen the selling of sports as a facet of the extension of imperial hegemony or the capitalist way of life, work, and consumption. The problem is that the same imperial way of life in some places permitted different social classes or ethnic groups to compete for hegemony at least within the ludic sphere. And such participation is at the very least a form of enactive subjunctivity, with all its implied optimism and fantasies about the possibilities of success.

What is equally interesting anthropologically is that sometimes the conquered group simply refuses to play the games of the overlord and puts more emphasis on its own original folk forms or its preferred alternatives. We might call this the rhetoric of *counterludic identity*. The distinctive older folk games of the Irish (Irish football, hurling), the Belgians (popinjay shooting, crosse, closh), and the Italians (bocce ball) are modern cases in which countries, or ethnic groups, long subordinated by foreigners, have maintained their own identity in part by intensifying their regard for their own folk forms. In the contemporary rhetoric of multiculturalism there is a great interest in rehabilitating older forms of play. It is not hard to believe that the international political culture of the future will allow for more local and nationalistic ludic expression, even while seeking a kind of worldwide international economic and social order.

Many minor efforts of this kind are occurring. In Louvain, Belgium, the Sports Institute at the University of Louvain has for more than twenty years, under the leadership of Roland Renson (1991), been researching, preserving, and reinstating in museums and play parks Belgium's own traditional games, many of which date back to the medieval period. Brueghel still lives there. Not surprisingly perhaps, some members of the regular sports faculty at the same university have vehemently opposed this investment in their own national past, preferring to compete only in terms of the current international forms of play. In the past several years a Europe-wide movement has also developed for the preservation of traditional games or folk sports throughout Europe. In France the Rainbow Movement at the University of Toulouse gathers children from all over the Third World every three years to play their own traditional games, in an attempt to sustain those games through such acceptance. Speakers at these concourses regularly lament the loss of the older games, just as at present the parochial craft toymakers throughout the world are lamenting the loss of their own toys in the face of the international toy trade. Another group, the international World Organization for Preschool Education, has sought to establish a new curriculum for elementary school children's play based on examples of traditional games from around the world (Ivic and Marjanovic, 1986). An American example is the attempt to substitute cooperative games for competitive ones, for both children and adults. The New Games

Movement was founded in California in the sixties with the aim of bringing families together for forms of cooperative play or for competitive play of a frivolous kind (Fluegelman 1976). Another somewhat similar phenomenon is the international Gymnastrada, a kind of Olympics of dance held every five years, at which participants from most of the countries of the world gather to watch each other's dances. What is really novel here is that each country displays a synthesis of traditional and modern dances, which is to say of national and international dances.

These last few examples show how games can be specifically managed so that they generate the rhetoric of the world or parish as having a potentially cooperative identity. In *The Well Played Game* Bernard De Koven (1978), one of the founders of the new games movement, votes strenuously for subordinating games to the community of players, which he says is larger than any game. When the game is played only for the good of the larger community that plays it, then it can be well played. If not so subordinated, games may run away with their players and cause friction and conflict. Quite often the rhetoric on behalf of a community is accompanied by a bitter rhetoric against the rhetorics of contest. For some, what is wrong with the world is too much emphasis on the play of power and contest (the tragic mode, it is said) and insufficient emphasis on the play of love and belonging (the comic mode) (Meeker, 1995; Donaldson, 1993).

Perhaps more interesting than these examples are those *inversive ludic identities* in which the local group, having been introduced to the dominant play form, totally transforms it, so it becomes an upside-down synthesis with its own preexisting forms. An example of this is recorded in the film *Trobriand Cricket,* a pictorial account of the way in which, after the Second World War, the Australian government banned head-hunting in the Trobriand Islands off New Guinea and the missionaries introduced cricket to take its place (Leach, 1976). As the years went by, many of the tribes in the hinterland developed a game in which they played in their traditional war costumes with head feathers and body markings (instead of the traditional British white shirts and long white pants). Every good hit or out in the game is accompanied by a war dance by the competing teams. The game takes place, as had the head hunts, at the time of the harvest contests and feasting. The host side is expected to win and to provide a plenteous supply of food and gifts to the visitors. A lack of sufficiency is likely to promote hostility. Intoxicating betel nuts, erotic dancing, and sexual revelries are among the bacchanalian accompaniments of the game (Weiner, 1988). At the same time, the chief and his matrilineage, who prove their superiority by hosting this potlatch-like event, are also likely to attract the jealousy of others. Thus cricket has became an uneasy mollifier of continuing traditional hostilities. The story would not be complete without mentioning that the film *Trobriand Cricket* was made by the Ph.D.-holding son of a murdered chief, as his part of a rhetoric intended to build more progressive leadership in the villages which would in turn be useful in forging a different identity for the people (Leach, 1976). There are many such examples of transformations of modern sports in terms of older ways of life (Blanchard and Cheska, 1985; Blanchard, 1981).

Another order of ludic events has involved a reverse flow of influence, with the landlords, as it were, usurping the play of their dependents, which can be called *usurpative ludic identity*. This occurs when politicians or governments take over the local or national folklore to foster their own ideological ends. It was perhaps most noticeable in the communist era in Eastern Europe, but it occurs in all countries in which some recognition is granted in the official ideologies to the play forms of the lower or minority orders, as when, for example, presidents in this country throw out the first baseball of the season, or rugby football players in New Zealand preface their games with an imitation of a Maori war *haka*, usually led by Maoris on the team. Sometimes the inverse subsumptions are of only token significance. But in other cases a whole culture is transformed by such adoptions, as in the effects of African-American jazz and singing in the United States and the world. This latter profound upward contribution was prefaced by smaller-scale imitative parodies by white performers in the prior century, such as blackface minstrel shows and dancing in the slave style, which are said to have derived ultimately from corn-shucking ceremonies in the pre–Civil War period, according to folklore authority Roger Abrahams in *Singing the Master* (1992). These shucking ceremonies staged by the plantation owners, partly to get the shucking done and partly to display their munificence, became occasions in which whites and blacks took heed of each other's modes of entertainment and parodied each other.

These largely anecdotal examples call a halt to the notion of contestive or other festival play forms as fundamentally separate from the general society or trivial within it. Here the notion founders that play is only an escape or a diversion (the rhetoric of play as frivolous). Play forms often seem to be more of a fulcrum of conflict for the assertion of this or that transcending identity. In normal times there may be few opportunities for an intensive investment in national identity such as there is during wars and crusades. Perhaps contestive and festival play are a special province for such rhetorical assertions of identity in times of peace, providing a means for its continued exercise or even, among the young, for the rhetorical rehearsal of such larger group fantasies and commitments. Play is perhaps what you do during recess or when you are waiting or when you have time between mundane occasions, and what it does is maintain your chosen identity by exercising commentary on that identity. Play in this rhetorical case would be seen as an exercise in keeping your morale in tune, as Erving Goffman has suggested, because it is, after all, "where the action is" (1962). Still, this is all speculative. The major point is that, publically speaking as well as intellectually speaking, the character of contestive and festival play has largely been interpreted in terms of the political rhetorics of power and identity. What is said to be a theory of play as contest, hegemony, or resistance, is usually also an example of some group's assertion of its immemorial "traditions."

Implicit in this system of classifying power-oriented ludic identities as direct, contestive, counteractive, inversive, and usurpative is the view that the resistance of those who are being culturally assimilated expresses itself directly in terms of the way in which they play or refuse to play the games of the powerful colonizers. One presumes that when they voice their ludic antagonism to their overlords, they follow a rhetoric of resistance in terms of which they both interpret the games and shape the way they play them. Rhetoric and the play motive become somewhat fused in these rebellious cases, just as they do in the most jingoistic ones.

Traditional Identity as Noncontestive

Much of the above discussion as been preoccupied with communities in conflict and has biased this chapter toward being a footnote to the chapter on power. Historically that is probably a fair representation of the hegemony of sports in Western society. But it is not fair to the present claim that a concern for communal identity, regardless of power relationships, is also a rhetoric of play. The accounts of intimate play within which the lovers are reputed to establish their new sexual selves through play forms might be regarded as an example of the play rhetoric of a dyadic community identity (Betcher, 1987). The rhetoric of how sexual identity is better as a result of these play forms and games is a very modern exercise in persuasion. There is in sex play an idealization of the appropriate kinds of "joint" play that seems often to be the case in identity rhetorics. Some have even suggested that all of sexual behavior is a form of adult play (Frey, 1991). Others might be inclined to think that this is letting the sexual identity rhetoric run away with itself.

On a similar note, some feminist literature seeks to use play as pleasure, as against play as contest, as a statement of the desirable female identity. In the 1980s some declared women's essential being to lie in play. The "theology" of play is said to allow for a distinctive female spirituality and to be central to the goddess religion. Oriard describes this movement as "fundamentally communal, a vision of sisterhood harmoniously playing out individual and collective desires" (1991, p. 482). "In these [feminist] novels, play stands variously opposed to rigidity, control, alienation from one's true self; to rationality; to competition and violence; to oppressive earnestness and work; to power and domination . . . they reject dehumanizing 'games'; play stands instead for the 'dance' of enlightenment or for communal celebration . . . these feminists expressed a familiar fantasy of freedom through play" (ibid., p. 483).

Lest these various advocacies seem a little strange, I should mention that they are very much in tune with the experience of many children, particularly girls, who find that the most important thing about play is to be included and not excluded from the group's activities. Much of female play is itself about the play of exclusion, as in the examples from gossip given earlier. Exclusion and inclusion are also the power tactics that differentiate preschool girls from boys, who spend their time on more obvious aggressive power tactics (Savasta and Sutton-Smith, 1979). And as a motive throughout childhood it seems almost as powerful as the motive for play itself. The play motive for many girls is to be included in the play, almost regardless of the character of the play itself. The society of traditional female play subsumes the substance of play almost as De Koven wished it would in *The Well Played Game* (Nicolopoulou, 1997).

In sum, play as traditional community identity can be seen as not inevitably allied to play as power, as it has been in the great majority of the examples above. Empirical support for this, and therefore for the importance of distinguishing the rhetorics of community from those of power, comes from the anthropological record of the great dominance of cooperative forms of play over competitive forms in most earlier tribal societies. In smaller human groupings where co-operation is essential for survival, it is more likely that cooperative games will be more important than competitive games. In our own individualistic society, affluence and the need for originality make such competition affordable. In smaller societies such modern competitive rhetorics might well disintegrate the group's way of life (Sutton-Smith, 1980b).

Social Context of Identity

In general the anthropological evidence also suggests that familial or other cultural contexts affect the basic identity of the players as players. There is abundant evidence available from social science research to indicate the *relativity* of the forms of play to culture (Roberts, Arth, and Bush, 1959; Roberts and Sutton-Smith, 1962; Whiting, 1963; Whiting and Whiting, 1975; Whiting and Edwards, 1988; Schwartzman, 1978; Sutton-Smith, 1981b; Gaskins and Goncu, 1992; Greenfield and Cocking, 1994). In many cultures child play is suppressed or highly directed, sometimes actively, in terms of punishment or admonition for its presence, but more often play is intruded on because adults need the assistance of the children with chores (Lancy, 1996). There are, however, reports of cultures in which children so restricted nevertheless play surreptitiously, out of the sight of adults (Miracle, 1977). Fantasy play seems more susceptible to such adult restriction than does physical play (Feitelson, 1977; Smilanksy, 1968).

The modern Western tendency to promote object play so extensively (toys), and child independence in imaginative play, seems to be relatively unusual in the human condition and is probably an outcome of the kind of literary and technological entrepreneurial developments in the West. More typically, outside the West, there is high cultural *interdependence,* where adult family members favor respect, responsibility, obedience, helpfulness, and physical closeness to and from their infants and children (Greenfield and Cocking, 1994). This leads to tighter cultural patterning of fantasy in support of the social status and mythic systems that prevail in the culture (Sutton-Smith and Heath, 1981). These more obedience-oriented cultural systems have clearer patterns of collective play and narrative or mythic forms with less of the anarchic variability that is taken for granted in the Western concept of the imagination. Modern play seems to have much to do with individualized narrative, whereas that of these forebears has more to do with communal myth. The latter suggests stronger cultural constraints on the individual playful mind but not on the playful mind that is in service of communal and traditional forms of festival play (Drewal, 1992; Arnoldi, 1995). Early socialization clearly has a direct impact on the kind of identity that players will have and helps to account for the considerable differences in play forms across cultures. One should also note at this point the great stress some cultures place on the way the identity of children is shaped by their participation in the festivals of the culture, as is recorded by Noyes (1995) in her comments on Catalan festivals. This socialization evidence makes it clear that escape from cultural rhetoric is well nigh impossible. It is doubtful that any play is unspoken for. Only animal play untrespassed by language could possible exist without ideological framing. But as I have already shown, this trespass can have either a heavy or a light influence on the play itself. Furthermore the community of players (within the communities in which they live) also develops its own intrinsic play rhetoric, which in the long run has the more important influence, because it is constitutive of the play from within. This is what Linda Hughes calls their "gaming."

The Independent Cultures of Play

It has been shown that sometimes players play primarily to be with others. Or they parade because they wish to see their ethnic group proudly identified. Or they enjoy sports because they are interspersed with moments of ideological self-glorification. Having demonstrated some such links between play and social rhetorics, it must now contrarily be stressed that there are multiple cultures of play, games, sports, festivals, and so on within society, just as there are multiple cultures of music, art, literature. All of these are forms of human engagement that provide participants with solidarity, identity, and pleasure. The constant modern tendency to think of play as simply a function of some other more important cultural process (psychological or sociological) tends to underestimate the autonomy of such play cultures. It makes it difficult to understand that the major obvious function of play is the enjoyment of playing or being playful within a specific culture of play. The most important identity for players is typically the role that they are playing (first baseman, "it," trickster). Whatever else might be subserved by that identity is generally a secondary matter during the moments of play.

Players enjoy participating in social play because it makes them a part of the collective social dreams that are called games, sports, and festivals. When playing, whether play improves skills for nonplay functions is not central. Play is about the ontology of being a player and the dreams that that sustains. It is only indirectly about the epistemology of creating other forms of competence. Social science needs a rhetoric for the theatrics of play identity more than it needs a lesson in the way play subserves any particular other communal identity. Perhaps a rhetoric like that suggested by Sawyer, where the focus is on the improvisational processes of the playing group (1996)—a point of view that derives from treating the play community at any age level as being mainly concerned with its own play functions. This is not to say that players play the game only for the game's sake, because that is a statement that requires the abstraction of the game from its play group context. Any game requires a gaming society, and any society has norms and hierarchies that interpenetrate the game. Talking about the game independently of the life of the group playing it is an abstraction (Gruneau, 1980; Hughes, 1983). In sum, there are the rhetorics of the larger culture that have their own socializing influence, then there is the game-relevant rhetoric of the group that plays the game (see Chapter 7), and then, within both of these, there is the game itself.

Validations and Definitions

This identity rhetoric has its historical basis in community traditions; its players and advocates are adults, male and female; and their play is usually some kind of festival. The scholars of this rhetoric are typically historians, anthropologists, folklorists, and femininists. And as just stated, there is a very strong interplay between the meaning of the identity to be gained through festivals and the group life of those who engage in them. Considering the preceding chapter about power, as well as this one about identity, it is fair to see these rhetorics as normatively incessant attempts to assimilate play phenomena into preexisting value systems. The great developmental scholar Piaget suggested that the job of play was to assimilate the logic of necessity into the individuality of experience, whereas what is seen here is the necessity of public logic to assimilate play into the community of value. That process is what I call the rhetoric of communal identity. Rhetorics do not stand separate and apart from play but work constantly for the interplay that gives play significance in the public mind, regardless of what play might be doing in the private mind. Nevertheless, in this rhetoric as in the others, play, like sex, seems to go on regardless. Its lability allows for a cacophony of such identity rhetorics on the margins, a cacophony that some scholars mistake for the play itself. It almost seems that scholars, as well as "traditions," can hardly abide the intensity of the play phenomena without subsuming it to their own rhetorical excesses.

The hegemony in this rhetoric is enjoyed by those who control the events and exclude the unwanted, as is currently exemplified in ethnic parades and their exclusion of the outsiders they do not want, and by almost all the members of almost all known groups against those whom they seem to need as their "outsiders." Unlike those who believe that contest is the key to play, the denizens of this rhetoric believe that bonding and belonging are the key to play, even though most maintain this apparent virtue in an exclusive fashion.

Festival definitions are varied. Putting aside the fact that modern Western festivals now have their religious ritual side separated from their festive side, and that most of the latter is generally differentiated into calendrical customs (Christmas, for example), ethnic and commercial parades, or sporting events, and only occasionally into carnivals such as Mardi Gras, the following comments apply to the residual festival sentiments as they still exist in modern societies even if often only in private parties and gatherings.

The participants talk about festivals in terms of the public excitement, merriment, and freedom from work. Falassi (1967) titled his book on festivals *Time Out of Time* to suggest the quality of being apart from all everyday events, which is what the players may come to experience. Noyes describes this phenomenon in a Catalan festival: "As the five days of the festival progress, as the dances are repeated over and over, as the great drum keeps beating 'Pa-tum' into your head, and the band and your neighbours force your feet to dance, as you drink more and more and sleep less and less, as the smoke from the firecrackers blackens your face and the crush of the bodies takes from you the control of your movements . . . You lose your everyday name and position; no longer distinguished by them, you are a part of the sweating dark mass" (Noyes, 1995, p. 476). Festival participants point to the aspects of European and Mardi Gras festivals that have effects on their behavior and that they enjoy, such as the masks; the orderly and disorderly fools, jesters, and clowns; the grotesque costumes, the singing and dancing; the food and gifts freely received and freely distributed; those dressed as witches and demons; the opening and closing ceremonies, with parades in between and with dramatics and contests for prizes. Most of all, in the festivals there could be nonsense. As Falassi sums it up: "At festival times, people do something they normally do not; they abstain from something they normally do; they carry to the extreme behaviors that are usually regulated by measure; they invert patterns of daily social life. Reversal, intensification, trespassing, and abstinence are the four cardinals of festive behavior" (1967, p. 3).

For some theorists the meaning of the festival is that it provides a wholeness and a feeling of total presence more complete than can be found in other areas of life. Life is here said to be more coherent than it is at any other time. Even in the relatively detached festivals of the modern Western world, such as Thanksgiving, Christmas, New Year's Eve, there can be a somewhat similar striving for a more complete unity with others of the family, neighborhood, church, or work group, and for some there is considerable depression when this special time is over. For those who plan and organize festivals and have their own festival clubs, however, the companionship of the group continues through most of the year. It is a feature of festivals that they are a form of play that extends through long periods of time. While this is most obvious with the festival clubs of Europe and elsewhere, where members meet on numbers of special festive occasions on their temporal route toward the final Fat Tuesday or Ash Wednesday festival, in the modern world this has become true in another way for the patrons of sports clubs, who meet regularly during the season in their taverns to celebrate the playing of their teams. This is especially so when teams make their way toward the final championship in local or international competitions. It is possible to see these forms of identification as play motivations that are recurrent over long periods of time, just as they once were in the older seasonal festivals.

There are endless claims for the underlying meaning and function of festivals. Most simply, it is said by the Catalans, for example, that through participating in the festivals the children learn the very foundations of their own culture; that their culture is more unified then than it is at any other time (Noyes, 1995). Other explanations are more far-reaching and probably more tenuous. Many like to provide the phenomena with political interpretations. Thus it is said that the meaning of the festival is to create a fantasy hierarchy of the players, behind which lies a real hierarchy of those who organize the games for their own purposes, as suggested in the volume by Aercke (1994) about the festivals of the seventeenth-century kings in Europe. In similar terms it is said that Mardi Gras, whether that of New Orleans or Rio de Janeiro, is anything but an egalitarian institution, even though that is a part of the feeling among the crowds who turn out to witness the spectacles. The politics of carnivals can be analyzed in terms of the way they are carefully controlled by governments or, conversely, by the way they are used by those who see them as a place for latent subversion. There are also ways in which scholars, with their own preconceptions, sometimes even have an influence on what the people themselves come to feel about their own authentic "traditions," particularly when they are rehabilitated after a period of decline (Stewart, 1991). Then there are the larger speculations on what the very existence of carnivals can mean throughout the history of the world, as when Falassi says: "If we consider that the primary most general function of the festival is to renounce and then to announce culture, to renew periodically the lifestream of the community by creating new energy, and to give sanction to its institutions, the symbolic means to achieve it is to represent the primordial chaos before creation, or a historical disorder before the establishment of culture, society, or regime where the festival happens to take place" (1967, p. 3).

Ultimately, perhaps such a romantic view of the festival as representing some kind of universally shared primeval chaos can be held as the basis for the present chapter's quite partial rhetorical view that festivals bring a renewal of communal identity. What is never sufficiently mentioned by the apologists of play as identity is that a play community is like a musical or dance community, each being a form of culture that provides shared enjoyment for its members through the kinds of music, movement, or festivity that are central to their cultural occasions. All of these activities are ultimate cultural values, not primarily explained by their sometimes useful or earlier relationships to other forms of human functioning.

As to ambiguity, we have here one major claim, at least, that festivals are used to proclaim the identity of their originators and to reduce the ambiguity about them that is otherwise present. Ambiguity in this formulation is a primary reason for the rhetoric. Furthermore it is the communalizing orgy of the festival as a play form that itself creates feelings of identity in the participants. So in this case there is an unusual degree of compatibility between rhetoric and play form. Ambiguity creates the rhetoric, the rhetoric creates the festival, and the festival reduces the ambiguity.

7

Child Power and Identity

Play is beyond all rationality and ethics.
Friedrich Wilhelm Nietzsche

If girls get only 10 percent of the playground space during recess,
is that because they are 90 percent less playful?

after Mrs. Frech

Given the public play events discussed in the past two chapters and
their high profile in modern life, it would not be surprising if the
power and identity rhetorics were found to have relevance for children's lives. In this chapter I make the case that they are indeed
applicable to children. However, I am in a peculiar position: whereas
in prior chapters the task was to reveal and sometimes to lament the
influence of ideological rhetorics, the task here is to suggest that
power and identity rhetorics are given too little influence, that they
are largely repressed or ignored in their application to children.
Generally, the focus on the rhetoric of progress has tended to obscure the time that children give to their own affairs of power. Perhaps the adult progress rhetoric has actually disguised the
understanding of what childhood is about as a way of maintaining
adult power over children. There does not appear to be a generally
accepted power rhetoric or theory of play for children as there is for
adults. Though a few exceptions to this generality are emerging, as
in King's important discussion of the prevalence of "illicit play" in
elementary school classrooms, where children doodle, pass notes,
whisper, make faces, giggle, mock and satirize adults, with the bright
students doing it all more covertly and the backward students doing

it overtly and disruptively, sometimes teasing the teacher by pretending to stage actual fights (King, 1987). And there is also power-relevant discussion in the treatments of children's cruel play on school playgrounds (Sutton-Smith, 1982f; Sutton-Smith and Kelly-Byrne, 1984), bullies (Hart, 1993), and male hegemony over females on the same playgrounds, as reflected in the above epigraph (Thorne, 1993).

There are several weak child-power alternatives within existing play theories (Schiller, 1965). The oldest of all is the *surplus energy theory*, which had quite an audience in the nineteenth century when, with the first compulsory schooling, it seemed difficult to keep children in their seats and quiet. The way they leaped out of their classrooms to join in frenetic playground activity certainly seemed to suggest that energy was the key form of power involved in play. There was a surplus to be expended after classroom confinement, or, as was framed by an anonymous theoretician at a later historical stage, "after response deprivation there was an increased tendency to fire off the nonused response systems." Actually, in light of Pellegrini's recent work, if the theory had any credibility (which it doesn't), one might rather frame the theory as relevant to boys' playground activities but not to those of girls. A period of activity on the playground seems to get boys back to attending to their schoolwork, whereas for girls it was found to make no difference, because in Pellegrini's Alabama (hot climate) study, the girls didn't run around much expending energy (Pellegrini, 1995b). But as it stands, the surplus energy notion is too vague, because it doesn't distinguish play as "a surplus" from any other avocations, such as the arts or religion. It was, in Schiller's day in the eighteenth century, an interesting trope borrowed from the major power motif of "energy" in contemporary industrial civilization.

Nietzsche and Children

The metaphor of child play as a kind of irrational power rises to its acme in the writings of Nietzsche, where it is couched as a central illustration of human willfulness and chaos. (I am indebted to Spariosu [1989, pp. 69–88] for bringing these quotations together.) In Nietzsche's words:

The child throws its toys away from time to time and starts again in innocent caprice.

Absolute free will can only be imagined as purposeless roughly like a child's game or an artist's creative play impulse.

Innocence is the child, and forgetfulness, a new beginning, a game, a self-rolling wheel, a first movement . . . Aye for the game of creating which is at the same time a game of destroying.

And this child is the child not of Christ but of Heraclitus. It is the innocent power as eternity, beginning its game of creation and destruction each time anew, without remorse, in blissful self-forgetfulness.

Now if all of this is not just Nietzsche speaking as a kind of metaphysical drunkard but actually truly describes the human and childish possibility of being grandly irrational through play, then there might indeed be a desire by some to subsume or repress it under the rational promise of human progress. In this plight progress might be not just a utopian dream, it could be a jailer's necessity. A first question has to be about the evidence we have that children, like adults, find their agonistic motifs expressed through competitive play. What is known about their being affected by power and identity rhetorics? One answer can be found in the team sports played by girls and boys. With some exceptions these public events have had a much smaller impact on play scholarship than the progress rhetoric issues outlined in Chapters 2 through 4 (Redekop, 1988). Still, the controversies over the power roles of coaches, the interference in games by parents, whether all players should be treated equally, or whether the less proficient children should be excluded, and the view that all the fun is taken out of this kind of organized play by an overemphasis on winning, as well as the issues of the legality of girls' access to boys' sports teams and the physically and psychologically harmful effects of early sports' pressure, are familiar in the literature. With so many conflicts and all the attendant publicity, it is not far-fetched to suggest that this domain of children's play is an area of power crisis in modern parent-child relationships. Consider, for example, the title of Rainer Martens's 1978 survey; *Joy and Sadness in Children's Sports* (see also Magill, Ash, and Smoll, 1982).

The relevant question, however, may be not so much about adult power over controlled team sports for children, where most of the rationalizations are of a progress rhetoric character, but rather about children's own spontaneous and traditional play and games. The issue is whether the nature of these games allows them to be embraced by power and identity rhetorics. If so, would that substantially change the notion of what childhood play is all about? Can a power or identity rhetoric say something about a theory of children's play that is less misleading than the progress rhetoric seems to have been?

Children's Folklore as Hidden Rhetoric

Jay Mechling, Tom Thompson, Felicia F. McMahon, and I recently published *Children's Folklore: A Sourcebook* (1995). This material can be examined for support or refutation of the view that power has much to do with what is going on in the traditional play materials of childhood. In general, what we examine is whether the content of children's play derives from their relative disempowerment as compared with adults. It is a commonplace in play theory to suggest that much of what children do in play is a compensation for their general life conditions. As Erikson says, they "hallucinate" the very mastery that they do not have ordinarily (1950). He suggests that in play children can be autonomous in a way that they cannot be anywhere else. This is not a surprising thesis, only one that has seldom been fully explored or accepted, outside of therapy circles, as the child's way of life. The focus in *Children's Folklore* is on play and games in the interpersonal context within which issues of hegemony and hierarchy become significant. This is not a discussion of power or autonomy in some intrapsychic sense as an individual need. This is about how children, as well as adults, must arrange themselves hierarchically (leaders and followers) so that they can get on with the business of play. They do this by socially constructing a society in which the play can take place, as play sociologists Denzin (1977), Corsaro (1985), and Sawyer (1996) might have said. What the sourcebook argues practically is that children can have their own autonomous play culture that attempts to be independent of adult cultural forms, insofar as the children are the ones who organize and maintain it through their own interactions, metacommunications, and framings, such as play and games. It is noticeable that in the current discussion of children who are bullies and children who are their victims, the focus tends to be on the individual psychology of individuals rather than the more universal processes of group hierarchization that the individuals serve. These hierarchical processes are found in childhood as well as in animals and in adult groups (Olweus, 1993).

The chief theoretical guide here will be James C. Scott, whose book *Domination and the Arts of Resistance* (1990) is about subjugated persons and the ways in which they have learned to deal with those in power in a public way while at the same time expressing themselves privately. Scott says:

> What I do wish to assert . . . is that to the degree that the structures of domination can be demonstrated to operate in comparable ways, they will, other things equal, elicit reactions and patterns of resistance that are also broadly comparable. Thus, slaves and serfs ordinarily dare not contest the terms of their subordination openly. Behind the scenes, though, they are likely to create and defend a social space in which offstage dissent to the official transcript of power relations may be voiced. (p. xi)

> Every subordinate group creates, out of its ordeal, a "hidden transcript" that represents a critique of power spoken behind the back of the dominant. The powerful, for their part, also develop a hidden transcript representing the practices and claims of their rule that cannot be openly avowed. (p. xii; see also McMahon, 1993b)

> I suggest, along these lines, how we might interpret the rumor, gossip, folktales, songs, gestures, jokes, and theater of the powerless as vehicles by which, among other things, they insinuate a critique of power while hiding behind anonymity or behind innocuous understandings of their conduct . . . Together these forms of insubordination might suitably be called the infrapolitics of the powerless. (p. xiii)

For the greater part, children in Western society are no longer serfs, nor are they a race or class set apart. Yet as I have shown, the disjunction of childhood innocence and adult maturity is nevertheless an essential part of modern ideology. Children are a social stratum that is set apart. The public transcript of adults is the rhetoric of progress, which is a justification for educating and disciplining children for their future part in the adult world. The hidden transcript of adults has to do with disguising children's and adults' own irrationalities and sexuality (Kelly-Byrne, 1989; Rose, 1993). The public transcript of children is their good behavior and their good grades in school. What I wish to investigate is the extent to which their own folklore reveals some part of their hidden transcript.*

Following Scott, children's folklore can be considered hypothetically as a series of hidden transcripts of the nonpowerful segment of the population known as children. One can ask whether the collective fantasies of this childhood group represent an implicit protest against their world fate.

> The distinctiveness of subordinate group cultural expression is created in large part by the fact that in this realm at least, the process of cultural selection is relatively democratic. Their members in effect select those songs, tales, dances, texts, and rituals that they choose to emphasize, they adopt them for their own use, and they of course create new cultural practices and artifacts to meet their felt needs. . . . [T]he existing cultural hierarchy (adults) holds out a model of behavior for civilized man that the peasantry (children in this case) lacks the cultural and material resources to emulate . . . Finally, what permits subordinate groups to undercut the authorized cultural norms is the fact that cultural expression by virtue of its polyvalent symbolism and metaphor lends itself to disguise . . . for any subordinate group. There is a tremendous desire and will to express publically what is in the hidden transcript, even if that form of expression must use metaphors and allusions in the interest of safety. The hidden transcript, as it were, presses against and tests the limits of what may be safely ventured in terms

---

*As a reflexive comment, it may be important to admit that some of my own prior research has consisted in investigating the nonidealized character of children's play, including the role of power in their games. The relevant items are Sutton-Smith 1953b, 1959c, 1960, 1970d, 1972a, 1973c, 1977a, 1981b, 1982f, 1983a, 1984b, 1987g, 1989a, 1989b, 1989e, 1990b, 1994b; and Sutton-Smith and Abrams, 1978.

of a reply to the public transcript of deference and conformity. (Scott 1990, pp. 157, 158)

Children love to tell their childlore to sympathetic collectors, at the same time often disclaiming any responsibility for its origins. What is exciting about this rhetorical interpretation of children's folklore is that it raises the possibility that their traditional play is not just composed of remnants of the past but also often embodies a rhetoric they use to hold off the adult-oriented rhetorics that usually surround them (McMahon and Sutton-Smith, 1995). The players, in these terms, subvert the rhetorics of the adults by creating their own play as pragmatic rhetoric against those adults. Is this possible? Can we regard a mixture of pranks, teases, denigratory terms, and antagonistic laughter as a pragmatic child rhetoric? If it is, all of sudden rhetoric that has so far been presented in this work as infiltrating play from the outside becomes fused with the subversive play itself from the inside. The children's use of play in this case is not only for enjoyment but also for protest. This is probably the most extreme example in this book of a rhetoric fusing with play enactment, and the fact that it can occur in one case means it can occur in others and explains, furthermore, why the distinction between rhetoric and play form is not always easily achieved.

Children's Folklore: A Sourcebook contains a number of examples that certainly seem to support this thesis; some seem strident, others more playful. For example Mechling, in a chapter entitled "Children's Folklore in Residential Institutions: Summer Camps, Boarding Schools, Hospitals and Custodial Facilities," says:

Even when they are not literally so, young people in American culture sometimes feel like prisoners in the institutions controlled by adult caretakers. Their primary institutional experience during the course of the day is one of being in "the custody of" adults, from parents to teachers to athletic coaches to Scout leaders and beyond. To be sure, there are islands of autonomous children's cultures that offer refuge from adult supervision, islands located behind the locked door of the child's bedroom, within the dark hideout of the school bathrooms, or in the open space of the vacant lot, fields or woods. But generally, our children are an underclass perpetually in the one down power position. (Sutton-Smith, Mechling, Thompson, and McMahon, p. 273)

One could hardly want a better example of a Scott-oriented script than this one, though at the time of writing, Mechling was basing his sensitivities in part on the earlier work of Erving Goffman on asylums (1961b). Not surprisingly, then, he discusses the multiple ways in which children in these conditions form their own society and indulge in multiple expressions of their resistance through their manipulations of ritual and play. They develop their own institutional lingo; their own insults, jokes, toasts, initiations, and narratives; their legends and ghost stories; their pranks and practical joking; their riots; their unique games; their forbidden rituals (drugs, sexual behaviors); and their material culture (knives, totems, clothing). In addition they respond in their own mocking way to the institutional ceremonies, the house newspaper, self-government, parties, theatricals, open houses, intramural sports, Sunday services and amusements, and assemblies. They have their own rituals of incorporation and separation. Naturally summer camps are the most benign of these institutions, as Mechling says, "fitting most closely the adult's romantic notion of what the child's folk culture should be." At the other end of the spectrum, children's custodial facilities are near-perfect representations of the world of public and private transcripts in relationships between controlling and subordinate identities as Scott describes them. What this continuum reveals is that in all of these cases there is always some organized subordinate group life that is expressed partly through open and partly through covert play and ritual. It is as if public and private transcripts are an inevitable duality when there is a distinction in power between two groups of any kind, even though in the milder cases, where there is considerable autonomous opportunity, most of the resistance is of a potential or fantasized kind. One must remember, of course, that Mechling is considering only groups that are sequestered together for periods of time. Children living at home without siblings, for example, might find it very difficult to find collegial support in their resistance to highly authoritarian parents.

In general Scott can assume that his nonpriveleged groups are fairly unified in their organization, because in general he deals with those whose experience is of common isolation, homogeneity of conditions, and mutual dependence—like the experience of miners, longshoremen, lumberjacks, merchant seamen. Such groups are high on scales of militant cohesion. However, if children are organized, the results are in no way comparable to this kind of phenomenon. What children usually have to deal with is a public adult transcript that says they are not capable of organizing themselves at all. This is so strongly taken for granted that many parents become extremely upset when their children are affected in common and contagiously by the cultural fantasies manufactured for them by commercial agencies. The public transcript in child psychology is also largely about socialization, about how children are turned into social beings as a result of what their parents do. The study of how they make themselves into their own social beings is very much a recent and a minority concern in this field of scholarship, though studies of peer relations, sex typing, play and aggression are making that less true (Hetherington, 1983). Child sociology, by contrast, has a longer tradition of examining how children organize themselves through their peer and symbolic interactions (Mead, 1934; Denzin, 1977; Corsaro, 1985). Probably the most remarkable example of how subtle and complex is their social organization is the Goffman-inspired work of M. H. Goodwin entitled *He said, she said* (1990), which is about the complex social organization of black girls in their neighborhood play.

Recently the first coherent account of the way in which hundreds of children organize themselves in a playground at recess time was published (Beresin, 1993). Using film, video, and audio recordings, Beresin examined the complexity of children's ability to behave as a large community, in a situation framed by adults but by and large left to themselves. Her work clarifies what to date has been only partially understood (Eifermann, 1970a, 1970b, 1971a, 1971b, 1973; Smith and Connolly, 1980; Slukin, 1981; Pellegrini, 1988, 1995b; Sutton-Smith, 1990b; Hart, 1993), recording more than six months of interactions between the types of games played and the categories of players, such as African Americans, Asian Americans, European Americans, boys, and girls. Some games integrate across ages and some across these group categorizations. Beresin offers a complex series of findings illustrating that games are selective social microcosms within the frame of the schoolyard. It is a story that leaves in no doubt children's capacity for complex organization of the available resources to create their own independent play cultures. One notable finding was that, in the study's circumstances, African-American girls integrated across age levels and boys integrated across races, presumably because the girls were relatively more interested in the nurturance of younger girls and the boys relatively more interested in play skill, regardless of race.

Beresin's work complements the intensive and subtle studies by Hughes of a group of girls playing one particular game, foursquare, over a period of several years (Hughes, 1993a, 1993b). Hughes shows how the game rules that prescribe the scene, actions, and central meaning must interact with social rules, which are what the children believe about cheating, fairness, niceness, and friendships. In turn these two together must generate the non-context-specific higher-order gaming rules, which govern how the players themselves, moment by moment, know to respond appropriately to what is going on; how to interpret whether a response is nice or nasty; when to be serious; when not to be serious; when to defend friends, make allowances for the young, act deceptively toward those not in one's own group; when the player counts more than winning, or winning counts more than the player. In the course of this complex account, Hughes shows how cooperative friendships, though a major rhetoric of the Quaker school in this research case, as well as of traditional femininity, can be limited by the intrigues of a child's own claque, even though the pretense of cooperativeness is presented to other players. The appearance of "fairness" in the game represents the children's acceptance of the Quaker rhetoric, but their secretive conniving with each other is one way they manipulate that rhetoric. In all, this is a wonderful example of the ambivalent way in which the larger cultural rhetoric intrudes into children's games and then their own rhetoric partly subverts it. These girls run a fairly tight social ship, with complex hidden transcripts of their own. It is not possible to speak of play or games in abstraction from what Hughes calls the children's gaming of the games. Playing games for the sake of games is always playing games for the sake of games in a particular social context with its own particular social arrangements. There is no lasting social play without play culture.

Historical accounts of the way in which such self-governing children's play groups have developed over the past hundred years has been presented by various authorities. The overall situation is that, with the Industrial Revolution, children became increasingly separated from the world of work where they had operated like little adults and instead gradually acquired more and more markers of a distinctive subcultural group. It should not be forgotten, however, that since the Middle Ages the child-youth groups of European cultures had often enjoyed the role of those most involved in inversive rituals (Strutt, 1801) and social disorders (Gillis, 1981). The introduction of universal schooling was itself associated with a great deal of rioting by the children, who were "incarcerated" for the first time (Sutton-Smith, 1981b, 1985a). The acquisition by European children in the late eighteenth century of distinctive clothes, toys, and children's books is taken by some to be the first general evidence of their newly separate status (Stone, 1979). One can say that this group, disenfranchised from work by the Industrial Revolution, gradually developed its own markers—largely in leisure interests (sports and toys)—that converted it into the child and youth groups we know today. Mergen (1982, 1986) notes that in the first part of this century records indicate that the bulk of American children largely played in the streets or empty fields wherever they lived. Urban neighborhood gangs often required direct physical contests for males to establish their place in the hierarchy, a condition that also prevailed in many schools. The hidden character of the children's transcripts is indicated by such evidence as secret clubhouses and forbidden activities, such as stealing, vandalism, gambling, drinking, and watching prostitutes. In the second half of this century, with increasing attempts by adults to "domesticate" children through the introduction of playgrounds and playground equipment, organized sports, fenced-in school yards, organized clubs (Scouts), recreation (dancing, gymnastics), and supervision of play, the children's hidden agendas in the have become increasingly supine, as the categories of bus play, cafeteria play, under-the-desk play, note passing, giggling, doodling, satirical songs and rhymes, toilet play, mock fighting, and "illicit school play" all suggest (Block and King, 1987). Recent work on children's storytelling is another source of information about their largely hidden views of the adult world. The largest available collections of such stories are those by Pitcher and Prelinger (1963), Sutton-Smith (1981a), and McCosh (1979), the latter of whom writes, in a remarkable British collection, of the way in which humor and jokes are often obscene accounts of the world from the child's viewpoint.

It is in teasing and pranks, however, that contemporary children's groups cease to keep their transcripts hidden and begin to engage in more open warfare. Unlike rhymes, riddles, and stories, pranks can overflow into adult culture in a disruptive fashion, owing to their practical rather than verbal nature and also to the older age level of the perpetrators. While all taunts, teases, pranks, and tricks are deceptive in nature, some are benevolent and some are malicious. Although much pranking is done, spitefully or harmlessly, to other children, adults are mostly the targets in phone tricks, mischief nights, Halloween, and April Fool's Day. Teasing, tricks, and taunting are more often directed at younger children or at the opposite sex.

Just how serious these childish hidden transcripts can be is perhaps best illustrated by what happens to those who seek to study them. When one is dealing with child lore, the problem is that it is often arcane, antithetical, racist, cruel, obscene, and sexist, so that the investigators are themselves as much at risk of censure as are their informants. The progress rhetoric of childhood is likely to claim that, the very act of seeking such data from children is itself a kind of molestation. Seeing that in this progress rhetoric, children themselves are not supposed to be sexual and subversive, then discovering that they are sexual and subversive is itself a "molestation" by the adult investigator (Fine, 1981, 1988). Still, one can find in this official public attitude much of the reason why children's folklore necessarily is hidden, disguised, or indirect. A power rhetoric suggests that child culture and adult culture are inevitably in conflict about who may dominate the behavior of the other and how it will be done. But there is, as yet, no coherent rhetoric about the hidden transcripts of children. We have childhood from the opposing viewpoints of Piaget and Denzin, but not yet from the point of view of a Spariosu. We need a theory of the child-adult power relationships as they determine how rhetoric plays its part in children's play transcripts, both hidden and public. Sufficient evidence has been provided here to show that the hidden rhetoric of the children actually enters into and helps determine the very forms of much of their play. This hidden rhetoric has a direct influence on play, just as the public rhetoric about power and glory has a direct influence on the sports of adults.

The Rhetoric of Identity

Chapters 2 and 3 suggested that the progress rhetoric, the view that children's play is mainly about modern conventions of growth and progress, has not been strongly supported to date by the scientific evidence. Chapters 5 and 6 and this chapter have suggested, further, that there is strong support for the notion that play at both adult and child levels gives expression to concerns over power and identity. Although most of the attention thus far has been focused on power, either rational or irrational, a rhetoric of childhood identity has been implied. It is because there is an economic, social, cognitive, and affective child identity that is disjunctive with the adult identity that the inevitable struggle between the generations is taking place in Western society. The adult public transcript is to make children progress, the adult private transcript is to deny their sexual and aggressive impulses; the child public transcript is to be successful as family members and schoolchildren, and their private or hidden transcript is their play life, in which they can express both their special identity and their resentment at being a captive population.

In addition to their identity as children, however, they also have innumerable other play identities as siblings; friends; boys or girls; church and school members; club and gang members; town, state, and country members; and members of clubs and sports teams. In general these memberships define what it is appropriate to play or to view as play. Obviously home play with siblings and friends contains much of what is often called solitary play, and individuals often become noted for their proficiency in some of these forms, like video games and computer play, sandlot baseball, making models, and collecting trains or dolls (Sutton-Smith, 1986). School playground groups define another swathe of acceptable play forms; club memberships do likewise. The Boy Scouts have been notable since the turn of the century for organizing multiple forms of outdoor play as tests of competence that lead to personal awards, and ultimately to the rank of Eagle Scout. At the same time, the scouts themselves have developed their own profane hidden transcripts involving a wide range of obscenities, many of which have been catalogued by Mechling (1980) and listed in *Children's Folklore: A Sourcebook.*

The identity that has been of major rhetorical moment in recent years has been the gender identity of boys and girls. Roemer and Hughes, in *Children's Folklore,* present evidence to modify the simplicity of an earlier view of girls' play as relatively supine and simplistic as compared with that of boys (Sutton-Smith, Mechling, Thompson, and McMahon, 1995, chaps. 5 and 8). It has been suggested by some feminists that the more cooperative and ritualized rhythmic play of girls is not a good preparation for competitive executive life, but the girls' social skills, as shown in the Hughes and Roemer accounts, raise doubts about that interpretation. And while girls are coming to be perceived in some quarters as more "powerful" than had been supposed, there is a related emphasis on making boys less aggressive, with some advocating the censuring of all their rough-and-tumble play fighting (Carlsson-Paige and Levin, 1987). There is also a desire to modify their power and control of space in the playgrounds. Boys have ten times more space on school playgrounds, and yet they insist on interrupting and invading the games of girls, says Thorne (1993). One sees the beginning of a very strong rhetorical push to do away with school playground–based gender differences in identity, or at least to be tolerant of much more variety than the usual stereotypes suggest (Sutton-Smith, 1979f). Of course, phrasing play in terms of such a "battle between the sexes" would be seen in some quarters as yet another example of macho power-oriented, if inversive, rhetorical inclinations.

The rhetorics of power and identity explain a lot of what is going on in the play of children, and they seem to have more of a part in the actual substance of play than is the case with the progress rhetoric. This follows because hidden rhetorics and antagonisms enter into the substance of much of the play, as pranks and teases, for example. One group of theorists and researchers is gathered around play ideas that they presume help to bring progress into the lives of children; another much smaller group is gathered around ideas about power and identity that they hope will liberate or enhance the particular children's play forms or play groups that they study. Any attempt to study childhood that neglects both of these struggles is certainly unbalanced. The failure, to date, to have power theories of child development that match the abundant progress theories of child development is a measure of social science's acceptance of adult hegemony. What I wish to emphasize here is that children always seek to have their own separate play culture, and the proper study of childhood should begin with an acknowledgement of that.

Resistance against adult power and conventions is a hidden transcript of childhood, but that is not to say that it is a verbal rhetoric. It is a rhetoric often only by implication, as there is little overt verbal coherence to be found in children's subversions, except perhaps in the hands of vocal gangs in street corner societies. What is remarkable, however, is the strange synthesis that exists between such covert transcripts and the actual subversive play. In children's power play there exist some points where rhetoric and action are the same thing.

Validations and Definitions

In support of the notion that the child rhetorics of power and identity are hidden transcripts, unlike the public ones discussed in the preceding chapters, one can cite the history of adult-child discontinuity (Chapter 2) and the continuous subordination of children through the progress rhetoric (Chapters 2 and 3). The advocates of any such rhetoric of children's hidden scripts would include the folklorists and child sociologists as well as many others scattered throughout the literature. The theorists are all those novelists who have written about naughty or insubordinate children (Brand, 1963; Covenay, 1967; Carpenter and Pritchard, 1984) and, increasingly, folklorists. The play forms for this rhetoric are those described above as part of children's folklore, and the players include children and adolescents. The scholarly disciplines most concerned are those of children's folklore and also the history and sociology of childhood. Hegemony here is located either in adults, as the enemy, or in those children who are the leaders of the children's own groups. The interplay between this hidden rhetoric and children's play is clearly quite considerable, sometimes to be seen in open pranks but often muted in traditional rhymes. Obviously there will be great variability of this rhetorical influence according to age, sex, neighborhood, and school.

Children define their own play of this kind largely according to their names and actions: bus play, cafeteria play, desk play, toilet play, Halloween tricks, and April Fool's jokes; telling dirty rhymes, taunting, giggling, goofing off, doodling, whispering, teasing, bugging, making mischief, playfighting, stealing, vandalizing, gambling, telling ghost stories, pulling pranks, and making faces. It needs to be made clear that much of this folk play is an expression of children's traditional interests in movement and words (chasing and riddling), owing more to their common humanity than to their opposition with adult authority. Not all is so directly aimed at adults as in the pranks and obscenities mentioned above.

The intrinsic functions of these forms of play have been said to include illicit play, catharsis, hallucinating mastery, the pleasure of being a cause. The play's extrinsic functions have been defined as hidden transcripts, illicit play, cruel play, mockery, parody, satire, group hegemony, bullying. At this stage these are all social science rhetorics rather than well developed theories of childhood subversion.

Ambiguity is everywhere present in a discussion of the rhetorical area of the hidden and public transcripts of children and adults, and in the play areas of gaming as well as games, of play and play cultures, of gender differences, and, finally, of many the fusions of rhetoric and subversive play. Such fusions have already been claimed for some contesting (between jingoism and sport) and some festivals (between membership and orgiastic unification). It is most paradoxical that, whereas in the rest of this work the major focus is on the way rhetorics bias play theories, in this chapter, the focus is on generating rhetorics as a step on the way to generating theories. The implication seems to be that rhetorics precede theories, even if both follow forms of play themselves. What the monkeys begin, the folk rhetorize and the theorists make shapely.

8

Rhetorics of the Imaginary

Oft on the dappled turf at ease
I sit, and play with similes,
Loose type of things through all degrees.
William Wordsworth

When I'm playful I use the meridians of longitude and parallels of latitude for a seine, and drag the Atlantic Ocean for whales! I scratch my head with the lightning and purr myself to sleep with the thunder!

Mark Twain

Play may be paradox to play theorists, but to good friends, it's a sure thing.

after Trevarthen

The word *imaginary* means to be not real, to be fanciful and visionary. The mood here is in general lighter and more playful than that of the preceding rhetorics. Gathered here are all who believe that some kind of transformation is the most fundamental characteristic of play. Not surprisingly, therefore, artists of all kinds are here. The heterogeneity of this rhetoric is illustrated by listing many of the concepts relevant to its description: imagination, fancy, phantasmagoria, creativity, art, romanticism, flexibility, metaphor, mythology, serendipity, pretense, deconstruction, heteroglossia, the act of making what is present absent or what is absent present, and the play of signifiers. It was not easy to choose the name for this rhetoric, for the very reason that it is not a simple category. The most obvious term historically is *imagination,* but this has become too limited by its own rationalistic

127

history. *Creativity* as a term has become too confined by its history as a quantitative variable in psychology. The term *fancy* would be attractive because it was used as the negative term (as contrasted with the positive term *imagination*) by the idealist and romantic originators, Kant, Schiller, and Coleridge. *Flexibility* is a good term too and is used with animals, but it refers to a more limited function than is implied by this rhetoric. The term *imaginary* was chosen to encompass all of these, including imagination and fancy. In addition, because the history of children and the imagination is so much more clearly a history of rationalizing or idealizing repression, it has seemed a fair restitution to emphasize the wilder side of the childish imagination more than has been done for adults. Therefore, within the rhetoric of the imaginary I also include Chapter 9 on children's phantasmagoria, which is defined as a rapidly changing series of things seen or imagined, as the figures or events of a dream. An early preference was to call the overall rhetoric Proteus, to highlight the protean character of the imaginary and the fact, as in Bakhtin (1981), that there is in all our minds an internal dialogue of voices, just as in play and festivals there is a dialogue between the different characters, some of whom change their shape as the dialogue proceeds. Thus play can be both heavy and light, ritualistic and playful, earnest and frivolous. There is an ever changing heteroglossia of voices, and the realm is not polarized but always fluid.

Within this rhetoric proponents use metaphors for play (the play of the gods) and the play of metaphors (play as important, unimportant, serious, trivial, dallying, or contesting), rather than empirical examples of some group of players, such as children, sports persons, or a community. This rhetoric seems not so much concerned with play as an intellectual contest, a competitive bout, or a parade; rather, play and games are presented as ways of thinking about culture or as texts to be interpreted (Geertz, 1973). So there is talk about life as a game, or the play of the gods, or children's play as an example of metaphysical chaos, and these metaphors permit either depreciation or elevation of those phenomena (Mechling, 1989)—that is, they make for new thought about those categories (life, God, magic). So one aspect of this fifth rhetoric, the imaginary, that must be understood is how the play metaphor works and whether it really has anything much at all to do with playing persons.

At the same time, there are candidates for players in the rhetorics of the imaginary. After all, there are the players on stage who perform the play, those who play the piano, write fictions, perform as dancers, and those who are artists, composers, choreographers, and directors. Then there are those who are called imaginative or inventors, who create toys, games, fantasylands, movies, plays, symphonies, and other works of the imagination, and there are, of course, all the children of the world who are pretending and making believe. Of all of these only the pretending children, who are a relatively coherent cultural group, have been studied empirically as players (Fein, 1981; Bretherton, 1984; Singer, 1973; Singer and Singer, 1992). Few of these other cultural groups are studied as players, though they are, of course, studied endlessly as actors, musicians, dancers, artists, and novelists, which may perhaps be the same thing but the idea is not usually consciously entertained. Inventors seem to get somewhat less attention as cultural innovators, and next to none as players. It is clear that this is indeed going to be the most protean of the rhetorics, which is quite fitting, since that is what appears to be its essential character.

I will identify the rhetoric of the imaginary by looking at its origins and correlates in romanticism, art, literature, and semiotics and in the next chapter in the pretence and irrationality of childish phantasmagoria.

The Romantic Imagination

The romantic movement that began at the end of the eighteenth century is generally understood as a reaction against the rise of rampant industrialism and urbanity. It has been characterized as an attitude of mind that glorifies freedom, originality, genius, the arts, and the innocent and uncorrupted character of the childhood vision. The key phenomenon for play theorists is the new importance that was given to the central faculty of the imagination in human mentation. For two thousand years, since Plato and Aristotle, art and play had been confined to roles as secondary sources of knowledge (Spariosu, 1984). By making play essential to the aesthetic, and by attributing moral power to the aesthetic, play was potentially dignified for the first time in Western civilization.

As James Engell says in his classic, *The Creative Imagination, Enlightenment to Romanticism* (1981):

> The Enlightenment created the idea of the imagination. As the idea evolved in the eighteenth century, it became the vital principle for an expanding network of concepts and values. The understanding of genius, poetic power, and originality, of sympathy, individuality, knowledge, and even ethics grew and took lifeblood from the imagination . . . Seldom in Western Culture has one idea excited so many leading minds for such a stretch of time. It became the impelling force in artistic and intellectual life, in literature and philosophy, even in political and social thought, especially from 1750 onwards . . . The imagination became the way to grasp truth . . . Many of the individuals who fall in love with the concept of the imagination—Coleridge, Blake, Schelling, Shelley, Tetens—have such capacious identities of their own, or at least offer such new expansive views of the world, that each one of them is transformed and elevated . . . they exemplify . . . that imagination can free us from a self-centered world . . . *We wrestle with the problem of diversity and unity, a challenge that Whitehead called the great one confronting modern thought. The concept of the imagination was, and perhaps remains, the boldest reply to that challenge.* (pp. 3–10; italics are mine)

If this is not exciting enough as an announcement about the romantic period's new meaning for play as the imagination, consider Thomas McFarland in his 1985 work *Originality and Imagination,* in which he suggests that the concept of the imagination began to take the place of the concept of the soul. Why was it so urgent that it do so? he asks. His answer:

> The historical phenomenon that engages our attention is the enormous acceleration, in the late seventeenth and early eighteenth centuries, of the sense of imagination's importance. We may boldly present an answer in its largest outline: imagination became so important because soul had been so important and because soul could no longer carry its burden of significance. That significance was the assurance that there was meaning to life. No soul, no meaning. But even if the soul wilted under the onslaught of science and skepticism, so long as there was imagination as a secondary validator then at least there remained the possibility of meaning. This largest

truth is simple, as large truths tend to be. In its historical ramificat-
ion, it is exquisitely complex. (p. 151)

This new version of play as the imagination bore the promise of
being a broad top-down idea. Immanuel Kant (1724–1804) stipulated
that it was the imagination that mediated between sensory knowledge
and formal reasoning. It was the imaginative faculty that provided the
hypothesizing without which science would be impossible. The imagination was not merely a fanciful part of the mind, as the great British
empiricist David Hume had earlier suggested it was. This new and
novel idealization of play is first expressed most explicitly in the
famous statement by Friedrich Schiller (1759–1805) that "Man plays
only when he is in the full sense of the word a man, and he is only
wholly a Man when he is playing" (1965, p. 80). Schiller, the idealist,
was searching for a process that would actively unify human feelings,
perceptions, and passions into a whole worldview. He saw imagination as unifying both objective and subjective life (for my purposes
here, perhaps daydreams as well as imaginative plans). This is indeed
the *broad* view of the play function. As Engell says, "There was a
pleasant rhetorical shock produced by saying that play, not reason,
duty or religion, was the highest fulfillment of humanity" (1981,
p. 236). But the breadth of this apparently top-down character of
human thought was immediately nullified for play itself by the key
role these writers gave to aesthetic intuition as the central moral
function, thus neglecting many kinds of play phenomena as irrational or mere play. Schiller exults only, we soon discover, about the
kind of play that could produce his own poem, the words to
Beethoven's chorale "The Ode to Joy," which, while having its quality
of wonder, is a highly idealized kind of play. What Schiller also had
in mind was the selective play represented by classical images of
Greek bodies in the supposedly bloodless beauty of the Olympics. His
idealization of play was part of his romanticization of the Hellenic
past. He was not in favor of the irrational and bloody play of the
Roman gladiators.

Somewhat later it was the educator Friedrich Froebel (1782–1852)
who developed the view that play was the highest phase of a child's
development, the function of the imagination being the peak of the
child's self-active inner representation. His unimpeached idealiza-

tion of play is the one that has persisted the longest in Western society, through his influence on preschool education. Froebel dignified all kinds of child play, even play with toys, to which he gave a spiritual significance. One hears again the voice of Schiller in Froebel's belief that it is possible to develop moral character and understanding through play activities and through contact with toys as symbols representing the principles of cosmic perfection. Dark play is not put down as it is by Schiller, it is just ignored.

Still, apart from Froebel, who had considerable influence on the kindergarten and playschool movements of the late nineteenth century, the new faculty of the imagination was not to persist in this idealized and comprehensive form. From the very beginning Kant, Schiller, and most others continued to make a distinction between the higher kinds of play, such as the imagination, and the lower and more nonsensical or crude kinds, most of which they termed "mere play." In the history of this school of the imagination, most subsequent philosophers and psychologists have likewise sought to tie imagination to rational functions such as problem solving. And another twist is that, although Froebel continued to be revered in the field of education, his comments on play were felt to be true at best only for children. In a way, then, the traditional dualism of top down (logic) and bottom up (play) was not recast. Play did get a new hearing, but among scientists only heuristic play was accepted, all other kinds being disregarded or treated as having value only in the lives of children. The concept of play might be a top-down one for children themselves, it was believed, but it might also be said in jest that children are nevertheless basically an infantile bottom-up group. Play was demeaned by its central association with them.

The title "Rhetorics of the Imaginary" has been chosen for the present chapter, in part to forestall the rationalizing tendency in Western thought that neglects some "lower" play functions (fantasy or phantasmagoria) in order to allow its idealizations (imagination) to be appreciated. As we have seen already in the words of Nietzsche and Schechner, there is abundant evidence that the human imagination can be used in quite diverse ways and can deal with the nonsensical, dark, and monstrous sides of thought as well as more poetic or scientific elaborations. In the review that follows, various uses of "play" in the arts and elsewhere will be examined in terms of how a choice is made between the top and the bottom or the broad and the narrow, and in the way in which the arts are said to represent play as a form of transformation.

The Conflation of Art and Play

The romantic theories left the world with an identification between art and play, as both involve the freedom, the autonomy, and the originality of the individual. Although not equal, according to Schiller, as free forms of expression, art and play are constantly paired in subsequent history. In psychology the pairing of the two enters social science through Herbert Spencer, who opines that an underlying surplus energy in the child drives them both. Spencer declares "play and art are the same activity because neither subserves, in any direct way, the processes conducive to life and neither refers to ulterior benefits, the proximate ends are the only ends" (1896, p. 694). He is the first influential social scientist in the Anglo-American tradition to consider child play and child art to be for scientific study.

What develops in the twentieth century is a complex of ideas in which the child's play and art are brought together with ideas about the imagination, about the child as a primitive, an innocent, an original, and, in effect, the true romantic, because he or she is untouched by the world and still capable of representing things in terms of an unfettered imagination. The result is a touch of Rousseau compounded with Schiller, the theory of recapitulation, and perhaps Lewis Carroll, constituting what I have termed elsewhere the paradigm of the imaginary child (1994c) and what Boas labeled the *The Cult of Childhood* (1966).

When we consider that children's art and modern art were constantly paralleled from the turn of this century, the strength of the linkage between the child's imagination and the child as artist becomes apparent. Partly this interest is due to the discovery of "primitive" art, which played a key role in the genesis of modern art and in turn led to further parallels between the child and the primitive (Rubin, 1984). Leading modern artists, such as Picasso, Matisse, Gris, Kandinsky, and Klee, avowed that they would like to be able to draw like children, because children draw what they imagine and not what they see. In children, the subjective and the objective are not as separate as they will become later. At the same time, whatever is seen is fresh and new to the child. "Now the one adjective which appears over and over again in praise of the child, as I hope is now clear, [is] 'innocent.' Infantile innocence was traditionally believed to be moral . . . When cultural primitivism was upheld in the field of art, the moment had come to praise the art of children" (Boas, 1966, p. 102).

Essentially what this "romantic" relationship between children's play and art did was to obscure whatever the true relationship between play and art actually is and to contribute instead the notion that what is most important about both of them is the freedom, originality, and autonomy they connote. Even today many educators act as if all forms of children's free expression are forms of play. Play is a name they give to a conglomerate of activities that have such other names as exploration, practice, manipulation, mastery, experimentation, reading and listening, making music, painting, dancing, roughhousing, and so on. In his classic work *Education through Art* (1944) Herbert Read conducts an internal argument with the famous play theorist of the time, Margaret Lowenfeld (1935). He concludes with the statement, "While Dr. Lowenfeld regards art as a form of play, I regard play as a form of art. This is not merely a verbal distinction because my order of words does in effect restore a teleological element which Dr. Lowenfeld has altogether rejected" (p. 110).

From the rhetorical point of view, this particular history of the play-art conflation as originality, autonomy, and innocence has to be a major reason why many think this is the most fundamental meaning of play. Looking at children's play in terms of freedom, or the play of poets as freedom, provides a powerful value system for this kind of play advocacy. The down side, however, is the undifferentiated identification of the two. Fortunately not all scholars continued with this naive line of thought. Several philosophers within the expressive traditions of thinking about art, Bosanquet, Croce, and Collingwood, for example, denied this conflation of play and art, although they were sympathetic to the similarities (Beardsley, 1981, p. xi). If we follow another branch of post-Kantian philosophy, that of Cassirer, Langer, and Goodman, in which symbolic forms carry their own objective codes, we get even less affirmation of the conflation. Cassirer, in his *Essay on Man* of 1944, emphasizes that what play and art have in common is invention and personification, and what they have at odds is the development of sensuous forms, as this is restricted to the arts. It is an interesting distinction, and by and large probably true, but limited inasmuch as many children's singing games, for example, have a formistic character, a distinction recognized by Cassirer's follower Langer in her work *Feeling and Form* (1953).

In psychology, since Groos at the turn of the century, occasional attempts have been made to separate play and art, usually in a more specific behavioral and less "essentialist" manner. For Groos, play is biology and art is culture (Groos, 1976). For Berlyne, in his major work *Aesthetics and Psychobiology* (1971), play is frivolous and art is revered, a dualism redolent of typical work ethic attitudes. More important, however, he identifies play as diversive exploration and art as specific exploration—which, within his epistemic theory, is a cogent distinction. Howard Gardner has done more than anyone in the recent years to make sense of the difference between play and art, and he devotes a chapter to each, operationalizing art and play separately, in his basic psychology textbook, in which inclusion of the art-play rhetoric is itself a remarkable event (1982a, 1982b). He sees play in terms of the mastery of anxiety, self, and the world, but art in terms of the mastery of symbolic systems. His analysis, and all the different statements made about play in the prior chapters on progress, power, and identity, indicate that in modern social science there is really not much relevance to the continued identification of play and art as a way of explaining play. The tradition of this identification, and therefore of the present rhetoric of the imaginary, has more to do with the "romantic tradition" of discourse than with empirical evidence.

Literature as Play

The associations of play with literature are in general even more diverse and heteroglossic than those with visual arts, though there is a point at which play and literature are the same thing, as when, at the height of romanticism, poetry and the lyrical are identified as the purest and most original form of play. This assertion is continued in the work of Huizinga, who says poetry (and therefore play) functions as a bridge between primitive and civilized man. He writes that poetry "lies beyond seriousness in the primordial domain peculiar to the child, the animal, the savage, the visionary, in the domain of dreams, of ecstasy, of intoxication, of laughter" (1955, p. 119). Here the romantic nostalgia for the primitive and for childhood continues. The paradox is that Huizinga says such play contributes to the transition from savage to civilization but that, as civilization proceeds, play becomes increasingly professional and therefore doesn't contribute to civilization, a contradiction that some have found ludicrous (Ehrmann, 1968, p. 49). One need only note that what is being said here of poetry and play parallels the earlier conflation of art and play, both being exemplars of romantic rhetoric rather than having much other verity, historical or scientific. But there are a number of ways in which literature and play do relate to each other, and these are worth examining, both as possible sources for the view that play and literature have something in common, and as clues to why play in literature should be thought of as a kind of transformation. First, there is the view that all literature is to some extent play; second, there is literature with playful content; third, there are play forms that are themselves literature; and fourth; literary metaphors or tropes can be a form of play.

The broad view that all literary writing is play has for centuries generated discussion among poets and philosophers, and, more recently, among cultural historians and psychoanalysts. To make some sense out of this concept, the writer or artist might be thought to draw incessantly from his or her own broadly or narrowly conceived play activity in the process of being an artist. This doesn't have to mean that art is play, it only means that the incessant activity of the playing mind is constantly present, intermixing with the processes of composition. The playing mind daydreams and fantasizes and cannot keep itself from so doing. The overt processes of writing need not themselves be play, because the materials and traditions of composition have their own inherent adaptive and formistic rigidities and call on the talents of the artist in rigorous problem-solving ways. At the end of each artistic venture the product stands alone and separate from the artist's deeper and broad mental life, but during the process of creation it cannot. In the narrow play-theory view, however, there may be no need for the broad conception of play to enter into the process. In the narrow view, the credit for problem solving might be given to the directed imagination. Obviously the extent to which the mind works playfully in undirected or directed ways in the background of one's problem solving is not easy to assess. And there is the added complexity that the artist can be thought of sometimes as playing with his skills and traditions as a way of solving problems with them.

A second way in which play and literature interact is through literature that contains explicitly playful content as a part of the art form itself. Thus Kathleen Blake (1974) sees Lewis Carroll (Dodgson) as a writer who plays an agonistic game with the reader, perhaps not unlike a writer of mystery novels. Carroll himself once said that "Alice was about malice." Blake contends that Carroll wishes that human activity in general could be formalized and bounded by the same kind of constraints that one finds in games (ibid., p. 20). Anthropologist of play Helen Schwartzman is much attracted to the writings of Carroll and uses them to illustrate the kind of "transformations" that play can accomplish. She cites the following remarkable example of playful yet agonistic transformation in *Through the Looking Glass:*

"You are sad," the Knight said in an anxious tone: "let me sing you a song to comfort you . . . The name of the song is called 'Haddock's Eyes,'"

"Oh, that's the name of the song, is it?" Alice said, trying to feel interested.

"No, you don't understand," the Knight said, looking a little vexed. "That's what the name is called. The name really is 'The Aged Aged Man.'"

"Then I ought to have said 'That's what the song is called?'" Alice corrected herself.

"No, you oughtn't: that's quite another thing! The song is called 'Ways and Means' but that's only what it is called, you know!"

"Well, what is the song, then?" said Alice, who was by this time completely bewildered.

"I was coming to that," the Knight said. "The song really is 'A-sitting on a Gate': and the tune's my own invention." (Schwartzman, 1978, p. 210)

Carroll has a competitive game mentality and shows how ambiguous this kind of play can be for Alice, although it is highly flexible and logical for the Knight, who appears to be a creature of some malice. This kind of playful content, versatile as it is in this example, is also the contestive kind of play that illustrates the rhetoric of power. Lewis Carroll, like Huizinga, believes in that rhetoric, but Schwartzman, who cites Carroll for his ingenuity, believes in play as the imaginary or as "transformations," which is the title of her classic work. All of which illustrates the general proposition of this book, that whatever play itself may be, it is generally subsumed in theories about it to one or other of these rhetorics. I should also add that, according to Sheehan's account (1993), Carroll was as much mocking the world of the Knight as punishing Alice. The implicit agonism may be between Carroll and the world's secular and scientific authorities.

Another example of play in literature is examined in Guiseppe Mazzotta's *The World at Play in Boccaccio's* Decameron (1986). *The Decameron* is the story of ten young people who retreat into the country outside of Florence to escape the plague of 1348, and who fill their time by playing and telling stories. On one level they escape their dilemma by using play as therapy, as comedy, through chess, spectacle, jousting, tricks, disguises, music, mimicry, and gambling. On another level there is the freedom of the imagination. As Mazzotta says in his analysis:

> The imagination is always forced by men of reason within recognizable forms of sensible living or it is dismissed by them as mere nonsense; at the same time, the imagination always exceeds the ordinary, rigid determinations of commonsense. The possibilities of the imagination, its fleeting shadows and dazzling fabrications are probed throughout this book . . .
> . . . It is this discrepancy and kinship between art and life, whereby the two can never be thought of as fully apart nor as fully coincident with each other, which is the subject of the present study . . . it is a mode drawn under the sovereignty of play, which is both a stance and a style of effacement of the boundaries between the real and the make believe . . .
> . . . The elusiveness is Boccaccio's irony, the perspective which gives a dark edge to his humor and which brings with it the disclo-

sure that simulations, jests, the turns of the imagination, are not mere interludes in the business of life but the shadow of the play of the world . . .

. . . In the *Decameron* the theology is absent or it is present as the object of laughter, but play is the category through which Boccaccio enjoins us to look at the world and at its suspected but also elusive secrets. (pp. 10, 11, 268, 269)

What is difficult to grasp in *The Decameron,* Mazzotta says, is that the ambiguity of play forms and their meanings is used to emphasize their precariousness and yet also their autonomy. Play can be an area where the despairs of life are mocked, where there is precarious but safe retreat, and yet where there are also only shadows of the other world. In short, *The Decameron* is a testament to the ironic uses of play in the content of a book. It is Boccaccio's implicit literary rhetoric to comment on the Church and on the plague that turns the group's games into a mockery of the real life and times.

The notion that play has sufficient ambiguity to allow such rhetoric was born in modern social science with the work of Gregory Bateson (1972). He points to the paradoxical and metacommunicative nature of play, showing that play is not just play but is also a message about itself (a metamessage), being both of the world and not of the world (paradox). The child playing mother is both a mother and yet not a mother. Thus one can enact something real in play while denying that one is saying anything about the world, and thus be both innocent or guilty at the same time; only the shared knowledge of secrets allows others to know which truth, if either, is most intended. The act of play is always by itself manqué, and is certainly opaque, but as such it can yield the most mysterious of transformations, and it seems to be this irony that makes Boccaccio use play not only as the content of his book but also as its form of metacommunication. In short, he can give his readers the illusion of literature, within which his characters tell stories (more literature), but then he adds that the characters are also playing or imagining when they tell and talk, so that it is no longer clear what is illusion and what is not. In Boccaccio, as in Carroll, the kind of play in the content lifts the literature to a new and more elusive commentary on reality. And in terms of our rhetorics, this is probably the most that one can claim in maintaining that play is among the most labile of forces available in human communication. No play theorist has claimed as much for play's transformational capacity as Boccaccio does in *The Decameron;* but then the moderns are plagued only by their own rhetorics, whereas he was facing the Black Death.

Another writer who uses a play form as his literature is Mikhail Bakhtin (1984), who, in writing about Rabelais, discourses on the play form of medieval festivals and carnivals. He describes the grotesque realism of Rabelais's serfs in their carnivals, with their laughter, blasphemy, cunning, coarseness, farting, nose picking, flatulence, dirtiness, scatology, gross gluttony, and sexuality. Bakhtin says these are their ways of coming back to life and rising above their most oppressed circumstances.

> In grotesque realism, therefore, the bodily element is deeply positive. It is represented not in a private, egoistic form, severed from other spheres of life, but as something universal representing all the people . . . We repeat: the body and the bodily life have here a cosmic and at the same time an all-people character; this is not the body and physiology in the modern sense of these words, because it is not individualized . . . This exaggeration has a positive, assertive character. The leading themes of these images of bodily life are fertility, growth and a brimming over abundance . . . The essential principle of grotesque realism is degradation, that is, the lowering of all that is high, spiritual, ideal, abstract; it is a transfer to the material level, to the sphere of earth and body in their indissoluble unity . . . Laughter degrades and materializes. (pp. 19–20)

As such the carnivals are a commentary, a transcript from the bottom up, on the domination of the masters whom the serfs despise, and in some cases their wild play is the seedbed of revolution. But over and above that, this work on medieval literature by Bakhtin is also a satire on the contemporary (1930s) socialist realism of Russia. He is in effect saying that the medieval play forms described by Rabelais tell us more about modern Russian peasants and their instincts than all the social-realistic gloss provided by their communist masters.

Whether the writer describes play as gamesmanship (Carroll) or irony (Boccaccio) or carnival (Bakhtin), each play form is used as a metaphor for the identification and persuasion of the group personified as the players in these fields of play. In the eyes of the authors, the play content become metaphor is a strong rhetoric for the transformation of the lives of both characters and readers. These authors use the rhetoric of the imaginary because they want us to identify with their perspective, as Burke would say (1950). The metaphors ally the readers with the writers, not unlike the way in which Fernandez says festive metaphors unite their players with their group membership and identity (1986).

The third kind of interaction of play and literature is that in which the literature itself takes a ludic form, as, for example, in the literature of nonsense and humor. Whether in reading Edward Lear's *The Complete Nonsense Book* (1912) or Stephen Leacock's *Nonsense Novels* (1929) or G. Legman's *The Limerick* (1969), to take but a handful of examples, the reader is immediately at play in an imaginary world of textually incongruous transformations. The playfulness of literary or other nonsense has been well described by Susan Stewart (1978):

> Nonsense becomes that which is irrelevant to context, that to which context is irrelevant. Nonsense becomes appropriate only to the everyday discourse of the socially purposeless, those on the peripheries of everyday life; the infant, the child, the mad and the senile, the chronically foolish and playful. Nonsense becomes a negative language, the language of an experience that does not count in the eyes of commonsense discourse . . . Nonsense wastes our time. It trips us up. It gets in the way. It makes a mess of things. (p. 5)

When nonsense happens in the behavioral and social sphere, it is a kind of frivolity that makes adults mad, as in the case of the hilarious disorders of infants, the obscene parodies of children, and the cruel mockeries of adolescents. When it is written down, however, it is immediately recognized as a play form. Anything that can be the negative of both standard behavior patterns and standard uses of language provides a large scope for flexible play. This kind of literary play is as much an empirical buttress to the rhetoric of imaginary as are sports to the rhetoric of power and the Olympics to the rhetoric of identity. Even more this kind of play is also central to rhetoric seven, the rhetorics of frivolity.

A second and even more momentous example might be Mikhail Bakhtin's other work, *The Dialogic Imagination* (1991), in which he treats the history of the novel as if it has been the register of an endless dialectical play within the human imagination. On the one hand there are the novel's heteroglossic, the polyphonic, and carnivalistic aspects, which pull meaning apart, and on the other, the delusion, illusion, or allusion of a centralized set of meanings that all can understand, which pulls everything together. Michael Holquist, in his introduction to *The Dialogic Imagination,* says, "This extraordinary sensitivity to the immense plurality of experience more than anything else distinguishes Bakhtin from other moderns who have been obsessed with language . . . Implicit in all this is the notion that all transcription systems—including the speaking voice in a living utterance—are inadequate to the multiplicity of meanings they seek to convey. My voice gives the illusion of unity to what I say; I am, in fact, constantly expressing a plenitude of meanings, some intended, others of which I am unaware" (p. xx). Bakhtin suggests that the openness of the novel to its own alterity is the dialogue of the imagination, which is central to the novel and, in the broad sense, to play, which could of course make imaginative play the heart of what the novel is about. The narrow sense of play would concede that the novel is a work of the imagination, but not that this necessarily makes it play. However, as inversion, carnivalia, laughter, travesty, and parody are always essential to the novelistic process, as Bakhtin emphasizes, there are good grounds for granting that we have here an illustration of Schechner's broad-play process expressing itself through the novel. On this reckoning the novel is the supreme play form of the Western world—at least according to Bakhtin's rhetoric of the imaginary.

Fourth, play can be seen as a literary trope, particularly as a metaphor for other things, and this is a preoccupation of the rhetoric of the imaginary. Play can be applied as a metaphor to other phenomena in multitudinous ways, sport alone providing seventeen hundred metaphors by one count (Palmatier and Ray, 1989). Play as some kind of figure of speech is itself a popular figure of speech. As I have said, Fernandez (1986) speaks of carnivals and festivals (play forms) as acted-out tropes standing for a group's desire to make statements it can believe in about its own identity. However, while his rendering supplies such festivals with yet another ingenious rhetorical purpose, this is all he can claim for such a theory; his view belongs with the rhetoric of identity, in the terms of this work. After all play, itself is not a figure of speech, not a trope, not a metaphor; play is at first a kind of biological, prelinguistic enactment with its own claims on human existence, no matter how metaphorized it is in other claims.

Marjanovic-Shane (1990) makes the distinction between the metaphoric statement that "Brian is a pig," and the play description that "Brian is a pig." In the first she is assimilating Brian negatively by allusion to various police authorities; in the second she is pointing to Brian moving around on hands and knees and grunting like a pig for the amusement of his children. The first pig is a proposition, a commentary, a metaphor implying something about the nature of Brian in the real world. But when Brian plays the role of a pig, he is in the fictive world, an imaginary world established by metacommunications and quite distinct from the real world. Being a pig in play is taking a fictive role. The pig is a prop or a role in the fictive world. It is not a commentary on someone's character in the real world (except in the eyes of psychoanalysts). Marjanovic-Shane suggests that if play is to be likened to a figure of speech, it would be more of an allegory than a metaphor. Quite a good case might be made that play is a primordial form of what later is represented as allegory, a story with symbolic meaning. Children often act out (play) what later they will be able to talk about as made-up stories (Garvey, 1977). Furthermore a structural analysis of both play and story can be almost identical (Eckler and Weininger, 1989). Perhaps this is indeed adopting the broad view of play, that play can flow into literature: what is first acted out as a kind of theater is later put into words as a kind of storying. So while play can be identified with its use as a metaphor, such metaphoric use is just one of multiple transformations that can be made of play, and that are revealed within play itself. Further, playing with metaphor is as legitimate as playing with anything else. But play itself, if indeed it has a self, is a metaphor—not.

In short, the variability of the many uses of play in literature matches the desire for a play rhetoric that truly expresses such variability. It is possible to sum up this variety of ludic usages by saying that perhaps, at least in literature, we are witnessing at the end of the twentieth century a ludic turn that begins to match the aesthetic turn at the end of the eighteenth century. Where once art was at the center of moral existence, it now seems possible that play, given all its variable meanings, given the imaginary, will have that central role. I would even suggest that if we desire students to learn about the ludic turn in literature, we begin with a curriculum that includes such places as Wonderland, *The Decameron*, carnival, nonsense, the novel, and the world of tropes—or, alternatively, the works of Carroll, Boccaccio, Bakhtin, Stewart, and Fernandez.

Play of Signifiers

The most radical account of the role of the ludic turn in modern thought has come from the pen of Jacques Derrida (1970), who, like Bakhtin, finds language to have always a multiplicity of meanings, to be constantly reinterpretable with no central, essential, or final meanings. His position, in effect, criticizes all prior literatures of criticism, theology, Marxism, and structuralism that have sought to tie the meaning of texts to their own theories about them. Those theories usually involve the stipulation of some "sacred" source that is above and beyond the machinations of language, such as Plato's beauty, truth, and goodness; Christianity's Jesus; Rousseau's "nature"; Marx's "productive forces"; or Saussure's linguistics. The written texts of these authorities, according to Derrida, are only a play of signifiers, always susceptible to multiple interpretations, always susceptible to "deconstruction." Because Derrida calls the text a play of signifiers, it might seem appropriate to call it a text at play—and to be satisfied that things are this way because the mind and speech and writing are always at play in the broad sense of play. From the narrow, orthodox play perspective, however, the word *play* itself might be thought of as merely a metaphor for some other process of variability, randomization, or chaos that is going on in all this plurality. Derrida can be understood to support the broader perspective, as when he says, "Free play is the disruption of presence . . . Free play is always an interplay of absence and presence, but if it is to be radically conceived, free play must be conceived of before the alternative of presence or absence; being must be conceived of as presence or absence beginning with the possibility of free play and not the other way around" (1970; p. 264).

In sum, everything begins as free play, though there seems to be something of a paradox in the assertion that free play is so central to a process in which no center has a fixed meaning. One might argue that Derrida deals with free play in text only as a kind of metaphysical indeterminism, because there is little sense of who the person is who deconstructs the texts and discovers their plays of meaning. We are not told that the plays of meaning are resident in that person as a presence. But where else could they be? A play of text without some kind of human presence is like that falling tree in the forest. The contrast between Bakhtin and Derrida seems to be that Bakhtin finds the source of his radical variability in the multiplicitous meanings that occur within the imagination as well as in the interactions between people, and he contends that the novel is the best literary instrument we have for the expression of that radical uncertainty—an uncertainty that is constantly transcending itself, as the names of almost any outstanding novelists will indicate, to take Joyce, Nabokov, Barth, and Barthelme as a small sample. Derrida is concerned primarily with uncertainty in the written text itself. His focus is on literature; Bakhtin's is on people. Derrida is only one of a number of postmodern or poststructuralist writers who have expressed discontent with earlier ways of looking at the fundamental character of knowledge, and have suggested that life is much more generally play- or game-like than has generally been acknowledged in the earlier, more deterministic scenarios of a functional kind, such as are still found in abundance in the social sciences (Culler, 1988).

There are a number of other moderns who can be mentioned as further evidence of the spreading desire to find in the ludic some of the important answers to the nature of knowledge in the modern world. For example, William Stephenson, in his singular work, *The Play Theory of Mass Communication* (1967), presents the view that all media constitute play forms, and that when we are watching or receiving them we are essentially at play (in the broad sense). Even when you see an event on television, or read about it in the news, you are not actually there. It is not "Alive at five," as they say, it is rather the presentation of scenarios or interpretations about some event that is not present, and even when it is somewhat present—as, say, in the case of O.J. Simpson's "getaway" car on the Los Angeles freeway—the presentation is something that can be turned on or off.

One can suspend it at any moment and can like it or leave it. This is a characteristic of play, not of everyday adaptation.

French writer Jean Baudrillard has taken this point even more seriously, suggesting that most of us now live in a consumer-oriented-media world, where we are divorced from reality and suffering most of the time. Things are not what they seem, on a very large scale. We live most of the time in a world of pretending in which we relate to media figures without any accountability to them or to anyone else, nor do they have particular accountability to us. We are invited to play with this relationship in any way we wish, though advertisers naturally hope that they will have some effect on the daydreams they sponsor (Poster, 1990). Others have made much of the even more detached character of the person using a computer network, where the degree of accountability is also very low and a greater degree of freedom for playfulness, pretense, and multiple language games is possible (Turkle, 1995; Aycock, 1993, 1995). It is even suggested that in a culture dominated by such images, without personal account-ability, the imagination itself is imperiled. There is the paradox that we live in an empire of pretense, "a civilization of the image," as Barthes says, but without seeing much of the individuals who create the pretense. Obviously someone somewhere still has to be creative; but most of the play experienced by the recipients of the mass media is a play of images over which they have no control and for which the sponsors take little responsibility. What they see and participate in is an endless play of simulation or parody. It is called parody because each image is an imitation or exaggeration of some other image. There is no point of origin, no authentic beginning or authentic end point, or so it is said (Kearney, 1991). What such analyses underesti-mate, however, is the brain of the receiver sitting on his couch, who is never being just a potato. In most of these dire analyses of mass media there is an implicit copyist, tabula rasa notion of the brain of the receiver, whether that person be child or adult. If the brain is endlessly chattering to itself, as has been alleged by neurologists, it is simply not as malleable as the worst cynics imagine.

It follows that some writers will make efforts to escape what they see as the power of this endless circulation of simulated images through the mass media. Some intellectuals, indeed, have resorted to using play to escape the very power of language itself, which they see as being as bad as the media because it is also full of implicit stereo-typic hegemonies—economic, racist, and sexist—that are relatively inescapable and that control all of our thought (Foucault, 1972, 1973). Derrida's proposal of deconstruction was one tactic for end-lessly finding further interpretations not yet revealed and thus defeat-ing orthodox understandings. Roland Barthes is likewise famous for his notion of playing imaginatively with any text so that, by raising all of its possibilities, he can take the reader out of its given textual hegemony. One must open up the pleasures of the texts against the fetishes contained in them, he says. If this play is not undertaken, the texts are an encratic political force. And finally Derrida again, as if saving himself from the control that language takes in those who leave it as it is, has undertaken an extensive campaign of appearing to rewrite classics, as in his works *The Postcard from Socrates to Freud and Beyond* (1987) and, more self-evidently, *The Archeology of the Frivolous* (1980), both books that treat their subject with considerable if ab-struse playfulness. In these works Derrida becomes the kind of pres-ence that his corpus of writing is intended to deny. After all, where everything is at play and there are no players, who is Derrida?

Play, the Playful, and Metaplay

Play is sometimes defined in terms of the content of the forms it takes, such as children's play, games, sports, festivals, and so on, most of which are well-organized entities within human culture and are pursued with great earnestness, while *playful* refers more to a mood of frolicsomeness, lightheartedness, and wit. But there is nothing fixed about the distinction, because play is also usually thought to include the playful. At the same time, there is also a modern ten-dency to idealize the playful but to say that the more routine forms of games, sports, recreations, entertainments are only play. The dual-ity of play and the playful tends, in these cases, to be assimilated by the duality of work and play, the adult and the child, the serious and the nonserious, the heavy and the light, the corrupted and the innocent.

It is suggested here that these ambiguities of usage might be clarified by reserving the concept of playful for that which is meta-play, that which plays with normal expectations of play itself, as does nonsense, parody, paradox, and ridiculousness. Playful would be that which plays with the frames of play. Play, by contrast, would be that which plays with the frames of the mundane and sticks to its purpose of being a stylized form of house play, truck play, contest, or carnival in which the expected routines or rules guide and frame the action in a steady way throughout. Always granting, of course, that even in such sober play, some of the players may indulge in playful asides or disruptions, as when they make jokes about what is going on. Susan Stewart's work on nonsense, mentioned above, is the most profound discourse currently available on the character of what is playful. While it is a book on nonsense, she says all of the nonsense forms have as their basis the message, "This is Play" (1978, p. 199). She describes in great detail how these playful forms depend on such elements as reversal and inversion, exaggeration, paradox, playing with boundaries, playing with infinity, playing with space and playing with time. Some of the genres included by Stewart and others as obviously playful manipulations of established expectations are tricks, pranks, teasing, riddles, puzzles, sound play, spelling play, grammar play, genre play, and puns (McCarthur, 1992, p. 787). The key is that the playful is disruptive of settled expectations. It is the genre of comedians and tricksters, of wits and dilettantes. Indeed there are contests in some cases to see who can be more outrageously disturbing of expectations in wit or pranks. By contrast, the common fact of play life is that most players are deadly serious about their undertakings and do not typically make light of others who play around with their play meanings and their play pursuits. The playful is the modern way we idealize play. Play is the way we used to speak of ritual.

Validations and Definitions

The imaginary is a rhetoric derived from the historical movement known as romanticism. Its advocates and its players tend to be creative persons of literary and artistic competence, or the performers of their works. Its forms of play are those used by writers and thinkers as they go about their metaphoric and artistic tasks. The performers are writers, artists, composers, auteurs, and all other imaginative people. The scholars of imaginary play are found in all disciplines, but theorists of such mind play tend more often to use the term *play* metaphorically than as a part of any very systematic accounting. The members of this group have a tendency to denigrate the more physical kinds of play and to show perhaps too much readiness to consider themselves mind players of very large dimensions. Nevertheless the power of all the examples cited from art and literature, as well as from modern computer networking, strongly suggests that whatever may be the real science of the matter, the next generation is going to believe that our minds are always at play, regardless of whether there is any such vital play presence in our midst. The rhetoric of the imaginary seems likely to overwhelm the evidence. There will be a rhetoric of ludicism in the future, whether or not there is much substantial ludicmindedness. Participants acknowledge that as performers they are frequently at play in their work; they are artists only when they are at play, or perhaps they are ideally human only when they are at play, as Schiller meant to say.

Intrinsic definitions by theorists of this rhetoric of play would include the disputes over play as narrow or broad, top down or bottom up, aesthetic or mere play; play as art or as poetry; play as originality, autonomy, freedom, or innocence; play as only sometimes playful or metaplay; play as sober and the playful as facetious. See also the prior remarks of Bateson and Susan Stewart, about play as metacommunication and nonsense.

Extrinsic definitions might be that play is about heteroglossic cultural dialogues over gamesmanship, irony, humor, the novel, and the imagination; that the imagination makes unique models of the world, some of which lead us to anticipate useful changes, and some of which provide freedom in their mockery of the constraints of the ordinary world; that the flexibility of the imagination, of play, and of the playful is the ultimate guarantor of our survival.

Whatever ambiguity was found in the earlier rhetorics and their companion play forms is clearly much multiplied here. Play is used in so many ways in the arts, literature and semiotics, and is made to enter into so many relationships with metaphor, that there is no way these varieties can be contained in one simple ludic category. Nor, for that matter, can we fit Carroll, Boccaccio, Bakhtin, and the many others mentioned into one unified category. Furthermore, quite apart from all the ambiguities in the discourses about the form of play that I am here calling the imaginary, play itself is inherently ambiguous and unpredictable. That is its nature. Take, for example, even the interesting suggestion that play and the playful are a duality. Perhaps instead they are more subtly the ends of some continuum, one end of which has play genres that are framed, follow the rules, and have relatively predictable expectations (as in games and sports), and the other end of which doesn't play within the rules but with the rules, doesn't play within frames but with the frames, as in farce and comedy. A neat contrast, but then of course it follows that if the playful, witty, trickster person plays with the frames and the rules and defies conventional expectations, then that trickster is playing by some other rules. He who is breaking the play rules is being ruled by some other rules of play. The rest of us know he won't play by the usual rules of decorum or according to the usual meanings of words, but he will in general stay metaphorically "on stage" when he shocks us with his fantasies. We "frame" him as a "comedian" and he can play with material that most of us do not play with in the same irreverent way, but he is nevertheless confined by the rules of public presentation. That is, he may be playful as a comedian, but to be a comedian is to be "in play," that is, to be in a known, rule-bound play context. So to be playful most of the time requires that it be known that this is only play. Where that is not known, the player risks embarrassment or outrage. Having said that, however, it is also true that one of the ways of being playful is to play with even that expectation, so that people respond with "I hope you are only pretending." Still, one who plays with the ambiguity of his own pretense must ultimately be perceived as being at play in some form. Playing with just that ambiguity—whether he really means it or is just playing—is the most ambiguous form of play.

9

Child Phantasmagoria

He who dies with the most toys wins.
T-shirt

Play may not be literal, but it is very tangible.
after Frech

In Chapter 8, the examples from many disciplines suggest that Western society is beginning to take play more seriously as an important form of culture. Attempts are being made to extend the range of what is meant by play, so that a much broader definition seems applicable. From the progress rhetoric material on childhood, however, the argument could be made that the central historical effort these past two hundred years has been to suppress recognizing either of these broad play possibilities so far as children are concerned. Even with adult theories of play, no matter how far ranging, Spariosu still finds that, with few exceptions, the broadening of the view of play is usually accompanied by some ultimate belief that such knowledge will give us a more orderly grasp of the nature of things human and nonhuman. Thus, with the exception of Nietzsche, and possibly Feyerabend, if irrationality is brought into our purview, its recognition is only temporary, because in the long run it is used once again to broaden the boundaries of rational control and understanding.

It seems that the history of the imagination in childhood is a history of ever greater suppression and rationalization of the irrational. Paradoxically children, who are supposed to be the players among us, are allowed much less freedom for irrational, wild, dark, or deep play in Western culture than are adults, who are thought not to play at all. Studies of child fantasy are largely about the control, domestication, and direction of childhood. So in a sense the rhetoric of the imaginary, with its emphasis on so many varied possible rational and irrational play transformations, is not much used for childhood. At the same time, the words *imagination* and *fancy* are constantly associated with childhood in some lesser and idealizing manner, as is exemplified by the great body of children's literature, and the Disney- and Nickelodeon-like character of most media for children.

This leads, paradoxically, to the contention that there is a need to develop a rhetoric that will apply to the widest array of childhood imaginary potentialities. But this would be an anomaly, because the other rhetorics presented in this work are historically well established value systems, whereas any such special rhetoric of the imaginary for children would have to represent our own personal invented rhetoric at this time. In Chapter 7 a beginning was made as to what such a child-oriented power rhetoric might look like. The term *phantasmagorical rhetoric* will be used here to distinguish how one might also schematize a rhetoric of the Imaginary for children that is oriented toward irrationality as well as rationality.

Toys and Television as Phantasmagoria

The progress rhetoric dominates most of the early Western discussion of toys. Toys are designed as learning devices in the eighteenth and nineteenth centuries. They are meant to teach something about the world. In the twentieth century, however, they increasingly inherit the contexts of both romanticism and commercialism. Romanticism gives us Wordsworth's belief that his capacity to be a creative adult derived from his early memories and the fantasies of his childhood (Wordsworth, Jaye, and Woof, 1987). In so declaring he brings childhood into the concourse of Romanticized history otherwise symbolized by such icons as the "primitive" and the "noble savage," and subsequently memorialized in children's literature by Alice, by *The Secret Garden,* by Peter Pan, and by Pooh (Kuznets, 1994). These late nineteenth and early twentieth-century literary works stress the timeless imagination of childhood and increasingly led parents to permit their children to participate in that state of mind.

Connecting toys with this wonderland on any large scale may not have occurred, according to Gross (1996), until handcrafted toys were replaced by better-made commercially produced symbols of childhood innocence, such as the teddy bear, which may have been the first toy to permit the symbolization of overt affection by children in the presence of their parents. Thus we have the paradox that commercial toys, currently identified with the extinction of romanticism, along with children's literature, may have been one of romanticisms major cultural carriers. The cultural interpretation of the toy in children's imaginary life has, in this century, been a paradoxical battle between the fears of mass commercial stereotyping of children's play and the ability of the toys to expand on the emotional life of the children who get to play with them. In this interpretation, while toy manufacturers do flood the world with their stereotypic images, their success or failure depends on their making a toy that presents some dynamic underlying human fantasy. The Barbie Doll, at first so deplored for her glamour stereotype, is now discussed as the first permissible symbol of the emergence of interest in a sexualized body for young girls (Brougère, 1992). It is said that Barbies satisfy girls' elementary lust for an active discourse with the body. Even if the doll represents only one of the body's sexual discourse possibilities, it seems to be the first made available for small girls in mass iconology.

Although Kline, in *Out of the Garden* (1993), his important survey of the modern state of toys, has interpreted the commercialization of toys as no longer sustaining the innocent and secret childlike fantasies that resonated in children's literary classics, in the light of the studies by Cross and Brougère, apparently what might be occurring between commercial product and private fantasy is somewhat more complex. The players' minds are clearly not entirely the stereotypic tabulae rasae of the modern commercial world; children still have their private imaginary gardens, even if the content of those gardens is not always as sweetly Victorian as the prior era might have supposed. Jerome and Dorothy Singer, in their work *The House of Make-believe* (1992), spend considerable time discussing and promulgating, in a Wordsworthian way, the importance of encouraging children in their early imaginings. They find that imagination plays a large role in the lives of some children and, furthermore, that those who are more imaginative, other skills being equal, seem to manage their school lives with more persistence, self-control, and enjoyment and are less of a problem to others (Singer, 1966, 1973). Whether imagination is a cure for all or only for certain personalities is not yet clear, but the latter seems to be the case in the cute study by Silvey and MacKeith (1988) of what they call "paracosms," and in the study by Cohen and MacKeith (1991). Apparently a small percentage of children grow up, as Wordsworth thought only poets could, treasuring forever afterward their memories of some recurrent fantasy that preoccupied them in their infancy, childhood, or youth. In examining some of these modern paracosms, the authors show them to be quite as phantasmagorical as one might expect.

An additional example from Brougère shows that even when children try their hardest to match their own play behavior to that modeled for them by television—in this case, to the actions of the *Power Rangers* television show—they are forced by their need for cooperation to make all kinds of compromises, such as bargaining for who takes the negative roles, deciding how they can adapt their unique "power" feelings to the scenario, devising costumes, weapons, gestures, and sequences. What they reproduce is a playful theatric adaptation. There is no tabula rasa. The point is, no matter what the cultural stimuli might be (toys or television shows), they have to be mediated by children's fantasy in order to be accepted, and adjusted to their play norms and social competence in order to be assimilated into the active theatric play forms of childhood. Commercial stimuli that meet these requirements will be adopted, and will dismay parents who do not want to believe their children are responsive to such fantasies, phantasmagorical and violent as so many of them are today.

Increasingly the producers of these commercial phenomena successfully create and distribute material that indicates that children are as polymorphously perverse in their fantasies as are their parents. The programming seminars conducted by children's television studios, in the meantime, such as those of Nickelodeon and Rupert Murdoch's networks, rage with contests between those who are more emotionally labile and perverse and those who are more constricted, those who are more macho and those more humane. Some of the members of these groups are phenomenally creative, and some keep their eye on respect for parental values—although not to such an extent as to lose children's attention and reduce advertising income.

Furthermore, the modern realm of child phantasmagoria is increasingly being staged in solitary play rather than in the collective play discussed above. In an earlier work, *Toys as Culture* (Sutton-Smith, 1986b), I present the case that one of the major implicit cultural functions of toys in the past 200 years has been as props to support relatively solitary play. Play in most societies throughout most of history has been a collective activity. But in modern societies, which require massive amounts of individualized symbolic skill from their members, habituating children to solitary preoccupations has been a primary function of toys. Though most educators emphasize the cognitive, educational, or motoric worth of toys, it is as probable that toys' solitary function is actually like that of "homework," that is, to habituate children to the "solitariness" of a preoccupation with personal "imaginary" skill. But toys are also remarkable in the modern world because they are decreasingly self-evident tools. The more traditional the society, the more likely the toy is a simulacrum of an adult occupation (a miniature spear, a doll); the more modern the society, the more likely it is a negation of everyday realism. It is fundamentally inversively symbolic. One can consider, as a simple example, the Play Path toys of the Johnson and Johnson Company, most of which have more to do with the mental fantasies of the great genetic philosopher Piaget about infant cognitive development than about the more mundane forms of reality. The infant toys even look like Bauhaus plumbing. At the other end of the age span, children are being increasingly immersed in the virtual realities of video games, computers, and virtual worlds. These are all admittedly crutches for the development and standardization of fantasy, but they also permit the promotion of internal (and therefore unpredictable) solitary fantasy. Some commentators speculate most positively about the value of the changes occurring in children as a result of these modern forms of play (Rushkoff, 1996).

It is important to emphasize at this point that in solitary or private play children create cultures of play that are virtual worlds not mundane worlds, and often with not much obligation to the latter. The "paracosms" are only an extreme form of the capacity all children normally have for creating their own virtual worlds, even if these often reflect larger cultural worlds (as in daydreaming about fantasy heroes). Most adults look at children's play with toys with a kind of amazement at how they can be preoccupied so well with them, and they also look with amazement at the millions of "strange" adults who still collect toys and presumably still fantasize about them. But it may be that all of us, child and adult, work at fantasizing metaphysical paracosms all our days. We are eternally making over the world in our minds, and much of it is fantasy. The difference is that while children have toys, adults usually have images, words, music, and daydreams, which perform much the same function as toys. Our fantasies are the microworlds of inner life that all of us manipulate in our own way to come to terms with feelings, conflicts, realities, and aspirations as they enter into our lives. Children and adults may not really be so different in their use of fantasy play. The difference lies in the concreteness of the symbols, and in the maturity of their purpose, not in the universal existence of fantasied inner lives (Kuznets, 1994).

Childhood Pretense

In general psychologists have not done a great deal with the imagination of children. They have been more concerned with the supposedly serious functions of problem solving, learning, and exploration, as well as with quantifiable kinds of creativity. There are exceptions, of course, because a great deal has been said about the childish aberrant imagination in works on child play therapy and child psychodynamics. But in those sources the imagination is typically examined as a psychological defense against conflict rather than as a creative power of the mind. There are literally thousands of articles and books of this kind; a few must suffice here for reference purposes (Schaefer and O'Connor, 1983; Solnit, Cohen, and Neubauer, 1993; Herron and Sutton-Smith, 1971).

Despite the immense amount of scientific work on child development, there has as yet been no encouragement to see in children's imaginations and playfulness the willful variety of possibilities that motivate adults' use of the play concept, as discussed in the preceding chapter. Yet there is enough evidence of variegation in the chapter on child power and identity (Chapter 7), including the hidden transcripts of children's play groups, to show that the material is there. The material on riddles, rhymes, gaming, play-grounds, jokes, pranks, tales, and legends, as well as on institutional life, show that in their collective life children often have access to a wild array of carnivalesque fancy. Fantasy, mundane or fantastic, has always been only a small part of research in developmental psychology from the earliest years, even if never a major theme. It would be disrespectful not to pay some belated tribute to at least a few of the original writings on imagination and fantasy, by such investigators as Bach (1945); Griffiths (1935); Hartley, Frank, and Goldenson (1952); Murphy (1957). In the past twenty years, how-ever, in the nontherapy areas, most of this small stream of interest in child fantasy has been channeled into cognitive studies on the nature of pretense. What is left of Nietzsche's metaphoric dream of the ravaging child is a small number of studies on the origins and development of the capacity for pretense in preschool chil-dren—all of which is excellent and scientific in its own right, but is an indication of the further limited and contained exploration of these child powers in the academic world. This also brings up what is faulty about much of the work on children's imagination. Most thinking on children's imagination is in terms of its degrees of abstraction (the number of transformations, the complexity of the role structure, the degrees of nonrealism, the forms of decon-textualization). This is legitimate when we wish to think about play in the light of logic and information (categories and hierarchies), but it processes the imagination only in terms of complexity. It does not explain why children must dream such dreams; why some dream them forcefully and continually and others very little. This is again an argument against a solely progress rhetoric oriented concern. Nevertheless these studies do show that children can com-prehend and sustain very complex play macrocosms together and paracosms by themselves, and that is indeed a testimony to play's independence, without which viable ludic transformations would probably not be possible (Fein, 1981; Leslie, 1987; Howes, 1992; Bornstein and O'Reilly, 1993; Goncu, 1993; Harris and Kavanaugh, 1993; Lillard, 1993; McCune, 1995).

Suffice to say that it has been a hard fight for early childhood psychologists such as Greta Fein to establish that play is motivated primarily by feelings and not just by images of reality, and that children's fantastic exaggerations are their storied interpretations of the world (Fein, 1981, 1984, 1987). As she says:

> Although divergent thinking is characterized by novel and original associations, most theorists exclude bizarre or inappropriate associations from the definitions of novelty and originality. In pretend play, however, there is often ludicrous distortion, exaggeration, and extravagance at times bordering on the bizarre. At the same time, the distortion, exaggeration and extravagance reveal a considerable degree of affective force but cognitive theorists have all but ignored the affective side of pretense . . .
>   . . . These affective units, which constitute affect-binding representational templates, yield the "motivated" symbols of Piagetian theory. These motivated symbols are always present in pretense, from the infant's rendering of a physiological state in pretending to sleep, to the older child's rendering of intricate emotional overtones in pretending about being sent to bed. (1987, pp. 291, 293)

Children's play fantasies are not meant only to replicate the world, nor to be only its therapy; they are meant to fabricate another world that lives alongside the first one and carries on its own kind of life, a life often much more emotionally vivid than mundane reality. According to Fein, children give their play a structure, which is based on experiencing in a safe way the intense and even potentially disturbing emotional relationships of actuality or fantasy. Their play is not based primarily on a representation of everyday real events—as many prior investigators have supposed—so much as it is based on a fantasy of emotional events. The logic of play is the logic of dealing with emotions such as anger, approval, or fear, and it has to do with how these may be expressed and reacted to in any mundane or fantastic way that the players choose. What is remarkable about the Fein account (and it is much more complex than can be detailed here) is that it parallels the efforts of biologists who tell us that animal play also is not about realistic representations, that it is, rather, fragmentary, disorderly, and exaggerative, which are not forms of "realism." Similarly, folklorist Roger Abrahams says adult festivals, are not mirrors of reality but are purposely made intense through distortions of everyday events, by including huge or dwarf creatures, firecrackers, ragtag costumes, grotesque masks, tricksters, and clowns. The unreal worlds of play and festival are like that of the novel or the theater. They are about how to react emotionally to the experience of living in the world and how to temporarily vivify that experience by transcending its usual limits. Life in the ludic lane can never be understood simply in terms of that which it interprets realistically, the so-called real world. It must be about mockery as well as mimicry.

When there is well-developed imaginative play, there must always be some entry into nonliteral behavior, which leads to the introduction of acts or objects that are only for pretend purposes. Further, with time these play actions become increasingly original and unpredictable. Children know that they are manipulating their thoughts about reality, not reality itself; and they know that their play self is not the same as their everyday self. Also it is generally agreed that children's play life has its own distinct gestures and language forms, many of which have been documented by Catherine Garvey (1977, 1993). Players also have their own well-developed techniques of stage management. To understand a group of well-acquainted children at play, it is often useful to think of them like a traveling troupe of medieval players who arrive, set up their theater, and then begin performing (Bretherton, 1984; Giffin, 1984). It is a world that is run more like a theater is run than like an everyday world. Children play the parts of stage managers, directors, and actors all at the same time, moving freely about the parts as they get ready to put together their own shows for themselves, and even if the show never gets off the ground, all of these activities are known to them as their "play" or their "games" (Magee, 1987). One has to concede that in the face of an adult world that wants to think children's play is not important—or if important, it is so because it imitates the adult world, and if excusable, it is so because it does that politely—the very solid evidence established in these pretense studies contributes to our appreciation of the autonomy of the play life in childhood. This is true even though most of the studies are confined to the cleaned-up world of the kindergarten and do not much reflect the kinds of phantasmagoria of which children are capable when in places under their own control. We are once again in that halfway world between fantasy being feeble or fantasy being too much to tolerate. But whatever we call it, children quickly establish their own autonomous cultures of play.

Childhood Narratives as Phantasmagoria

To demonstrate that children have a capacity for rendering their lives in theatric and fantastic ways, we have the massive body of therapy-derived evidence, the slighter mass of collective folklore evidence, and the sparse anecdotal evidence in developmental psychology. There is little else of a normative character to help us make an empirical determination of the varieties and importance of the wilder kinds of the childish imagination. What we do have of worth, however, are some systematic collections of children's own made-up stories, and in these one finds abundant phantasmagoria. There is similar evidence in the work on children's dreaming, which I referred to in Chapter 4, but there seems little need to demonstrate that the childish contents of dreaming and daydreaming are similarly phantasmagorical (McCale-Small, 1994).

Stories are not themselves play, but it seems that many of the themes that appear in the stories of preschoolers are first found in their play, such as being chased, fighting, and crashing automobiles. Thus a case may be made that what emerges as story can be drawn from prior experiences in play. Major antecedents of childhood storied art forms may be prior play forms, rather than so-called real experience, although reality obviously also has some hand in these emergent cultural forms. This is an important point, because it challenges the Cartesian readiness of most social science thinkers to make so-called reality the more fundamental sphere in the life-versus-play relationship, rather than seeing that these play phenomena always exist as a separate system with their own inherent developmental sequences. If this is not at first sight obvious, think of development in music, or development in graphics, and how much it has to do formally with the norms of music and art, and how little to do with everyday behavior.

Peterson and McCabe (1983) say of their collection of children's stories, "In a nutshell, children are interested in pain, gore, and Keystone Cop–style mishaps, as cartoonists and scriptwriters have known for years" (p. 27). This conclusion is easily supported by the Pitcher and Prelinger collection, *Children Tell Stories* (1963) and from my own collection, *The Folkstories of Children* (1981a). The typical actions in orally told stories by young children include being lost, being stolen, being bitten, dying, being stepped on, being angry, calling the police, running way, or falling down. In their stories they portray a world of great flux, anarchy, and disaster, not unlike that imagined by Nietzsche in his portrayal of childhood. Nietzsche was apparently right about their fabulations, if not about their behavior. Very young children's preference for these tales of relative disaster, often without any resolution, has to be a major reason why their stories are either avoided or strongly modified in most school situations. The stories in my collection were drawn from a special New York City school where, at that time, there was considerable license for free expression of any art-oriented kind. I should also emphasize that the stories were taken down over a three-year period, without moralistic commentary and with recipient enjoyment, so that the tellers came to trust and feel free in the presence of the story takers.*

If you add to young children's story disasters their repetitive episodic plots, their preferences for rhyme and alliteration, their nonsense, their obscenity, their crazy titles, morals, and characters, it is not surprising that most adults, even those who believe they are favorable to creative expression, tend to avoid them. Our Western belief in rationality is so important to us that tolerance for such clear bouts of apparent irrationality is limited, even though one could point out that in these cases the irrationality is only of a literary kind, not a behavioral one.

There follow two illustrations of childish phantasmagoria from *The Folkstories of Children*, a collection of 500 stories from some fifty children. Told by a four-year-old boy:

> Once there was a dragon who went poo poo on a house and the house broke
> then when the house broke the people died
> and when the people died their bones came out and broke and got together again and turned into a skeleton
> and then the skeletons came along and scared the people out of the town
> and then when all the people got scared out of the town then

*My story collections would not have been possible without the support of a remarkably progressive-thinking school principal, the late John Melser, a colleague from New Zealand.

skeleton babies were born
and then everyone called it skeleton town
and when they called it skeleton town the people came back and
then they got scared away again
and then when they all got scared away again the skeletons died
no one came to the town
so there was no people in that town ever again.

Told by a seven-year-old boy:

Once there was two babies and they hung from the ceiling naked
and their weenies was so long their mother needed 300 and 20
rooms to fit half of it in. But they had to chop half of it off. And the
baby had to go to the bathroom. So since they didn't have no
bathroom big enough for his weener to fit, so he put his weener out
of the window and Nixon happened to be walking along. And he
said "Flying hotdogs, I never heard of it." And then he said "Well I
might have one, it looks good." So the baby had to go to the
bathroom and Nixon took a big bite . . .

(Descriptions of the original materials referred to here are to be
found in Sutton-Smith, 1981; Abrams and Sutton-Smith, 1977; Botvin
and Sutton-Smith, 1977; Sutton-Smith and Abrams, 1978; Sutton-
Smith and Heath, 1981).

Inventing crazy and perverse stories is not the only way children
play with disorder in their lives. The youngest play at knocking down
blocks, destroying sand castles, jumping off furniture, rolling down
hills, falling over, laughing or screaming just for the sake of it. The
logic of some of this has to be that the very young so often suffer from
mistakes, accidents, clumsiness, food spilling, and enuresis that it is
not surprising if personal or perceived disaster should be alluded to
in their play and narrative lives. Adults have similar apprehensions
and allow theatric disaster to enter into their own recreations, as with
carnivals, festivals, roller coasters, clowns, contact sports, rock concerts, bungee jumping, and gambling. Children may have their real
small-scale disasters, but adults have their own very large ones: war,
catastrophe, accidents, hurricanes, riots, sickness, and death. The
play of disorder and phantasmagoria would then seem to be a universal aspect of all free play, for both child and adult. It is noticeable that

there is a very great distance between the real-life disaster and the ludic "disaster." There is not too much resemblance between a war and a circus.

As a footnote of caution Nicolopoulou has shown in her collections of the stories of four- and five-year-old children that boys are more prone to delight in disorder and girls in order. "The girls' stories are more likely to be marked by a stable set of characters located in stable and specified physical settings . . . In contrast the boys' are more marked by movement and disruption, and often by associative chains of exuberant imagery" (Nicolopoulou, 1997). Given that in my own study of children's obscene stories (Sutton-Smith and Abrams, 1978) more were garnered from boys than girls by both the male and female story takers, it seems highly probable that this theme of phantasmagoria has gender overtones. That is, both sexes truly pretend in play or story, but boys may be more prone to the exaggerative and the bizarre. Phantasmagoria as contrasted with imagination may still show a traditional gender difference.

It is useful to note that in the now well recorded presleep monologues of two-year-olds, there are no disasters to parallel those recorded above (Kuczaj, 1983). The two-year-olds' conversations with themselves represent the content of more everyday events; they are not dramatic as these stories are. This demonstrates that the stories are not just some unwitting Freudian emergence from the unconscious, because if they were would they not also appear at bedtime in the monologues? It seems these stories are socially dramatic performances designed with listeners in mind. They are part of the collective cultural genres of narrative to which children have had access from the earliest years in the storytelling of parents, in books, and nowadays in television. Such stories certainly commanded the attention of other children when we were collecting them. They would gather around the storyteller with much laughter and exclamation. Phantasmagoria, parodied or realistic, usually does command such attention.

Given the above description of the chaotic stories of children up to about seven years of age, and their parallels with many of the trickster stories in the folklore of other peoples (Abrams and Sutton-Smith, 1977), it is possible to suppose that these early childhood stories are very basic, perhaps universal, narratives of the human mind. Often called chronicles, they have been interpreted as *cyclic*

narratives of a tragic and comic character that voice a fatalistic response to the world (Appleyard, 1990). They are either mystically
religious (in ancient terms) or personally therapeutic (in modern
terms), because they take the teller and the listeners out of everyday
life into an "immortal" or "virtual" imaginative realm. The transformation of everyday emotion into virtual reality is often an elevating
event. It is possible to contend that much of the storied repetitiveness
of these cyclical tales is like that which occurs in religious liturgy,
where the redundancy accompanies a spiritual sense of being ele-
vated into another world. It may be pertinent to think of all early
stories and all early play in this way, as cyclical forms of virtual
transcendency. They all signal a leap into a different form of consciousness, and the repetitiveness retains that state of elevation.

At this elementary level there may not indeed be much difference
between story and play. Obviously, playful repetitiveness is the earlier
form of the two, at least in behavior (as in animals), unless we are to
grant dreams to animals, which we may have to do. Either way,
perhaps it is better to say that play, both as repeated behaviors and as
repeated stories, arises from an undifferentiated state. What may be
intriguing for biological theologians (Burkett, 1996) is the possible
primacy of play and dreams as the earliest expressions of the virtuality
that will later be required as an underpinning for the domain of the
soul. Presumably a virtual soul—that is, a playful soul—must emerge
in the animal kingdom before a derivative of the same can emerge as
a transcendent phenomenon, such as the soul in human affairs. The
copresence of play and ritual in much tribal custom certainly suggests
an earlier or at least different condition, in which the two were much
more easily linked in cultural consciousness than they have been in
modern civilization (Drewal, 1992). One wonders whether the moment in history has arrived when the uneasiness between play and
religion will be revised; whether the time has come when the joyful-
ness of play and the awesomeness of religion will be transcended in
some new form of human enjoyment and devotion.

But to continue with the present plot, these basic, primal, cyclic
narratives need to be contrasted with the more linear, plot-oriented
kind that we usually understand as stories within the Western tradition. Children, by the age of seven years, despite continuing disasters
in their stories, begin to create central characters that are more

reactive to their fate. They do not simply suffer it like nameless victims, they make some attempt to overcome it. And by seven to nine years of age, children begin to make up characters that actually overcome the villains or the deficiencies in their stories—though we are never too sure whether, after their victories, the characters may not be in trouble once more. Its only at the end of childhood, at about eleven years, that children finally tell stories with such miraculous transformations that everyone can live happily ever after without fear of regression. Thus, through the main vein of their self-told stories of disaster, the hero and heroine figures are gradually rising. In their own personal fantastic worlds they are forging their own quest for emotional truth. In narrative, as in social organization, they are capable of self-construction, even when the medium is phantasmagorical. The central childhood period is, then, occupied largely by hero tales or tales of romance that are a part of the traditional Western narrative pattern of overcoming adversity, which is not apparent in all human societies. Most Western narratologists assume that this ethnocentric linear form is a human universal, which it is not. And it is legitimate to say that the great majority of Western children's games are also of this type. They are games of romance, games in which someone overcomes adversity or is made into a leader or a winner. The games, on the one hand, and the linear stories, on the other, are two of the major ways in which Western children grow up with increasing confidence in their ability to fulfill some kind of quest.

The third type of story we find in childhood is that of nonsense, parody, and satire. This begins in the chaos of the earlier years but in childhood takes on a more formal character, as in riddle parodies, bathroom jokes, cruel jokes, gross jokes, elephant jokes, Dolly Parton jokes, Christa McAuliffe jokes, and stories that center on absurdity. These are all part of a childish play world in which, there is so much pressure for good grades, good behavior, and popularity that absurdity may be the only response. It would not be too outlandish to say that much of the phantasmagoria of midchildhood has to do with learning how to cope with failure by playing with parodies of failing. It has already been noted that the largest expenditures on adult games are on games of chance and gambling, where failure is guaranteed, and these have also been interpreted as a way of mastering failure by failing on one's own terms. Games of chance are known to be more popular with those who have experienced relative failure in the socioeconomic sense. At the same time, these parodic play forms are also to be found in adult festivals (Chapter 6) and in adult frivolity (Chapter 11). Clearly the parody has its own life and times.

In sum, narratives and play of a cyclic (tragic-comic), linear (romance), and parodic (satirical) kind show that there is pattern to the phantasmagorias of childhood and that it behooves those who would study childhood to understand the relatively autonomous nature of these imaginative play forms. There is order as well as disorder in these records, and our children deserve an adult rhetoric that will pay respect to their use of play for both power purposes and phantasmagorical puposes. At the moment, the rhetoric of progress blots out the possibilities for such a larger child-oriented humanism.

The Ludic Construction and Deconstruction of Irreality

What has been established thus far is that children's own play society, because it is about their feelings about reality and not about the direct representation of reality as such, is a deconstruction of that realistic society. It takes the world apart in a way that suits their own emotional responses to it. As such, their play is a deconstruction of the world in which they live. If the world is a text, the play is a reader's response to that text. There are endless possible reader responses to the orthodox text of growing up in childhood. There is an endless play of signifiers of which children and all other players are capable (Derrida, 1970). All players unravel in some way the accepted orthodoxies of the world in which they live, whether those orthodoxies have their source in adult or child peer groups.

So phantasmagoria exists on individual and social levels, and children are afflicted by it, as are adults. It is a common heritage. Still it is important to remember that all of the above information tends to be exemplified best by the play, daydreams, or stories of highly imaginative children. Looking at such selected children (called high players, high storytellers, responsive daydreamers) focuses attention on the imaginative brilliance that is possible in play. What tends to be underemphasized in such accounts is that ordinary children, in establishing their social play, must do many mundane things in order to play together. In this they are no different from animals or adults whose social play is highly repetitive and in a way highly conservative, even if also innovative in bringing about rearrangements of ordinary behavior and instigating quite novel behaviors, gestures, speech, and fantasies. There is a need to reach some deeper understanding of this paradox about social play, how it can be both conservative and innovative, a dilemma nowadays called Newall's paradox (Fine, 1980). Newall wrote the first ever book about children's games, *Games and Songs of American Children,* in 1883 and worried about this apparent contradiction between play's novelty and its ritualism.

Meckley (1994) undertook a five-month longitudinal videotaped study of 12 three- and four-year-old children at their daily play in order to learn how they were able to establish their own play society. She used multiple methods of data collection, including video and audio taping. As the study took place in a university preschool, it follows that the children's behavior was more orderly and less phantasmagorical than would likely be the case, say, among friends in a neighborhood (which would in turn be much less disorderly than some adults could imagine about children, as in the phantasmagoria of the *Lord of the Flies,* which is itself perhaps rivaled by the lives of street children in some parts of the Third World and in the slums of the first).

Meckley asked whether such young children can really construct their own play culture in the preschool setting and took as a standard of such construction the account of Berger and Luckmann (1966). According to Berger and Luckmann, if social play is to be regarded as a social construction made and maintained by the children themselves, then it would have to have as its features what adult society has, namely:

The community should have distinct, consistent, and predictable patterns of repeated actions, objects, players, and words.
The activities should occur in an ordered sequential manner over time and within consistent settings.
The varied play events should be interconnected.

Shared knowledge should be demonstrated.
Control and ownership of specific play events should be shown.
Children's play roles should reflect this collective reality.

Most nursery school teachers who allow their children considerable time to play will agree that the children can and do set up such a society. It is an ephemeral society, because it exists only for the duration allowed in the classroom day. A majority of teachers, however, do not set aside this time and thus prevent such a society from developing in any effective way. The children thus remain more dependent on adult socialization processes and have less of a chance to become autonomous and cooperative social beings themselves within play. The many studies of children's individual play competence or dyadic metacommunication skills, with parents or other children, do not allow us to make any judgment about what they can maintain or innovate socially in any collective sense. There is evidence that children get better and better at such imaginative social construction the longer they are allowed to play together and that usually by the age of three or four years they are quite capable of such group autonomy (Rubin, Fein, and Vandenberg, 1983). Studies of such collectivity that are important precedents for the present study are Corsaro, 1985, 1992; Schwartzman, 1978; Giffin, 1984; and Paley, 1981, 1984, 1990, 1992.

Over the five-month period, Meckley identified sixty-five play events in which one or more of the children participated, including varieties of play with or about the following: building blocks, castles, *bombs, prisons, floods,* trucks, *weapons, guns, police, clowns,* houses, dressing up, *blasters,* marriage, setting the table, kitchens, families, moving, babies, puppets, climbing, constructions, water, sand, clay, easels, *dinosaurs,* garages, necklaces, roads and railroads, planes, tractors, boats, reading, school, pegs, games, *chasing.* (The italicized events were intentionally phantasmagorical. Many others were also phantasmagorical on occasion.) These sixty-five events were then classified according to whether they were concurrent, intersecting, single, complex, collective, confrontational, evolved, diversive, linked, or transitional.

What emerges very quickly from the highly complex world created by these twelve children is that most of the games are played again and again at the same time each day, by the same players, in the same way. This is not the kind of information that one gets when studying the play of different children separately without calibrating activities across all children at the same times, as has been the case for practically all other studies of children's play. The unique character of this investigation lies in the monitoring of collective play. Researchers could return to the videotapes and score what each child was doing separately at the same time, minute by minute, during the play period. Despite the obvious originality of what the children were doing, despite their continuous negotiations and their shared knowledge, their repetition of the details indicates that they are highly conservative. What is at first glance innovative play is found to be a highly ritualized series of events. It is important to stress also that this was a group of children left to their own devices throughout the play period, so that the possibility of gradually forming a society of their own was open, and this is not typical in most playrooms, because adults often interfere and their intrusions inhibit the processes of autonomous social development.

Meckley's is a remarkable finding because in the general literature on adult play and ritual the two are often separated out as quite different kinds of phenomena, and one can indeed make such a distinction between, say, improvisational role-playing by theater students and a ritualistic religious ceremony conducted by a priest. In the early play of young children, however, play and ritual are handmaidens. Social play has to be both innovative and ritualistic to survive, though it is also clear from these data that some play events are more highly ritualistic than others. In the preschool group Meckley observed, for example, playing bombs and playing dolls were highly consistent, block events were of moderate consistency, water play and sand play were of very low consistency. Similar variability in consistency applied to the players; their use of actions, objects, and words; the interconnectedness of events; the times of day; the order of events within a day, across sessions, and across the five months of the study. Most of the children, when participating in events beyond those that they typically played, showed that they knew how the games were usually played by others and participated without trouble. In short, most of the children knew the routines of what was going on around them all the time, not just what they themselves usually focused on. Several of the more isolated or absence-prone children, however, did not show this knowledge and blundered with the games and their properties or sequences when joining in. Most events were controlled and "owned" by particular subgroups of children, and gender differences and individual styles of play were important. Some children preferred the quieter forms of play and some were louder, more dramatic, and more confrontational in their play forms. Not surprisingly more boys than girls were prone to the latter phantasmagoria, but not exclusively so.

Meckley had no difficulty demonstrating that most of Berger and Luckmann's requirements for the social construction of reality were to be found in the construction of the collective play life of these twelve children. Furthermore the boys' occasional phantasmagorias of blasting away the world of girls, or of the girls portraying ridiculous or disputative household events were fully matched by the routinization of their own roles and actions. In a sense it is very clear that no one can run a society without a great deal of routine or ritual, for otherwise it is impossible to act as a knowing group. Children don't want to have to invent their play life from scratch every day, and they probably need the ritual as a kind of time and behavior marker that allows new freedoms for their fantasy life. Further, all of the rituals the preschoolers established differentiated increasingly over time. That is, there was consistency but there was also growth.

The thing that is remarkable about this is that many of those who write about children's play see it as particularly flexible, spontaneous, and ambiguous, and see adult games as lacking in these characteristics. But what seems more obviously to be the case is that both children's social play and adults' sports and festivals are characterized by ritual as well as innovation. The innovations of these young children were no more notable than the constant innovation of tactics and strategies that goes on among professional athletes both in regular games and in warm-up games and practices. The more important point, however, is the revelation of the very real autonomy of children's play culture when they are given the opportunity to develop it. It is appropriate at this point to acknowledge the work of Corsaro (1985) and others who have also sought to show the autonomy of children in the developing of their own cultural routines in play—through framings, keyings, and embellishments, but most important through their own mutual negotiations.

Validations and Definitions

The rhetoric of this chapter and the previous one identifies the historical source of phantasmagoria as the romantic period in Western history. The notion of play as flexible, imaginative, and creative finds a supportive response from intellectuals in the arts and some of the sciences. In a much more constricted and idealized way, the notion is also applied to children. As shown here, however, children can also claim phantasmagoria and nonsense, while adults claim carnivalia and clowning. What this chapter establishes is that children have their own distinctive forms of phantasmagorical play. They have few advocates that study this focus, apart from some writers in children's literature and in children's folklore. The character of phantasmagorical play forms is alluded to by the material in children's folklore as well as that documented above for children's stories and daydreams. The child protagonists are certainly without any hegemony in this respect. Their rhetoric, if there is one beyond their praxis, has to be a hidden transcript just like their rhetorics of power.

But a more important point has been to establish that the adult imaginary rhetoric when applied to children tends to overemphasize the creative and innovative qualities of their play at the expense of both the contraries, the phantasmagorical and the ritualistic. The endless cycles of community sports, festivals, and parades, no more nor less than the endlessly repeated children' games or their play events, demonstrate that an understanding of play must be rooted in ritual as much as it is in innovation.

With respect to definition, there is as yet little evidence of how children feel about their phantasmagorical forms of play, apart from enjoying them (King, 1979, 1982); nor have there been extensive theoretical discussions about the parameters of such play or the way in which these dimensions vary and develop throughout childhood and among different children. What it all means to the larger society is as yet beyond reckoning, though I suspect it has something to do with the degree of innovation needed and permitted by that larger society. In all this phantasmagoria there is probably a systematic variation and control of emotion and imagery, along a wide range of parameters, that helps to decide the permissible creativity of the individuals and the resources of novel imagery they can make available to their societies. And this is as true of the creative people writing for Nickelodeon as it is for children themselves.

Ambiguity lies in the difficulties of understanding children's play in a culture as dualistic in terms of adults and children as ours is (Chapter 2). We appear to be frightened by children's phantasmagoria, and most of our work on children's play simply avoids such play forms rather than treating them as central to what play is about. Partly this is because when we allow children to fantasize freely with us they simply reverse the power relationship and insist that they be in charge. They can be despots until they learn that we can be trusted with their shared fantasies (Kelly-Byrne, 1989). As a result, adults generally prefer to play sports (which they can control) with their children than to share fantasies, for which they have few guidelines (Sutton-Smith, 1993a). Thus there is much ambiguity in the adult-child relationship about fantasy. At the same time, imaginative activity is itself often extremely ambiguous as to what it expresses, what it conceals, and what on earth it means. Clearly there is a real need for more intensive research and thought on the parameters of childhood phantasmagoria. There is a need also for a rhetoric that can reconcile the paradox of individualistic phantasmagoria with the clear conservatism of the way in which the child play culture runs its own society; both are evident in this chapter. As we seldom allow the first or acknowledge the second, the requirements for a new rhetoric are most ambiguous.

10

Rhetorics of Self

Most people put a distance between themselves and their surroundings. Western civilization as a whole turns humans into "individuals." I am I and you are you; we may love each other, but still I shall remain I and you will remain you. Like bullet glass . . .

Paul Feyerabend

When I live, I am not truly alive. But when I act I feel I exist.
Antonin Artaud

Play is intrinsically motivated, except if you don't do what the others tell you, they won't let you play.

after Frech

The invasion of play by the rhetoric of achievement.
Christopher Lasch

The rhetorics of the self in play theory focus on play as having its basis in the psychology of the individual player. They avoid the historical and anthropological contexts of play (Rojek, 1995). Sometimes the concepts deal with intrapsychic mechanisms, sometimes with neurology, but more recently reference to the quality of the player's play experience has become popular. This kind of play theorizing has its psychological origins with Freud and the various mental mechanisms that he and his followers ascribe to the individual as explaining play, such as abreaction, repetition compulsion, compensation, wish fulfillment, mastery of anxiety, tension release, stage-related conflict resolution, mastery through role reversal, reality testing, and the transitional interplay between subject and object. These are just a few of the functions and processes that have been discussed by psychoanalysts, who have probably written more about play than any other theoretical cohort in the twentieth century (Solnit, Cohen, and Neubauer, 1993).

More recent theories of play as a form of individual stimulus seeking, neurological arousal, and epistemic behavior could be included here also. The varieties of these theories are well summarized by Ellis (1974). The more popular recent theories are those that find the meaning of play in the quality of the player's experience. It is said to be, in one example, "playing by heart" (Donaldson, 1993). These theories interpret play in terms of subjective experiences of the player, as, for example, when proponents declare play is good because it is "fun"; it is an optimal experience, an escape, a release; it is intrinsically motivated; it is voluntary; it is an actualizing of one's potential; it brings arousal or excitement; it is conflict-free pleasure; it is free choice; it is autotelic or paratelic, to draw from a group of concepts that have been popularized in various academic theories. At a more descriptive, less interpretive level, there are also all the terms—like merry, joyful, lighthearted, carefree, aimless, joking, jesting, radiant, lightly engrossed, relaxed, amused, antic, bantering, capering, whimsical, cavorting, frisky, frivolous, frolicking, gamboling, galumphing, jumping for joy, jinking, kicking up heels, larking, sprightly, scampering, lolloping, sportive, monkey business, merrymaking, reveling, rollicking, and romping—that are said to describe what people are doing and how people often feel when they are playing, and which are an important part of their reason for playing. This rhetoric is the kind of view of play that says play is a state of mind, a way of seeing and being, a special mental "set" toward the world and one's actions in it. It is sometimes claimed in this rhetoric that it is therefore impossible to define play from the outside by relating it to particular activities or behaviors. "Golf is not necessarily play and research is not necessarily work" (Kerr and Apter, 1991, p. 14). Given its diversity, Susanna Millar, in one of the earliest comprehensive overviews of psychological play theories (1968) suggested that "there are advantages in regarding play as an attitude" (p. 20).

Like the rhetorics of the imaginary, the self rhetoric is more concerned with individuals than with groups. The rhetoric of the imaginary and the rhetoric of self are both a part of the great historical watershed of the romantic movement, and it is not always easy to keep them apart, though the keynote of the former is the imagination, and of this one, it is freedom. Just as power and identity share the common ground of victory and privilege, so do the imaginary and the self share the common ground of freedom. Unlike power and identity, these two are individualistic rather than communal. They share this individualism with the first rhetoric, that of progress. In this book, the archaeology of the discourses of fate, power, identity, and frivolity reveals more ancient and traditional social discourses about games, sports, and spectacles. The other three, progress, the imaginary, and the self, are relatively Western, relatively modern, and relatively utopian discourses about individualized forms of play.

The self rhetoric's retreat from institutional and cultural interpretations, which have dominated the history and anthropology of play, is quite remarkable and rare in human history. Why is the answer to the question, what is play? to be found in some superior form of subjectivity? The answer will be sought here in a number of sources: in individualism, capitalism, secularization, phenomenological philosophy, "amateur" sports metaphors, psychology, leisure theory, performance theory, narrative theory. There is throughout a focus on motivation, emotion, and the pragmatics and aesthetics of action.

Individualism

The basic answer is that the focus on the subjectivity of the individual as a way of explaining play is a latter-day expression of the increasing *individualization* of human life that has occurred throughout the past five hundred years of Western history. This change is spoken of in multiple ways, too many to be presented here. Most authorities place the beginning of the shift at the time of the Renaissance and analyze the increasing differentiation of the self as portrayed in the arts and literature of that time. Michael Beaujour (1984), for example, draws attention to the Renaissance literary theory of the play of selves, which was a revolt against the certainties of Church authority and the veneration of the ancients. He has in mind the kinds of rhetorical and parodic play exhibited in the writings of Rabelais, Machiavelli,

Castiglione, Cervantes, and Erasmus in the sixteenth century. He contrasts their notions of the individual's multiple selves with the dualistic, adult-child, progress-oriented play theories of our own time. Nardo's *The Ludic Self in Seventeenth-Century English Literature* (1991) gives a similar account of the growth of what the author calls the ludic self in the literary activity of seventeenth-century England, citing Shakespeare's *Hamlet,* John Donne, George Herbert, Andrew Marvell, Robert Burton, and Sir Thomas Browne. Nardo says these authors make use of playfully different personal stances as a way of responding to the contradictions and conflicts of contemporary life. They take play out of festivals, where it has belonged, and put it into literature. Trilling (1971), in his *Sincerity and Authenticity,* draws parallel attention to the seventeenth-century efflorescence of autobiographies, diaries, and spiritual journals, and the endless self-scrutiny of Puritans as to their own motives and their own suitability for heavenly benediction. One finds in them apprehension about the difference between the private and public selves and the way in which only sincerity or authenticity could guarantee the public self protection against hypocrisy or deception. Rousseau in the late eighteenth century made a strenuous effort in his book *Emile* to do away with the discrepancy between private and public self, which he felt characterized the corrupt society of aristocratic France. He perceived the private self to be that of deceit and vanity. He wished his model child to be possessed of only a transparent singular self, to be always the same person wherever he was and with whomsoever he interacted—though in his own confessions of personal deceit, it seems that Rousseau himself behaved quite contrarily (Starobinksi, 1988). In the nineteenth century, Wordsworth, by contrast, took the step of romanticizing the role of his own private memories for the illumination of his poetic soul, regardless of his public posture. In a sense, the present century's preoccupation with the private experience of play owes its debt to Wordsworth and not to Rousseau.

The romantic period, with its emphasis on the individual's personal freedom to be original, provided perhaps the major impetus for the ideas underlying the preceding chapters on the imagination as well as the present one on the privileges of personal experience. Play and the freedom for private thought and action have come to be inexorably bound together. In *Sources of the Self: The Making of Modern*

Identity (1989), Charles Taylor suggests that, increasingly, in the search for what makes life worth living, twentieth-century persons have moved from finding their implicit ontologies in religious and even scientific sources and have substituted instead their own secular pursuits and experiences. He says: "With the development of the post-Romantic notion of individual difference, this expands to the demand that we give people the freedom to develop their personality in their own way, however repugnant to ourselves and even to our moral sense—the thesis developed so persuasively by J. S. Mill" (p. 12). Credit, or debit, has to be given also to the amazing influence of Freud and followers in accounting for society and history almost totally in terms of theories of intrapsychic processes. Play as therapy gradually becomes a precursor to the notion of play as a worthy experience. The later twentieth century's widespread commercialization of therapeutic group-process training as a regular kind of useful experience takes this much further. What was once group play therapy gradually became an expectation of higher quality experience for almost anyone seeking personal development through means of play.

Roger Abrahams (1986) aptly sums up these changes as follows:

> When words become the only basis for establishing meaningful relationships and other such egalitarian fictions, then the voices of authority are no longer given value or trust . . . Modishly we replace the vocabulary and the practices of vested authority with terms and procedures proclaiming equality of mankind and the need to make a place in our systematic analyses for the achievement of authenticity by the individual, as each person becomes part of the community and society . . . We gather to mark the demotion of the key terms of authoritative rhetoric, "tradition," "custom," even "institution," as we make one further effort at finding in everyday speech a vocabulary that will assist in celebrating the new project of self possession, self fashioning, self expression . . . This has been the holy project of secular humanism: the ritualization of the construction of one's self. (pp. 45–46)

Modern literature records that responses to this new freedom to pursue the essential self have also led to the alienation of that self from public life (for example, as in the writings of T. S. Eliot or Samuel Beckett), or contrarily, to an optimism about the viable new religious or sexual roles available for the self in the twentieth century, as in Yeats and Lawrence (Langbaum, 1982). Social science, in particular psychology, has in more recent decades engaged in a frenzy of concern over the endless empirical variety of selves that can be researched, as in the concepts of self-esteem, self-awareness, self-presentation, self-verification, self-schemas, self-concepts, self-monitoring (Baumeister, 1986, 1991). There are in psychology those who see this embroilment with the self in negative terms, as in Gergen's *The Saturated Self: Dilemmas of Identity in Contemporary Life* (1991), and those who, contrarily, see it as a positive challenge, as in Giddens's *Modernity and Identity: Self and Society in the Late Modern Age* (1991). Excitement about the possibilities for the flexible or pluralistic self in the modern world has been heightened by the discovery that one can play with one's virtual selves in computer communication with endless others (Turkle, 1995). What was once hidden as daydreams now takes on the mask of the computer screen for anticipations and rehearsals. It is interesting to contrast the large and heavy traditional wooden masks of German festival participants, still today seen lumbering through the pre-Lenten streets, with the flitting virtuosity of multiply-masked identities on the computer screen. There can be no doubt that virtual worlds are a new play form allowing adults to play almost as amorphously as children.

For those of a more skeptical and Marxist persuasion, the most important reason that self-differentiation and subjectivity of one sort or another has become increasingly powerful as a way of explaining the meaning of human life in the twentieth century is that capitalism has changed life's economic character. Whereas in the prior several centuries an individual's productivity was the key to the development of the economy, and therefore one's valued self was reflected in one's work ethic, in this century one's ability to make free choices in consumer goods, and to enjoy that particular kind of material participation in the economy, has become the privileged form of personal worth. Freedom has become not just the freedom from work but also the freedom to be a conspicuous consumer, and to participate in the material riches of consumer civilization. The emphasis on subjectivity in play follows, from this account, the emphasis on subjectivity in the economy. Marketing constantly suggests in its fads and fashions that the consumers can and should make choices among the wares presented before them. Habituation to this materially oriented life leads to the belief that being able to make one's own choices is what life is all about. Play, in these terms, is found to be an especially suitable and often relatively cheap form of such free-choice consumerism. Not surprisingly, the contemporary construction of childhood as a consumer subculture, with its own buying power and susceptibility to media advertising and enticement, can be taken as a further illustration of this economic development and its effects on child play. The mass of toys now available to children, and discoverable underfoot in the living rooms of the country, are easily regarded by some as an effect of this Marxist consumer curse.

Metaphors of Play as Freedom

In a remarkable book entitled *Sporting with the Gods,* Michael Oriard (1991) traces the metaphors that have dominated the discussion of play and games throughout American history. He says of his work, "The subject, to repeat, is not the play element in American Culture but the specific rhetoric of sport, play and game, and my sense of that rhetoric's most significant functions" (p. x). He is concerned with the explicit rhetorics to be found in the language of sporting metaphors, whereas I am concerned here with the implicit cultural rhetorics to be found in the language of play theory. Oriard's investigations, largely of literature and the media, provide a remarkable parallel, and perhaps a validation, of those suggested by the present seven rhetorics of theory.

In general he tells a story of the American sporting literature, which, beginning in the nineteenth century, is dominated by the rhetorics of progress, power, and status, and which in the twentieth century increasingly changes to rhetorics dominated by the concepts of freedom and self-actualization. Writes Oriard: "American sporting rhetoric in all its variety ultimately has been concerned with status and power and opportunity, both material and spiritual, within the American system of industrial capitalism" (p. 477). There has been a "widely acknowledged shift in America from work-centred culture to one that has increasingly privileged the values of play," he says; the "modern 'mass culture' or 'consumer culture' is rooted in conspicuous playfulness" (pp. ix, x). Oriard states further that "the desire to play, and to transform work into a 'game,' has increased dramatically over the past century and a half. . . . In professional football and baseball in the 1970's and 1980's, for example, one can see a significant shift towards the values of self-fulfillment against the demands of the team . . . all the elements and consequences of the mediated culture of celebrity—are signs that sport has increasingly become an arena for self-actualization rather than male bonding" (pp. 478, 479). According to Oriard's historical analysis,

> The problem has remained constant since the 1830's: the inability to ground American social reality in a more satisfying integration of work and play. But the terms change, as do the prospects for success. In relation to earlier phases of American culture our contemporary 'postmodernism' is distinctly the culture of play; play with conventional forms in the arts, of play with the products of our economic prosperity in everyday life, yet while American culture has become markedly more playful, critics of that culture have continued to decry the absence of true freedom or creativity. Postmodern consumer culture, they argue, converts play into the engine of insatiable consumption, which drives the economy without leading to personal fulfillment. (p. 484)

In an earlier, similar work with a smaller scope, *Sport and the Spirit of Play in American Fiction* (1981), Christian Messenger approaches American novelists from Hawthorne to Hemingway in terms of the role they give to play in American sporting life. In his analysis of fictional American sports heroes, Messenger finds a dialectic between the discipline provided by sports and the freedom essentially associated with play throughout American history, once it evolved from its Puritan beginnings. From my point of view his analysis of the spirit of play, like that of Oriard, revolves around the interaction between the rhetorics of power and the self, except that in Messenger there is a more complete abandonment to the rhetoric of the self. "For in play, the ultimate issue is always freedom: how to live through play toward freedom, how to play the dominion that grants freedom. This quest is at the core of the desire to play" (Messenger, 1981, p. 313).

If one shifts radically from such twentieth-century literary analyses of these rhetorics to the contemporary leisure sciences, it becomes

apparent that some of the thinkers in the latter discipline have come
to similar conclusions, less by way of such recent historical analyses
than from reading Greek philosophy, particularly Aristotle. Sebastian
De Grazia in particular, in *Of Time, Work and Leisure* (1962), adopts
an elitist Greek view of play in his suggestion that leisure is not just
time off but primarily time off for playful speculation. He says, "The
world is divided into two classes. Not three, or five or twenty. Just two.
One is a great majority; the other is the leisure kind, not those of
wealth or position or birth, but those who love ideas and the imagination . . . The pleasures of this handful of persons differ sharply
from those of the rest" (p. 377). They alone are at play in their
leisure. What is important, says De Grazia's follower Neulinger
(1974), in a somewhat similar but possibly less restrictive vein, is that
"the primary dimension of leisure, then, is the freedom or, to be
more specific, the perceived freedom. By this we simply mean a state
in which the person feels that what he is doing, he is doing by choice
and because he wants to" (p. 15). He says that freedom means to
engage in activity freely, with spontaneity, as one's own master, accompanied by an aura of pleasantness, unhurriedness, and relaxation (p. 158). There is, once again, the echo here that play is seen as
having to do with the free choices and experiences of the self, though
in De Grazia's case there is intimation of the rhetoric of the imaginary as well as that of the freedom of the self.

Subjectivity

Individualism is not enough to explain these modern self-oriented
rhetorics of play, because individualism and Puritanism both originally had an antiludic view. But when in romanticism personal freedom for subjectively chosen experiences became a desirable
criterion for living, then such rhetorics could arise. A major philosophical source for the modern rhetorics of the self as player has
been historical phenomenology, which for its own anti-Cartesian
reasons sought to establish the self as not just an unscientific emotional residue out of touch with science, but as having its own "objective" validity, more real and true than those validities usually
associated with science. The major philosophers in this tradition
have been Husserl, Heidegger, and Gadamer, all of whom have per-

sistently sought to convert philosophy from "realism" and "positivism" into a concern for the "objective" character of the nature of being. Everyone has a "life world," it is said, and that is their ontological reality. Knowing this reality, however, usually requires a special kind of empathy manifested most clearly by the arts, including poetry. So here we are once again, superficially at least, with the romantics (Schiller, Wordsworth, et al.), giving a special place to the play of poetry in life (Jones, 1952).

Of these three major phenomenologists, Gadamer deals most explicitly with play, and he uses it to demonstrate the objective reality of the state of being to be found in play. The player doesn't play the game, he insists; it is, rather, that the game plays the player. Once you begin playing, you are taken over by the things that are serious within the game, regardless of how serious that same game is estimated to be in the eyes of the nonplaying world. The experience of play (and, therefore, art) "becomes an experience changing the person who experiences it . . . For play has its own essence, independent of the consciousness of those who play. Play also exists—indeed, properly . . . where there are no subjects who are behaving 'playfully' . . . The players are not the subjects of play; instead the play merely reaches representation through the player" (Gadamer, 1982, p. 92).

This is implicitly a pronouncement that play offers a particularly good way to talk about the objectivity of states of being, regardless of our apprehension of them. But Gadamer has more to say about play, which shows that he is actually interested in play itself, not simply as a metaphor for his idea of the objectivity of being. He writes:

> If we examine how the word "play" is used and concentrate on its so-called transferred meanings we find talk of the play of light, the play of the waves, the play of the components in a bearing case, the inner play of limbs, the play of forces, the play of gnats, even a play on words. In each case what is intended is the to-and-fro movement which is not tied to any goal which would bring it to an end. This accords with the original meaning of the word "spiel" as "dance," which is still found in many word forms . . . This movement which is play has no goal which brings it to an end; rather it renews itself in constant repetition. The movement backwards and forwards is obviously so central for the definition of a game that it is not

important who or what performs this movement . . .

. . . [A]ll playing is being played. The attraction of a game, the fascination it exerts consists precisely in the fact that the game tends to master the players . . . whoever tries is in fact the one who is tried . . . the game is a risk for the player . . . The game is what holds the player in its spell, draws him into play and keeps him there. (pp. 93, 95, 96)

Obviously there is some ordinary kind of truth to all of this, as anyone who has had to react to balls thrown and kicked by other persons, and who has been confined by the rules of a game, can attest. These phenomena do show that much of the pleasure of playing lies in the fact that the game plays you; that your reactions are often more reflexive or involuntary than voluntary; that the game takes you out of yourself. It frees you from one self by binding you to another. One cannot talk loosely about play meaning freedom without also taking into account the specific kind of bonding that then reigns over the player's being. To say something is play because it is free or voluntary seems to be an insufficient explanation, and that at least is what Gadamer makes clear.

Gadamer also adds that there are different kinds of play and therefore different kinds of "play spirit" or "play essences." These are multiple states of play being or mentality in which the player can feel himself surpassed by the reality. There is a paradox here, because clearly a rhetoric of self is not the same as this notion of the essential and objective "being" of play, which is outside oneself rather than inside oneself. Gadamer says quite clearly that play exists out there, it does not depend on our subjective choice or involvement. Still, irrespective of the validity of his formulation, his focus on play as an independent state of being is a focus on something that in our century is taken as having to do with the reality of the play for the individual or groups of players choosing to do it. Gadamer's definition of play as repetitive encapsulation of the self by the game feeds the rhetoric of the centrality of the self, even if it does derive from a more ambiguous, objectivist kind of ontology. What Gadamer and "self psychology" have in common is the well-known supposition that play is a thing unto itself and independent of external goals. Both have a kinship with the "amateur" sports theory of the late nineteenth century, in which only certain privileged games were said to be truly play, because they were played for their own sake and not for money. In games played for their own sake, courtly or gentlemanly virtues could prevail (as depicted in the movie, *Chariots of Fire*), whereas in games played for money, the desire to win prevailed over all other considerations. It was an aristocratic attitude designed to preserve the wealthy from association with the sweaty poorer classes. The current emphasis on play as fun can be seen to have similar connections to more affluent, or at least more elitist, perceptions of the good life. I am indebted to my student Michael King for suggesting that Gadamer's to-and-fro views of play are probably also a metaphor for his open-ended, ever-recycling theory of the nature of human "hermeneutic" understanding.*

The theory of play most relevant to the self rhetoric, and the one that has had the greatest impact in the past twenty years, has been that of Mihaly Csikszentmihalyi, who, though not directly influenced by the above-mentioned phenomenologists, was indirectly affected by them through the writings of Maslow on self-actualization. Csikszentmihalyi says he was influenced as well by the writing of psychologists such as Berlyne and White on intrinsic motivation and competence motivation. He defines his approach as that of phenomenological structuralism (Csikszentmihalyi and Csikszentmihalyi, 1988, p. 366). In his work, he seeks to account for why people are so highly motivated by their experiences of personal enjoyment, whether they find them in play, the arts, ritual, meditation, work, or elsewhere. After his research on the "peak experiences" of chess players, rock climbers, rock dancers, and surgeons, he came to believe that their descriptions of their peak experiences were basically similar (1977, 1979). He discovered that these people described their own peak inner states in very similar terms, which he decided to call being in "flow," and he says they have the following universal characteristics:

---

*Michael King was one of sixteen students with whom I conducted a seminar on this text at New College in Sarasota, Florida, in the fall of 1995. These students' greatest impact, apart from the pleasure of working with them, was in revealing the need for more material about rhetorics. It is very hard for the empirically minded to embrace the Kuhnian and Burkean theses.

1. First there is a merging of action and awareness . . . A tennis player pays undivided attention to the ball.
2. This merging results from the centering of attention on a limited stimulus field, a process of narrowing the consciousness . . . In games the rules define what is relevant and exclude everything else as well as provide the motives and risks, which keeps attention within the game. These motives are intrinsic to the game or "paratelic," as it has been called.
3. A consequence of the first two is a loss of self-consciousness during the play, a forgetfulness of other realities.
4. Another characteristic of a person in flow is that he is in control of his actions and of the environment.
5. Another quality of the flow experience is that it usually contains coherent, noncontradictory demands for actions and provides clear, unambiguous feedback to a person's actions.
6. A final characteristic is its "autotelic" nature . . . It needs no goals or rewards external to itself. (1977, pp. 38–46)

Csikszentmihalyi and his wife and coauthor, Isabella Csikszentmihalyi, suppose that this state of mind is universal across cultures and that it can occur in work or play (1988). If they are correct, one might assume perhaps that there is some underlying neurological wiring that is roughly the same for all humans and animals in their multiple activities, even though the character of the events being described seems quite different on the surface. Such a contention certainly runs against the claim that there are relativities of behavior and experience from culture to culture. Anthropology has been obsessed with such relativism throughout this century. The Csikszentmihalyis' own collected data also show persistent cultural and individual differences, which suggest that flow may not be a universal but rather a value that can be learned by some and not by others (1988). To say flow is universal might be like saying that all peak sex is everywhere the same, and that "flow" is to play what orgasm is to sex. But who would be innocent enough of all the different contexts and acts that make sex meaningful to say something like that? Another interpretation might be that in the West, and increasingly elsewhere, there is a widespread twentieth-century value system that seeks to find human meaning in the secular pleasures of individual people. The "flow" description of enjoyable activities is there-fore eagerly grasped, because it is in vogue in modern psychological explanation. As well, it gives a justification for personal proclivities, typically rating them much more highly than traditional value sys-tems. From a play theorist's point of view, a criticism might be that in these terms play at its best, at its peak, would no longer be distinct from work at its best, at its peak—something that hardly seems cred-ible, even if we are told by the Csikszentmihalyis that though their content may be different, play and work can be structurally similar in terms of points one through six above. Because there are so many institutional, spatial, action-oriented, person-interactive, and tempo-ral ways in which the grammars of work and play seem to be quite different, and so many ways that the grammars of play are different among themselves, more seems to be lost by such a universal notion than is gained. One cannot gainsay, however, the remarkable rhe-torical appeal of this concept of flow, as the popular success of the Csikszentmihalyis' venture makes very clear. It is very much the most well worked out exemplar of modern notions of play under the banner of the rhetoric of self. It is also remarkable for attempting to bridge the dualism of work and play with which our society is obsessed and which on all accounts seems to be quite ethnocentric (Lancy and Tindall, 1976).

Brian Vandenberg, the contemporary play psychologist who has taken most explicitly the attitudes of the Heideggerian existentialist phenomenology and applied them to play, was earlier well estab-lished in psychology for both his experimental and his clinical work with child play (Rubin, Fein, and Vandenberg, 1983). He points out that the three philosophical phenomenologists, Husserl, Heidegger, and Gadamer, give primacy in their explanations of human behavior (and therefore play) not to epistemological issues (logic and reason) but to ontological ones, such as freedom, anxiety, death, and authen-ticity. As a result, he says, "Play takes on new meanings within this framework. Most contemporary perspectives of play consider it as a means for the acquisition of information, the exercise of cognitive functions, or a domain for the elaboration of social skills. The pas-sionate aspects of play are seen as epiphenomena, or accompani-ments to these purportedly more fundamental aspects of play" (1988, p. 205). However, the essence of being a human being, he says, is that we optimistically project our possibilities into the future. For example, he says,

> a four year old friend of mine frequently pretends that she is a cheerleader. She dances, jumps, and twirls in youthful imitation of her older heroines. Certainly the situation can be considered as an opportunity to learn and practice social roles and physical skills, and [it] creates new information that may be used in later situations. However, none of these reasons explain why she has chosen this particular role to practice or why she plays it with so much gusto. A clue to a more complete explanation is that her mother was a cheerleader, and has talked to her daughter about it. Thus her daughter is attempting to construct a possible future for herself as she plays with the meanings of maturity and adulthood that have been presented to her by her mother. In its meanings, its immediacy and its emotional richness, her play is closer to wish and hope than learning and rehearsal . . .
>
> Play is an instance of projecting one's future and the thrill is derived from exploring possibilities. This view of play is contrary to the Freudian notion of play as mastery of past traumatic events. This is not to argue that children don't play out and play over events that have occurred in the past . . . This view based on Heidegger suggests that we are our future and we are concerned with the past only because it influences our projections into the future (ibid., pp. 207–208).

In sum, I have described three somewhat different approaches to play in the recent period, those of Gadamer, Csikszentmihalyi, and Vandenberg, all of which end up, one way or another, focusing the discussion about play on the relationship between players and their play choices and experiences. The important issue is that play be explained in terms of that relationship between self and play, not in terms of extrinsic issues about progress, power, and status.

Fun as the Essence

What seems to be happening is that many of those who advocate quite different rhetorics (progress, imagination, freedom, fate, power, community, or frivolity) and, therefore, describe their kinds of play in quite different ways, are nevertheless fairly parallel in describing why their players like to play. Quite surprisingly, for example, the psychologists Rubin, Fein, and Vandenberg, who summarized the state of the research in the field of child play in 1983, chose to describe it in a way that corresponds less with typical research concerns in their field, about play as a kind of development or progress, and more in terms of the player's disposition, which is the approach taken in most of the examples above. Obviously Vandenberg's phenomenological predisposition is showing. What these authors say is:

A feature that is almost unanimously acknowledged to be *the hallmark of play is that it is intrinsically motivated* (that it is "fun"). But the authorities they cite are nearly all psychologists, so apparently the unanimity they speak of is restricted to some members of that scholarly group. As mentioned earlier, many anthropologists and historians would have trouble with this account, since most play throughout the ages has been extrinsically motivated by village requirements.

Play is characterized by attention to means rather than ends. This is a notion derived from the history of the work ethic and the related abrupt distinction between work and play in that ideology. The dualistic Cartesian distinction that play is to be play and work is to be work, and that they are to be quite separate from each other, is collapsed in Csikszentmihalyi's work on flow as well as in the research on children playing. Current evidence shows that play always involves multiple personal and social goals as well as solely instrumental play behaviors. The game is not only an end in itself; many other goals are also achieved within the playing group (Hughes, 1991). This is true even in the engaging work by Bernard Suits entitled *The Grasshopper: Games, Life and Utopia* (1978), in which the distinction of play behavior for its own sake is said to make games the one remaining Utopia.

Play is guided by organism-dominated questions rather than context-dominated questions. This concept is used to distinguish between play so defined and exploration, in which the character of the object to be explored is said to dominate behavior. The problem is, in the course of everyday play these distinctions hardly exist; there is a vacillation between both kinds of behavior, and children will say all of it is "play." Nor is it possible in adult life always to say that what is happening at the work desk is work, when what is happening in the mind is often play. The intertwining of these aspects of behavior makes their separation possible only in abstract terms. The realities of play involve a more complex mixture of organismic and contextual behavior.

Play behaviors are not instrumental. Play is supposed to be nonproductive and not to intend serious consequences. Unfortunately this definition is again a derivative of our cultural attempt to make play and work quite distinct. Play has its own instrumental behaviors, and its consequences are quite real and consequential to the players. The conventional concept of instrumentality is a highly narrow one usually confined to work schedules with clear-cut, externally imposed "goal targets." The historical and economic basis for this dualistic metaphor is quite insufficient to deal with the complex intentionalities of everyday life, including play life.

Freedom from externally imposed rules is necessary. But the Meckley study (1994) shows that rules are imposed on children playing by other players (see Chapter 9). Nor can one deny that children in externally imposed organized games and sports usually see themselves as playing and enjoy themselves as players. So again this is a relatively useless distinction, because the notion of "rule imposition" allows for no subtlety in the gradients of imposition in everyday life, nor in its various meanings within each context. Some of the most exciting moments of play come because of such imposition (in blind man's bluff, for example). Being imposed upon is for some people a form of joy. Gadamer says the game plays us, we don't play the game, a notion that also completely inverts this proposition.

Finally, it is said that *players are actively engaged in their activity.* Does this then cut out vicarious play (where children are perceptually "actively" engaged)? Does it cut out daydreams or dreams? Does it cut out playful musings and ruminations? Or is the stress on "being active" a survival of the Protestant work ethic, now applied to all play to rhetorically increase its value?

Still, the importance of this list lies less in the scientific issues than in the readiness of these psychologists to define play as many leisure scientists often do, as recreationists often do, as sportswriters often do, in a way that has become increasingly popular in modern thought—that is, to find play's definitions in some attributes of the self's own experience or even perhaps in the autonomous characteristics of the chosen play form itself (Smith and Vollstedt, 1985). As it turns out, even children of the twentieth century, not surprisingly, believe, like their parents, that this is indeed what play is about: pleasure, voluntariness, friends, the outdoors, and not work (King, 1979; Fein, 1985).

Who Is the Self in the Rhetoric of the Playing Self?

By and large the self emphasized thus far has been variable. Sometimes it is the individual player's sensitivity or reflexivity; or the player is seen as an autonomous person or a free person; or the emphasis is on the historical shift toward seeing play as a kind of ideal, or at least rewarding, consumer freedom. But who is the self that plays? Here I turn to Spariosu, who has recently added to his work on the rhetorics of power, *Dionysus Reborn* (1989), further works on the rhetorics of self, namely *God of Many Names* (1991), and, with Ronald Bogue, a new and extraordinary work entitled *The Playing Self* (1994). Spariosu poses the question, does the self that plays have the kind of *archaic mentality*, or irrationality, that enjoys disorder and power over others, which he shows was an early Greek as well as the Nietzschean option, or does the player have the kind of median or Apollonian self that seeks order and rationality in the exercise of power during play? To put it in Freudian terms, do players play for their Id or for their Ego? Or, asks Spariosu in his more recent books, is the playing self to be one who rejects these concerns with power and seeks some other alternative? "Play, which along with power is a main theme in this book, may well be one of those phenomena that ultimately elude power and point to an anarchical, nonviolent kind of mentality which, from the perspective of Western history, seems to be on the order of Utopia. But play in this sense appears to have had a rather limited place in the Hellenic (and the Western) world, and the history which I have attempted to trace here is that of play as an instrument of power" (1991, p. xii). But, he continues, "Power, for me, is a man-made, historical principle rather than an inevitable, 'natural' phenomenon. Unlike Nietzsche and his heirs (such as Freud, Heidegger, Fink, Plessner, Foucault, Deleuze, and others), I believe that power is only one of the ways, and not necessarily the best way, in which humans can construct their world and relate to it" (ibid., p. xvi).

What Spariosu is alluding to as a nonviolent and indeed utopian kind of mentality is a characteristic of most of the material laid out here and in Chapter 8 on the rhetorics of the imaginary. Perhaps the widespread choice of these kinds of variables within these rhetorics reveals the urgency of the modern desire to use play as an expression of peaceful pursuits. This is quite explicit in feminist usages both for children and for women themselves (Oriard, 1991, p. 481). Spariosu goes further, in effect converting what was his account of the archaic, or anarchic, ancient power mentality into an open-ended autoformation of the world and the self according, he says, to Irenic rather than agonistic principles (Bogue and Spariosu, 1994). He sees this peaceful self as a nontotalizing, integrative personality that makes up the world as it goes, which is a highly creative notion of the self in play. In so doing, he calls to mind an earlier Heidegger-inspired work by Hans, *The Play of the World* (1981), which also emphasizes play as the basic ongoing vehicle for the construction of meanings. This is a broad and romantic interpretation at the very least. It is a surprising turn to this author to find Spariosu, the authority on play rhetoric as power, rational and irrational, now in search of such humanistic and utopian meanings for play. It shows the "power" of the rhetoric of humanistically intended and utopian wishes for play in modern times.

What is lost in this appealing twentieth-century romanticizing of the self is the quite different sense of self that is found in play throughout history and across cultures. As Geertz says: "The Western conception of the person as a bounded, unique, more or less integrated motivational and cognitive universe, a dynamic centre of awareness, emotion, judgment, and action organized into a distinctive whole and set contrastively both against other such wholes and against its social and natural background, is, however incorrigible it may seem to us, a rather peculiar idea within the context of the world's cultures" (1983, p. 59). The other selves he describes, Javanese, Balinese, and Moroccan, are organized on quite different and more distributive principles, and none of them has the sort of unity required for such singular, self-focused concepts as "flow" and "intrinsic motivation." In much of the world, the self is defined primarily not in terms of its own experience but as an aspect of collective family or tribal life. "Personal goals are subordinated to those of the collective; norms, duties and obligations regulate most social behavior" (Triandis, 1996, p. 409).

Play as Ecstatic Performance

Most of these approaches to the self concentrate on the feelings and meanings of play for the individual player; they focus on freedom, fun, intrinsic motivation, attitude, subjectivity, hope, optimism, autonomy. One wonders why there is so little emphasis on the importance to the players of *their own specific actions* in the kinds of games in which they participate. It doesn't take much reflection to remember that the players' own skilled movements, from babies playing with nipples to monkeys jumping out of trees to children erecting block towers that do not fall over to adults putting "birdies" into holes in golf, are extraordinarily exciting to the players, and that a lot of the self-esteem that is associated with play and games has to do with these molecular personal aspects of performance. Where, it might be asked, is the appropriate ludic *performance theory* or *action theory* to account for such motivated actions? Existing folklore performance theory emphasizes performance as aesthetic communication and also owes its lineage to romanticism and the linkages between art and play discussed earlier. That theory should be promising for understanding the centrality of the actions in play. But as Bauman puts it, "Performance usually suggests an aesthetically marked and heightened mode of communication, framed in a special way and put on display for an audience" (1992, p. 41), which on the surface means that the theory is limited to artistic performance, rather than being useful for the understanding of play at large. It is true that performance play (playing music, being in the play, and so on) can be an important subcategory of play; true, also, that much of the pleasure of actions in play can be said to have an aesthetic quality, when one makes the right move at the right time, in the most graceful, skillful, and appropriate way. And, further, it is true that most social play is not without the audience at least of the other players, who, as research shows, constantly monitor one another's play (Magee, 1987). The normal group of child players is typically a troupe rather than just a group. Still, Bauman probably wouldn't include ordinary players in his specifications for performance theory, concerned as he is about communication relationships and aesthetic performances in groups with audiences. Roger Abrahams, also a folklorist, in a paper entitled, "Toward an Enactment-Centered Theory of Folklore" (1977), indicated his awareness of the need to stretch the concept of performance to cover ordinary play and games, which are not centrally aesthetic nor necessarily performed for audiences, but would include any public cultural events in which community members come together to participate. He stresses that these events of play, games, and festivals will be more highly focused and framed, yet more redundant and stylized than other areas of experience. These are very useful concepts, to which I will return.

It is necessary, however, to take one step further to develop a performance theory of play that is about individual as well as social play, so that the performances can then be regarded as the reason for the player's own solitary self-involvement in these kinds of play, whatever they are. The need for such studies is filled in part by the mundane yet valuable empirical work on the character of children's performances as they play, work that has been accumulating in recent years. These studies show, at least, that play is not simply to be described in global terms as a matter of attitude or fun. Players do what they do in play in ways that are quite distinct from ordinary life. Catherine Garvey, over a long period of study, has been demonstrating with her colleagues that playing has a distinct linguistic registrar, different verbal tenses being used for different play functions, like those of emplotment, enactment, and so on (1993). Part of play's enjoyment, she says, is in these "stylized" speech forms and paralinguistics.

An example of research relevant to Garvey's work is the study by Gerstmyer, "Toward a Theory of Play as Performance: An Analysis of Videotaped Episodes of a Toddler's Play Performance" (1991). Gerstmyer videotaped his daughter playing in front of him from the age of one year and nine months to two years and eight months. Using mostly Garvey's categories, with some new ones of his own, he found the child used, for example, the following kinds of stylized categories of enactment when she was performing her play for her father.

1. She used paralinguistically appropriate "in role" speech, such as "motherese" when she was pretending to be a mother. "Motherese" is the kind of high-pitch, dramatically toned, but slow and emphatic speech mothers use with their babies.
2. She used vocalized sound effects to identify and enhance a nonverbal enactment, for example "vroom vroom" when pushing a toy car.
3. She used "magicking," which is a play "shorthand" whereby, for example, a brief nonverbal play action, such as shaking a pot accompanied by the verbalization "cook cook," might be used to represent a relatively sizable time segment of ongoing food preparation. It is typical for play to be a highly condensed representation of whatever it is about, which means that much can be covered with great brevity (Giffen, 1984). This is yet another kind of stylization.
4. She showed anticipatory and facilitative enactive behavior: for example, picking up the toy telephone before saying "hello."
5. There was, at times, brief out-of-role behavior that served the play action objective, as when she looked for a prop and retrieved it for ensuing action. Children combine ordinary behavior that is needed to keep the play going with what an observer might see more clearly as play, but when asked about it, they say that it is all "play."
6. There were brief affiliative, out-of-role facial expressions or gestures, which served to touch base between partners, such as giggling and laughing during, say, a pretend action of violence.
7. She prepared the onlooker for forthcoming climactic events by lower-volume confidential cues of a more intense kind: head nodding, pursed lips, lip smacking, and swallowing.

Garvey and Gerstmyer have many more examples, but these few give some sense of the microanalysis they deal with and that is needed to come to terms with play's actual stylized excitement. With the exception of animal theorists, most play researchers have preferred to rest their cases on highly generalized statements rather than seeking the first meanings of play in these small constituents of performance. Abstractions that describe play largely in terms of "fun" or "flow" or "attitude" do a great disservice to the incredible structural complexity of the intricate enactment of play and their consequential, quite specific enjoyments for the players. It is important to stress that there is a "language" of play, meaning its framing, its rituals, and its stylization in speech and gesture as well as in action.

Here one may also speak of mundane reality and virtual reality, where writers used to write of the real and the unreal. The latter duality privileged the real over the unreal, making the unreal usually a mimicry of the former. Now that we realize that human cultures are built out of imagination and fantasy, not just out of physical discoveries, the present duality of mundane and virtual is more appropriate. It concedes that the mundane and the virtual are both real worlds but in different ways, without in general privileging one over the other.

More centrally, in all of the above examples the play actions "play off" the mundane actions that they in part model, mimic, or mock. Every action in the above seven examples of observed play is an action about actions. It communicates by its own stylized character that it is a play reality, not an everyday reality, which is to say it is metacommunicative, as Bateson put it (1956). But underneath that, every action about other actions is also a meta-action. Between the original mundane action (looking after baby) and the ludic commentary (modeling, mimicry, or mockery of baby care with motherese), we have a binary tension that, it can be argued, is the initial source of the dialectical enjoyment of play. Play is novelty, but it also is typically at the beginning an incongruity (see the first three Gerstmyer examples, above). But as the play proceeds, one is impressed less with the initial incongruity and more with the enjoyable establishment of the internal incongruities of this separate kingdom of play (Gerstmyer examples five through seven). Play proceeds, as it were, within itself, every subsequent action playing off the preceding ones, sometimes with increasing transformation, even with increasing nonsense, from play to playful. To discuss play in this way is to imply that at the center of play's dynamism is a dialectical relationship between its enactments and their everyday references.

Play may be a paradox in communication terms (it is and it is not what it says it is), but play also involves maintaining the referential paradoxes throughout. Gerstmyer's daughter illustrates this with her motherese, her cuing of intended behavior, her affiliative faces, her sound effects. She shows supreme awareness of the two levels of being, the virtual and the mundane, and how she can interact with both of them. Her manipulation of that duality is central to the character of her play, and it is why I might call it here a dialectical phenomenon (Sutton-Smith, 1978a). There is the mundane and there is the virtual (as thesis and antithesis) and there is a synthesis in the ongoing play transformations that this duality then produces, and so, structurally, it is a dialectic.

Recall now the earlier discussion of the distinctions made between play and playful, where play was contained by frames and playful was disruptive of frames. When seven-year-olds tell riddles, for example, it is often a rule-bound, central-person game in which the one who asks the riddles stays in charge until someone guesses one of the answers, then that second person takes over and is the one to ask the riddles. Thus it is a rule-ordered social game. But the riddles themselves break the rules of language and behavior. "Why did the dog get out of the sun? He didn't want to be a hot dog." In the one game, therefore, we have both a series of plays (the game) and a series of playful alternatives (the riddles). Underpinning the dialectic between sensible play and nonsensical playfulness, however, is the dialectic just described between the mundane and the virtual worlds. The actions in the virtual worlds we call meta-actions because, while focused, framed, redundant, and stylized, they are actions about other actions in the mundane world. In the case of riddles, the real-world social origin is the general habit of parental and school authorities to be in a "one-to-many" power relationship with children. It is probable that childrens' central-person games (tag, hide-and-seek, Mother may I, farmer in the dell) model that one-to-many adult-child power relationship—and, in this case, a one-to-many verbal power relationship. This formulation receives some support from Roberts and Forman (1972), who, in a cross-cultural study, were able to show that such games of riddling are present in cultures in which oral interrogation is a method of child socialization.

So now we have, in effect, two dialectical relationships: the one between the mundane and virtual worlds that leads to the play transformations (which I will call the referential dialectic), and the one within the play form itself, between play and the playfulness it engenders (called the ludic dialectic). Involved in the structure of play, according to this thesis, is a referential dialectic and a ludic dialectic. The process from the mundane to the virtual leads to the meta-action of play, and the play itself sometimes evolves into the relationship of play and playfulness. What began in this section as a search for a performance theory of play, as a way of indicating the limits of simple self theories, has developed into a celebration of the molecular actions of play that bring delight to the players (and so are ecstatic performances)—and has then built upon that a general structural theory of play as a referential dialectic encapsulating a ludic dialectic. This gives play a structural conceptualization.

Validations and Definitions

This rhetoric requires us to understand something of the history of individualism, of phenomenology, of consumerism, of the psychology of optimal experience, the role of play as a kind of personal performance, and the effect of individual differences. A major limitation of this emphasis on the subjective self is that it concentrates almost totally on only the voluntaristic and internally motivated, an orientation that conflicts with the data from most historical and anthropological work indicating that play is often obligatory rather than optional. The phenomenologists, however, do introduce the notion that play is characterized more by desire than by freedom, more by wish and hope for the future and by optimism. They say play has more to do with ontology than epistemology. I mentioned earlier that in the current cognitive focus on play as an expression of the "subjunctive mood," the "mood" aspect of that subjunctivity is neglected. Wishing or envisaging possibilities for the future, which is the focus of subjunctivity, seems incomplete without acknowledgment that this subjunctivity is typically acted out by animals and humans with great vigor and excitement. If indeed play is an envisagement, it occurs in the mood of intense enactment. In play one is not like Hamlet, unsure whether "to be, or not to be" (the subjunctivity) but more like Henry V in saying, "Once more unto the breech, dear friends" (the affirmative mood). That meaning of play is symbolized in one way for us by the audience cheering the players onward or crying, "We're number one." There is always an intention to the play. There is always also an intensity of player action, and there is the belief that one can reach a resolution of the play form. This general state of play motivation was earlier labeled *enactive subjunctivity,* which is to say there is often more commitment and belief in play activity than in most other forms of human behavior. Perhaps this applies to all of us to some extent, and play is for us the action in which we truly live. One of the biases of an information-oriented age is the tendency to neglect the fact that, throughout history, the adaptive advantage has often gone to those who ventured upon their possibility with cries of exultant commitment. What is adaptive about play, therefore, may be not only the skills that are a part of it but also the willful belief in acting out one's own capacity for the future. The opposite of play, in these terms, is not a present reality or work, it is vacillation, or worse, it is depression. To play is to act out and be willful, as if one is assured of one's prospects. A weakness of many of the self-oriented play theories is that they often sound too much like vain consumerism instead of being about the more passionate and willful character of human play, which involves a willingness, even if a fantasy, to believe in the play venture itself.

I also speak of this compound of subjunctivity, belief, action, intensity, and commitment as *meta-action,* because it is an action that is central and stylized, and that creates incongruity through indirect allusion to the mundane world. The observations of children's pretense by Fein made the point that children are playing with interpreting their own feelings and thoughts, not primarily playing with representing the external world. Play is on the meta level, not the mimicry level. This is to suggest, further, that play not only contains Bateson's metacommunication, but also requires performance theory's meta-action. These have been summed up as the referential and ludic dialectics in this chapter. A concept of play as stylized but willful meta-action could be applied as well to the animal data.

In sum, this is a rhetoric derived from individualistic and consumer history. Its advocates are modern salespersons, preachers, psychological advisers, and almost all consumers. Its players are modern persons. Its play actions are usually those that are supposed to heighten individual experience, from group psychic participation to "extreme" games. Its scholarly disciplines appear to be those of leisure and recreation. Its theorists are followers of New Age thinking or the book *The Channeling Zone* (Brown, 1996). Its hegemony is the superiority of those who have access to the kind of places (aerobics classes, gymnasiums, ski slopes) where such experiences are available. The rhetoric as a form of self-belief and self-esteem is also highly correlated with the activities that are chosen to represent this rhetorical state. Much of the play rhetoric of the imaginary was only in the mind of the rhetoricians, it seemed. This is also true of much of the rhetoric of the playing self. Nevertheless, most people nowadays say they are playing for "fun," so they have adopted at least this part of the rhetoric and they do judge their play by whether it is fun or boring, both unimaginable notions in prior history. I finish with the paradox that this rhetoric has more to do with the autonomy of play than any other, though one might assume that such autonomy, if it exists, needs no rhetoric. Which means there is the present rhetoric about autonomy, and there are the neurological and physiological suggestions that play, like the arts, is indeed universal. One can say, then, that if monkeys do it, it can hardly require all this rhetorical artifice. Perhaps we humans do it rhetorically to persuade ourselves that we can give up the old Puritan uneasiness about the phenomena.

As a final cautionary note, I need to add that, though I have been strenuously showing the relativity of this self approach, this does not mean that such a focus is avoidable in today's age. It is quite impossible to frame a relevant modern play theory without saying something about these ever-present experiential concerns. Despite the twentieth-century relativity of the self rhetorics, we are all, inescapably, creatures of such individualism.

Definitions have been most abundant in this chapter, and I need not repeat them all here. Participants talk of fun, joy, caprice, and escape. When children are asked how they play their games, however, they tend to give extended descriptions of the specific actions involved in playing the games, like tagging or hiding or running. What they generally do not do is give accounts of the rules and the plot of the play, but if prodded, they show that they know this other more general information. From this it seems reasonable to conclude that their enjoyment lies primarily in the specific performances of the games, as Gerstmyer and others have opined. If the children are right, the self rhetoric should be not so much about personal experience as about personal performance (Peterson and McCabe, 1983, p. xvi)

Intrinsic theories include Csikszentmihalyi's flow characteristics; Rubin and colleagues' intrinsic motivation characteristics; emphasis on states of mind and on freedom; existential phenomenology; and enactive, dramatistic, metaperformance theory, which I have couched as an ontology of referential and ludic dialectics.

Extrinsic theories include Freudian play mechanisms (compensation and so on), and neurological arousal modulation theories.

The major rhetorical ambiguity in this chapter has to do with the multiple meanings of the self, which is supposed to be at the center of the play experience, through which play is to be defined. The shift from epistemological to ontological definitions is also a source of considerable perplexity to most social scientists. More profoundly, however, the present conceptualization of a structural and performance theory of play in terms of referential and ludic dialectics between mundane and virtual worlds, and involving both play and playfulness, puts incongruity and ambiguity at the very center of the ludic experience.

11

Rhetorics of Frivolity

Don't be afraid of talking nonsense, but you must pay attention to your nonsense.

Ludwig Wittgenstein

Play is fun
Sex is fun.
Jokes are fun.
Writing is fun.
Being funny is fun.
So what is fun?
after Mrs. Huizinga

This, the seventh and final rhetoric, is another ancient one, belonging with fate, power, and identity. But it has its own particular place as an opponent to the seriousness of all the other rhetorics, ancient or modern. The essences of play from this viewpoint are nonsense and inversion, hence their position at the end of this work. This chapter could be entitled "The Protestant Ethic and the Spirit of Capitalism" (Weber, 1930) and be about the role of both religion and the work ethic in the denigration of play as a waste of time, as idleness, as triviality, and as frivolity. But that oft-told tale need not be retold here, except to indicate that the Puritan ethic of play has been the strongest and most long lasting of all the rhetorics of play in the past four hundred years. It is the antithesis to all the other rhetorics. None of their assertions makes much sense unless seen as a denial of the proposition that play is essentially useless. Typically the work ethic view of play rests on making an absolutely fundamental distinction between play and work. Work is obligatory, sober, serious, and not fun, and play is the opposite of these. This distinction, while influenced by Protestant religion, derives its major impetus from the urban industrial view of time and work. In the Middle Ages in Europe, the temporal organization of the calendar was still largely agricultural. Festival time fit the interstices of agricultural time. There were as many festivals then (sacred, profane, or both) as there are weekends now (Endrei and Zolnay, 1986). With the growth of urban life, these miscellaneous intrusions on the work week became intolerable. Historically the festival play cycle was the enemy of the organized factory work week. So when play is opposed to work and is said to be optional, fun, nonserious, and nonproductive, this can be from the point of view of factory work and other forms of economic discipline. Play is obviously very serious to its participants; they strive very earnestly and with great effort at their play and sports, and their efforts produce important personal and social outcomes that cannot be gotten easily in any other way. In addition, there are many societies in which play is an integral part of religious and work ceremonies; where the duality of work versus play, so often taken for granted in Western eyes, is simply not valid (Lancy and Tindall, 1976).

Prime credit in play-theory terms for denying the puritanical and work contentions about play in modern times must go to Huizinga, who, in *Homo Ludens* (1955), argues that play is a most fundamental human function and has permeated all cultures from the beginning. Furthermore he says that social play, particularly contest, underlies and contributes to the characteristics of human culture as found in law, war, philosophy, poetry, religion, and art. In play, man creates a poetic world alongside the original world of nature. "Primitive society performs its sacred rites and sacrifices, consecrations and mysteries, all of which serve to guarantee the well-being of the world in a spirit of pure play, truly understood" (p. 5). Nobody has claimed as much for play before or since, nor has anyone had as much effect on humanistic play scholars in the twentieth century. Huizinga also shows that he knows play is often nasty, brutish, and short, and at times obligatory, not free, irrational and bloody. So in putting down the Puritan alternative, he does not at first appear to commit the mistake of making play the opposite of "triviality" by overidealizing its character.

And yet, on further analysis, it appears that in his efforts to state what the universals of play are, and how play must be "truly understood," he has actually adopted a quite rarified view of play and has indeed set it severely apart from everyday existence. The analyses of Ehrmann (1968), Gruneau (1983), and Duncan (1988) reflect that Huizinga has essentially adopted the aristocratic rhetoric of the late nineteenth century, which sought to see games as being played for the games' sake, just as it saw art as being practiced for art's sake, a point of view that can be sustained in practical terms only by a wealthy elite, or in modern terms by closely supervised schoolchildren. Thus by saying, as he did, that play is outside of ordinary life, that it is immaterial, disinterested, nonutilitarian, voluntary, spatially and temporally separate, childlike, nonprofane, governed by rules, and utterly involving, he idealizes and sacralizes play. These "essentialistic" statements not only contradict many of his own exemplars of play as nasty, brutish, and short but are also themselves conditions of play only in limited circumstances. There are some conditions of play life that approximate these specifications, but many that do not. If one substitutes the words *music* or *painting* or *novel writing* for *play* in the above statements, the one-sidedness of the supposed defining characteristics becomes even more apparent. By making the "truly understood" conditions of play so pure, Huizinga has, in effect, confirmed its puerility and triviality. He has countered the view that play is frivolous, but in his opposition he has so idealized it that he has vitiated its regular broad functioning in human life. But perhaps it should be said on Huizinga's behalf that in play's intellectual evolution from being despised to being idealized is a dialectical step on the way to a more adequate synthesis.

Given the view that play's frivolity continues and has its own history apart from the work ethic, I can now consider the ways in which play is frivolity, versus play as progress, fate, power, identity, and the self. The important issue is whether play's frivolity is necessary for the existence of all of these rhetorics. Children's own spontaneous play is still thought to be fairly useless by many educators and most parents who pursue the rhetoric of progress. Furthermore the behemoth of adult play, such as gambling, on which billions are spent, is seldom even acknowledged to exist as play but has a thousand other names, all of which serve to disguise its potential commonality with the "frivolity" of children's play. It can be ventured that the denigration of frivolous play actually subdivides itself into six different kinds of devalued play, each of which, in its own way, helps to sustain the six types of play that are lauded by these rhetorics: developmental play, fateful play, contestive play, festival play, imaginative play, and personal play. In these terms, when one form of play is emphasized, some other form of play is implicitly devalued. Each rhetoric involves an internal polarity between good play and bad play and uses the term *frivolous* for whatever kind is chosen as bad play. Such a line of thought would certainly make greater sense, however, if one could show that the rhetorics in this work exist largely because they serve the political posturing of some cultural groups against other cultural groups.

I noted earlier that the whole of Spariosu's remarkable work *Dionysus Reborn* (1989) is about the fight that has taken place, since ancient Greek society, between the Apollonian views of play as rational and the Dionysian views of play as irrational. What can now be added is that, if each of the present rhetorics does indeed contain a binary relationship between strong and weak play, and is thus in different ways a repeat of Spariosu's struggle, then the six forms of weak play may be seen to be the irrational, frivolous, and feeble opposites of progress, fate, power, identity, the imaginary, and the self. Showing that each rhetoric not only is a persuasive discourse but also implies a cultural hegemony of one group over others would provide the theory of rhetorics with much more substance than their mere description as value systems has done to this point. Each of the seven rhetorics can be examined as a representation of the way people value some kind of play, and also as a representation of the way these same people use play to maintain their control by denigrating other kinds of play.

Hegemonies

Of all the rhetorics, progress is the most explicit in terms of hegemony, and the organization of children's play in terms of the educational and psychological beliefs of adults has been discussed at length. The very point of the progress rhetoric has been to constrain child play in the service of growth, education, and progress (see

Chapters 2 and 3). The data on the paradigms of childhood, and on human and animal adaptation, reveal the great power and disciplining effects over children of these progress myths about play, as exercised by educators and play therapists, and indeed by adults in general. Most adults show great anxiety and fear that children's play behavior, if not rationalized in these ways, will escape their control and become frivolous or become an irrational representation of child power, child community, phantasmagoria, and childish ecstasies. Play as progress is an ideology for the conquest of children's behavior through organizing their play. What is put to one side, forgotten, neglected, denied, trivialized, or suppressed are all the other ways in which children play by themselves or together with other children. Treating all of this play as frivolousness, as something to be put aside, illustrates and adds momentum to the idea that adults should organize the kind of play through which children are believed to develop properly.

In general in Western history, other rhetorical play stances have dismissed the play of fate as frivolous and worse. There has in recent history been no hegemony of chance and gambling over other forms of play, except in covert terms among some of the very affluent. But in many other cultures, and within the underclass in our own, gambling has long had a priority over other forms of play. And in the past decade or so, the institution of gambling through government-sponsored lotteries and casinos, as a form of taxation, has allowed this form of play into the overt center of the entertainment culture. From a gambling addict's point of view, and in a world where money is central, all forms of play that are not for high stakes are trivial pursuits. Gambling is to play what the stock market is to economics. They are both the most serious concern in either area.

Much of the discussion in Chapters 6 through 8 on power and identity is about the use of games, sports, and festivals as an exercise of power by the potentates in charge of such games—by kings, princes, politicians, colonizing administrators, aristocracies, ethnic groups, heterosexuals, and men. What is important is that the games of the less powerful groups are implicitly excluded and even ridiculed. For example, much of the older sports data are about martial or war groups, and play was rationalized as being important to the training of such powerful groups, and what is clear in recent analyses is that women have generally been the most excluded group in the practice of these martial games. Throughout much of history, and in most cultures, women simply have not played a part in the most popular sports and contests. Women have sometimes, not always, been a part of community celebrations and spectacles, but not of contestive play. In the twentieth century, however, they have been creeping gradually into the picture, as their representation in the Olympics and some professional sports indicates. The "politically correct" rhetorical fight for members of excluded groups (women, homosexuals, minorities, the poor) to be included in larger community celebrations is a continuing one and one that is only sometimes successful. It is not possible, therefore, to think of these two rhetorics, power and identity, without recognizing that they have been and still are political homelands for the manifestation of the political power of the controlling communities. Gradually the games of girls, and the folklore and folk play of minority groups, are beginning to escape, at least partially in social science theory, and in publicly acceptable practices, from the diminished status that has for so long been an essential part of the power and identity rhetorics—remembering, of course, that with such encroachment the reigning powers and communities continually shift their focus to other forms of play from which those with less power and wealth can be excluded anew. As presently arranged, the divisions between the powerful and the powerless are also manifested by divisions between private and public play. In recent decades, the play of the more powerful and wealthy has been marked as much by inconspicuous play consumption as by conspicuous consumption (see Veblen, 1899), though the latter also continues robustly.

Those who have lauded the imaginary kinds of play are the social and intellectual elites, always concerned to differentiate their own sophisticated social or solitary playfulness from that of the masses. They often condemn organized sports for children (Little League) and nearly always condemn mass-market toys in contradistinction to homemade toys or wooden toys, which, according to Roland Barthes, in a romantic mood, carry ecological values that commercial plastic cannot (1972). There is a heightened attention in this group to the literature of the fanciful imagination, particularly the relatively nonviolent kinds, especially in opposition to the violent kinds of fantasy to be found on television and in movies. It begins to look as if the concepts of the imagination and pretense will gradually take the high ground in relation to the concepts of fantasy or phantasmagoria, which will be used for the low ground.

With respect to the experience of self in play, there is already a movement to distinguish the kinds of higher-level or peak experiences from the merely mundane or routine. We hear of play as peak experience, as flow, as autotelic, as authentic experience, as spiritual experience, as the well-played game (De Koven, 1978); as infinite games, not finite games; as playing with boundaries, not within boundaries; as being playful but not serious (Carse, 1986); as playing by heart (Donaldson, 1993). These are increasingly said to be better ways of playing for oneself. But it is probable that that self will have to be somewhat fortunate in having wealth, education, special training, or spiritual guidance, in order to have access to these "better" forms of play. We are living at a time when the concept of the "good" player, one who was probably a member of the new games movement (Fluegelman, 1976) and has subsequently participated endlessly in group-process play, is beginning to emerge as a person of higher ethical status. She or he can "flow" and can get others to flow, and in so doing help them evolve into ever more complex and sensitive beings as suggested in *The Evolving Self* (Csikszentmihalyi, 1993).

Frivolous Play Scholarship

Speculation about the different ways in which the grandiose rhetorics are rifted by their own implicit rhetorics of power leads to the conclusion that play is declared frivolous not only because of neglect or because frivolous play is the abstract opposite of some higher-level form of serious ludic activity. The label "frivolity" is, rather, an abuse of some kinds of play on behalf of other kinds of play, because that is what is politically suitable for some dominating groups. Not only are all players not the same but some are much more equal than others. So the issue of the equality of other people's pastimes comes to the forefront of our attention.

The frivolity of playfulness, which seemed at first to be just a mildly amusing relic of Puritanism, takes on a much more serious purpose when we view it as an implicit form of political or scholarly denigration. Much of the time most of us continue unwittingly with our frivolous play pursuits, unaware that we are despised by others except when the hegemony of those others suddenly makes itself felt as forms of rudeness, censorship, banishment, annulment, or cancellation. In scholarship the denigration of play in intellectual terms is shown by the absence of the key term *play* from the index of almost every book about the behavior of human beings. It is true that increased research attention has been given to play within psychology in recent decades, and within biology throughout this century, but there is still much more resistance to the subject than is justified, given its universal role in human behavior. From my point of view, regarding play as frivolous is itself a frivolous gesture. When one comes to deal with what has been treated as trivial or frivolous by the major six rhetorical groups—that is, the spontaneous play of children, women, minority groups, mass-media devotees, couch potatoes, and the folk wherever you find them—then suddenly this worm of frivolity takes yet another turn. All of these denigrated groups are generally as deadly serious and righteous about their own play as are those who denigrate them. They are not frivolous in their own eyes, they are seriously at play.

The academic discipline of folklore is a good example of a discipline that though dismissed by academia in general for its frivolousness, nevertheless pursues its own serious study of the playful goings-on of the folk. Its scholars spend their lives studying such "trivia" as folklore, humor, ethnopoetics, entertainment, oratory, ethnomusicology, oral history, oral culture, folktales, proverbs, riddles, speech play, insults, gossip, oratory, folk music, masks, mime, gesture, dance, artifacts, clothing, food, drama, puppetry, spectacles, rituals, festivals, and tourism (Bauman, 1992). There are only a few major academic programs in folklore in this country, at, for example, Indiana University, the University of Pennsylvania, the University of Texas at Austin, and the University of California at Berkeley and Los Angeles. These and other smaller folklore programs have generated a most serious and relatively coherent group of scholars and folk custodians, devotees of the "trivial" play habits of the world.

Perhaps a little further down the academic tree is the discipline of popular culture, itself a latter-day playful offshoot of folklore. This group, founded by Ray Browne at Bowling Green State University in Ohio, studies anything that is contemporary and interesting to ordinary people, including detective mysteries, box office hits, how much you can swallow, new legends, the cabinet of Dr. Seuss, songs of the unseen road, morality tales, myths of success, the myth of romantic love, Barbie dolls, soap operas, monster movies, and westerns, to take just a few items from a popular culture textbook (Nachbar and Lause, 1992). There are, in addition, a number of play associations throughout the world that study play as a serious scholarly or pragmatic subject. After all, in the United Nations Charter for Childhood, the child's right to play is one of the accepted articles. The Association for the Study of Play (TASP/USA) and the International Council for Children's Play (ICCP/Europe) are groups that study play in a scholarly manner. But even larger are the groups concerned with the practice of play, such as the Toy Library Association, the Association for the Child's Right to Play (formerly called the International Playground Association), the Association for Play Therapy, and the World Organization for Preschool Education. Finally, there are also innumerable scholarly and practical groups that study games, game simulation, sports, physical education, sports psychology, and sports sociology. All of these associations and societies consider their concerns to be most serious. But to the rest of the scholarly world, this array of interests is hardly to be taken with much seriousness. The focus is still seen as frivolous.

These groups that study play have their own minority rhetorics and academic journals of importance. Indeed they have their own hegemonies, from which it should follow that they themselves will treat something else as frivolous. But if they are not to be the lowest in the scholarly hierarchy being established here, who is to be the bottom dog? In folklore, the bottom dog is children's folklore. That's the easiest answer. Among scholarly associations for the study of play, the bottom dogs are the associations for the applied or practical study of play. And these attitudes are reversed and reciprocated by the latter groups. But perhaps there is yet some more general and playful frivolity that unites all the groups, both high and low, in their opposition. Putting aside adaptive play, agonistic play, territorial play, creative play, earnest play, and even play of low folk status, what kind of play is the least valued? A choice for the lowest of all forms might be dilettantist play, the form of play defined not as the play but as trifling with play. The dilettante is a dabbler, one who pursues his play just for amusement or in a desultory way. He or she plays with play itself. He is the personification of playfulness. I propose now to pursue this greatest folly.

The Festival as Frivolity

At this point I wish to shift focus from the way in which playfulness can be trivialized in Western society to examples from other societies that suggest that such "folly" can have a more central place than we have given it in modern times. A most excellent example is to be found in *Yoruba Ritual: Performers, Play, Agency* (1992) by Margaret Drewal, in which Drewal shows how fundamental improvisation or play is in this group's very serious collective ceremonies, such as burial, birth, and initiation rites. She makes the point that the most ritualistic and sacred parts of these festivals are not anywhere near as ritualistic and consistent as Westerners, with their biblical and liturgical backgrounds written down in books, typically expect. There is variability even in the most conservative aspects of the ceremonies. In addition, times are set aside for out-and-out improvisation, theater, or play, even in the burial celebrations. The Yoruba believe that the more people who participate and the better the improvisational play, the more power is passed to the departing spirit. Here play and ritual are deeply united in a way that is difficult for Westerners, with their traditions of work versus play, or sacred versus profane, to imagine. I have already discussed this fusion of play and ritual illustrated by children (Chapter 9).

In recent years many have written of festivals as rites of inversion, as in Barbara Babock's edited collection, *The Reversible World* (1978), the title coming from a notion introduced by Victor Turner in his earlier book, *The Ritual Process* (1969). Turner says: "One aspect of symbolic inversion maybe to break people out of their culturally defined, even biologically ascribed roles by making them play precisely the opposite roles . . . breaking down barriers of age, sex, status, family, clan, and so on to teach the meaning of the generic humanity; so that each person becomes the joker in the pack, the card who can be all cards, the method actor" (Turner, 1978, pp. 287–278). Others have argued that the folk character called the "trickster" need not be a rebel as some have claimed (although he can be); rather, he incorporates both the good and the bad, the sobriety and the insobriety, the body conventional and the body uncontrollable, and as such he occupies a dialectical status in culture (Koepping, 1985). He stands both for order and disorder at the same time. He is, in short, a truly dialectical being in the terms used to describe play in Chapters 8 and 9.

Contemporary modern examples of festival folly are still to be found in Europe, and among those much studied are the carnivals of Germany (Tokofsky, 1992). Many of these festivals are oriented around a season beginning in November and finishing with Fat Tuesday, the day before Ash Wednesday, the beginning of the season of Lenten restrictions. Hundreds of masked and costumed citizens parade, and the costumed are often various kinds of fools, all of whom play tricks on each other and the public. Some are mildly benevolent while others make a play of their malevolence. On the private occasions when the guilds, which have run these affairs for centuries, meet for periodic celebrations, there is a also a premium on folly. Apart from the typical cross-dressing nonsense where burly half-clad men simulate ballerinas, belly dancers, and Polynesian women—which is nonsense enough (or *Wahnsinn*)—there are kitchen bands in which the members simulate playing on various kitchen utensils, but without even a hint at either rhythm or melody, in an effort to bring nonsense into the most domestic of family realms. One listens in dismay and then suddenly realizes they are not making any kind of music but are in a realm of total folly (or *Unsinn*).

In many cultures and subcultures, the person known as fool, trickster, Frech, leprechaun, clown, harlequin, or comedian is held to be quite central to the theatric side of public affairs. All of the seriousness of regular play, or of regular play rhetoric or regular play theory, is susceptible to being made ludicrous by this inversively playful person, who trivializes all things most devastatingly, including trivialization itself. The true trickster is so frivolous he can invert frivolity. While in modern society one can still find the "official" fool in various places on the fringe of society, there have been times and there still are places where the fool has almost the position of the wisest person.

For example Barton Wright, in his work *Clowns of the Hopi: Tradition Keepers and Delight Makers* (1994), says of the Zuni sacred trickster:

> They found a little boy who was so full of life
> That he was never still. He laughed and joked
> And mimicked everyone and everything
> Around him, even the most sacred rituals.
> He said and did anything that came into
> His mind without regard for its effects. (p. 58)

Enid Welsford, in her classic of 1935, *The Fool*, struggles to explain why the most frivolous of modern persons, the fool or the comedian, though the "lowest" of us all, is yet in some way inversely the most serious of us all. She says that unlike the rest of us, who are all losers in most of the conventional senses, and most surely in the mortal sense, the fool transcends triviality.

> For the genius of the Fool is manifested by his power of deluding us into the belief that he can draw the sting of pain; by his power of surrounding us with an atmosphere of make-believe, in which nothing is serious, nothing is solid, nothing has abiding consequences. Under the dissolvent influence of his personality, the iron network of physical, social, and moral law, which enmeshes us from the cradle to the grave, seems—for the moment—negligible as a web of gossamer. The Fool does not lead a revolt against the law, he lures us into a region of the spirit where, as Lamb would put it, the writ does not run. (p. 321)

Both the fool and the playful person live in the place where the "writ does not run": a world where bad people are harmless, where stupid people are merry, where Fate is transformed into "Puck-like Chance" (ibid., p. 325). Perhaps the spirit of playfulness, never entirely foreign to all kinds of serious play, is ultimately the guarantee that all forms of play potentially promise that one can never quite lose while still at play. The promise is that the greater the frivolity, the greater the transcendence of the common writ. Which is to say that frivolity is potentially the most sacred play of all, a condition once recognized by the appointment of sacred tricksters and holy fools. But this is a play form that now must take up a more disguised and secular existence, in e-mail perhaps, where a surgency of spirit is all that is left of what once was the sacred message that only in the transformation that becomes a transgression is the immortal to be emulated (Makarius, 1970). This last remark sounds something like the discussion of games of chance and the way in which they are also challenges to fate. Apparently fate and frivolity share most closely the power to make players feel that they can transcend reality and indeed mortality.

Validations and Definitions

No theory of play would be adequate if it did not leave scope for its own deconstruction and distortion into nonsense. Any earnest definition of play has to be haunted by the possibility that playful enjoinders will render it invalid. And considering the regal role of some tricksters, who take the place of the vested power on festival days, the reverse can happen. Play is the fool that might become king, as once happened in legend when the king died in the brief festival period during which the fool was supposed to rule.

In the rhetoric of frivolity, we inherit the ambiguity of reversing all the other rhetorics and then calling that, too, a form of playfulness. But in so doing we find that such folly has had a sacred past and may indeed still today be a mirror of the desires for earthly transcendence that one finds in all other kinds of play. This mode of transcendence or transformation is most extreme in the way in which games of fate and games of frivolity deny both reality and mortality.

12

Conclusion

> No epilogue, I pray you, for your play needs no excuse. Never
> excuse.
>
> *William Shakespeare,* A Midsummer Night's Dream

This work begins with the announcement by experts that, theoretically speaking, play is difficult to understand because it is ambiguous. My focus is on the way in which these ambiguities are instigated
by the seven systems of value here called the ideological rhetorics
of progress, fate, power, identity, the imaginary, the self, and frivolity, and I offer reasons for claiming some valid internal coherence for each of these separate rhetorics, as well as for their
ambiguous effects on the theories of play. In general each rhetoric
has a historical source, a particular function, a distinctive ludic
form, and specialized players and advocates, and is the context for
particular academic disciplines. In addition its advocates and scholars manifest hegemonies both within their own form of play and
toward other forms. Some of the connections that give the rhetorics
their own distinctive validity are summarized in the accompanying
table.

The rhetorics are a source of various kinds of ambiguity. Obviously no rhetoric (the arguments made about a play form) is totally
identifiable with any play practice (the way the ludic form is played).
But because the rhetoric is making a statement about the value of
the play form, there is apt to be a conflation of the two. Those
who make statements about the value of the play are inclined to
imply that their statements are also descriptions of the behaviors

The Seven Rhetorics of Play

Rhetoric	History	Function	Form	Players	Discipline	Scholars
1. Progress	Enlightenment, evolution	Adaptation, growth, socialization	Play, games	Juveniles	Biology, psychology, education	Vygotsky, Erikson, Piaget, Berlyne
2. Fate	Animism, divination	Magic, luck	Chance	Gamblers	Math	Bergler, Fuller, Abt
3. Power	Politics, war	Status, victory	Skill, strategy, deep play	Athletes	Sociology, history	Spariosu, Huizinga, Scott, Von Neumann
4. Identity	Tradition	Communitas, cooperation	Festivals, parades, parties, new games	Folk	Anthropology, folklore	Turner, Falassi, De Koven, Abrahams
5. Imaginary	Romanticism	Creativity, flexibility	Fantasy, tropes	Actors	Art and literature	Bakhtin, Fagen, Bateson
6. Self	Individualism	Peak experience	Leisure, solitary, extreme games	Avant-garde, solitary players	Psychiatry	Csikszentmihalyi
7. Frivolity	Work ethic	Inversion, playfulness	Nonsense	Tricksters, comedians, jesters	Pop culture	Welsford, Stewart, Cox

or experiences taking place on the playing field. In some cases the identification is very close, as when a child's prank is itself the expression of the way in which the child embarrasses an adult figure. Here the child's hidden transcript (an implicit rhetoric) against authority is made overt. In sport, the agonistic cries of exultation over the opposition sometimes carry much the same attitude as the actual physical or strategic contests between the opposing players. Similarly there can be a closeness between verbal jingoistic exuberances and the forms, costumes, and music of a martial parade. Against all this, by contrast, it is clear that verbalizations about a ludic experience are not the same as that experience. When the adult says play is a developmental experience, for the child it may be nothing but hide-and-seek. What the Puritan says is character-destroying gambling may be, for the player, the one satisfying experience in the week. Because forms of play, like all other cultural forms, cannot be neutrally interpreted, it is impossible to keep ambiguity from creeping into the relationship between how they are perceived and how they are experienced. The rhetorical information in the preceding chapters certainly helps illuminate why there are so many scholars of play with quite divergent theories about what play actually is.

I cannot pass by this considerable exercise in the rhetorics of play, however, only in terms of the ambiguities to which it gives rise. Are the rhetorics of any other value? Roberts and Good (1993) hope that knowing that the rhetorics are what science presupposes will lead to a broader integration across disciplines and, in the present case, to a decrease in ambiguity about their common subject matter, play. But the present enterprise has been partly an unmasking of the tendentiousness and hegemony of these rhetorics. If in consequence there is less ambiguity about play, it would have to be because the sheer irreconcilability of these different play complexes is clearer than it was previously. From this study of some aspects of the way in which rhetorics in general are influential within the scholarly disciplines about play, it would have to be concluded that scholars also seem to have in common, wittingly or not, the way they manipulate these rhetorics to justify their own preoccupations with the different play forms. It is not just that play is susceptible to these ideological value systems but also that the scholars often need these rhetorics to license their own authority over the kinds of play with which they are concerned. If the interpretations given here have any validity, then this volume makes scholars more alike, but largely because of their shared tendentiousness and their use of "objective methods" in highly self-rationalizing and narrow ways as a part of their disciplinary identifications. This is not in itself a higher form of integration across the disciplines. That would require some new postmodern rhetoric of tolerance toward the variabilities of each other group's kinds of play and play rhetorics. One could imagine that it might become politically correct to see that there is increased opportunity for all players to go their own play ways and also to have more access to and understanding of the ambiguities of the others. Perhaps that is what a heteroglossic ludic rhetoric of the future might advocate. More simply, it is also possible that understanding the confusion of one's own rhetoric and one's own theories might lead to more useful general scientific theorizing. At the same time, some skeptics and romantics have commented that it might be kinder to leave play in the diffuse, inchoate conceptual shape in which it was found at the beginning of this inquiry. Then, ironically, all players could continue to have the satisfaction of making their own Rorschach interpretations without having to worry about academic redress. More fun, less stress.

Defining Play: Some Issues

Clearly a book of this kind is unsatisfying unless it can lead one beyond these particular rhetorics toward some more central definition or more universal rhetoric. A great variety of concepts and definitions of play have already been cited. Chapter 1 also provides the kind of material for those descriptive (ostensive) definitions of play that come about when knowledgeable members of a culture agree on the actions, persons, objects, places, times, and motives that they refer to when they use the word *play*. The reader might hope, however, that some attempt would be made here to overcome these more practical but narrow definitions. Given the varieties of play dimensions that have been raised, that seems difficult if not impossible. All the same, to just walk away from the theoretical disturbances that have been created in the preceding pages would also be a kind of betrayal of trust. One deserves to be roasted for presence as well as feted for absence.[1] The character of the problem is indicated by the following recital of many of the concepts that have been used to describe play in this century and in this volume. They are tentatively collected under the heading of each of the seven rhetorics. Obviously the fit is only approximate.[2]

In addition I must caution that the search for a definition at this time is a search only for metaphors that can act as a rhetoric for what might ultimately become adequate scientific processual accounts. While it is common to call such metaphors hypotheses to dignify the undertaking as a scientific one, the truth of the matter is that what I produce here is a metaphorical mélange, representing the possibility of a truth yet to be discovered. A cynic might say that most of social science is a play of metaphors aspiring to be measurable processes. Since the scholars who create these metaphors hope to take the next steps toward science, we cannot say that they are merely poets or players. Their intentions absolve them from the charge that this is only a language game.

A further point that must be made is that I have already shown in preceding chapters various biases, for example:

1. that play's definition must be broad rather than narrow, including passive or vicarious forms as well as the active participant forms, including daydreams as well as sports and festivals.
2. that it should apply to animals as well as humans, and children as well as adults.
3. that it should not be defined only in terms of the restricted modern Western values that say it is nonproductive, rational, voluntary, and fun. These are not concepts that can prevail as

---

[1] I have had the honor of being roasted on one occasion and feted on another by the Anthropological Association for the Study of Play, and in that sequence—an appropriately ambiguous reception for the author of this book.

[2] The authorities referred to are strongly associated with the concepts with which they are paired but are not necessarily their originators. Only the first author is mentioned in cases of multiple authorship. The "S-S" references are to neologisms emerging from the present work.

universals, given the larger historical and anthropological evidence to the contrary.

4. that play is not just an attitude or an experience; it is always characterized by its own distinct performances and stylizations.

5. that it can be as momentary as a piece of wit, or can endure as long as the one-year cycles of festivals or the four-year cycles of the Olympics. That it can be spatially either as diffuse as a daydream or as articulate as a sports stadium.

6. that play is like language: a system of communication and expression, not in itself either good or bad.

The contemporary concepts that follow are seldom sufficient to convey the complexity and variability implied by these assertions.

• Progress—Play as adaptation:

Biological concepts: preparation (Groos), recapitulation (Hall), instinct (McDougall), learning (Thorndike), skill training (P. Smith), metabolic restoration (Hutt), flexibility (Fagen), prax of subroutines (Bruner), neurological fabulation (Sacks), correlator brain model (Edelman), adaptive potentiation (S-S), holistic virtuality (S-S).

Psychological concepts: pure assimilation (Piaget), zone of proximal development (Vygotsky), transition (Winnicott), subjunctivity (Vaihinger), exploration (Berlyne), mastery (Erikson), divergent thinking (Lieberman), primordial negative (Burke), affect regulation (MacDonald), desire (Hans), enactive subjunctivity (S-S).

• Fate—Play as existential optimism:

Chance (Pascal), chaos (Gleick), indeterminism (Monod), the play of being (Heidegger), anarchism (Feyerabend), psychic masochism (Bergler), dark play (Schechner), existential optimism (S-S), unrealistic optimism, egocentricity, and lability (Bjorklund), neonatal ludicism (S-S).

• Power—Play as hegemony:

Adult forms: game theory (Von Neumann), playfighting (Aldis), rough-and-tumble (Panksepp), contest (Huizinga), conflict mediation (Turner), power (Spariosu), serious games (C. C. Abt), models of power (J. M. Roberts), deep play (Geertz), inversion

(Babcock), hegemony (MacAloon), gamesmanship (Maccoby), hidden transcripts (Scott), subversion (McMahon), agonistics (Loy), models, mimicry, and mockery (Handelman), dialectics (S-S).

Child forms: surplus energy (Schiller), pleasure of being a cause (Groos), willfulness (Nietzsche), compensation and abreaction (Freud), catharsis (Menninger), effectance (White), illicit play (King), hierarchization (Asher), cruel play (S-S), masks (S-S, Kelly-Byrne).

- Identity—Play as social context:

symbolic interactionism (Mead), bonding (Harlow), communitas (Turner), frame analysis (Goffman), intimate play (Betcher), communal play (De Koven), framing, focus, stylization, and intensification (Abrahams), gaming (Hughes), autonomous peer cultures (Corsaro), interdependent or independent social contexts (Greenfield), festival hazing (Noyes), orderly and disorderly genders (Nicolopoulou).

- Imaginary—Play as transformation

Animal forms: repetitive, fragmentary, reordered, reversive, unpredictable, exaggerative, and inhibitive play (Fagen).

Human forms: transformations (H. Schwartzman), vicarious play (Stephenson), dialogic imagination (Bakhtin), pretense (Fein), imagination (J. Singer), symbolic play (Bretherton), monstration (Spariosu), methexis (Huizinga), play of signifiers (Derrida), improvisation (Sawyer; Drewal), dark and light play (Schechner), metacommunication (Bateson), prototypic self-reflexive paradoxical mode (J. Schwartzman), panoply of tropes (Fernandez), narratological forms (Bruner).

- Self—Play as peak experience or microperformance:

consumer self (Veblen), relaxation (Patrick), arousal (Ellis), flow (Csikszentmihalyi), positive emotional state (Lewis), intrinsic motivation (Rubin), optimism (Vandenberg), the ludic self (Nardo), autotelia and paratelia (Kerr), ecstatic actions (Fink), affect regulation (McDonald), agentivity (Bruner), performance (Bauman, Garvey, Gerstmyer).

- Frivolity—Play as world upside down:

the trickster (Radin), the fool (Welsford), nonsense (Stewart), grotesque realism (Rabelais), the feast of fools (Cox).

A Rhetoric of Play as Adaptive Variability

What is most striking about the above lists is the multiplicity of the concepts that have been applied to play. If we add the extensive lists of play names in the first chapter, and the seven rhetorics with all their potentiality for further subdivisions and ambiguities of myriad kinds, it is the variability of the play phenomena which most impresses the present author. In looking for what is common to child and adult forms of play, to animal and human forms, to dreams, daydreams, play, games, sports and festivals, it is not hard to reach the conclusion that what they have in common, even cross culturally, is their amazing diversity and variability. The possibility then arises, that it is this variability that is central to the function of play throughout all species. Considering that variation is also a key concept within biological thought, this seems like the most profitable point to begin the inquiry.

A conception which makes such variability central to evolution is that of Stephen Jay Gould who in his recent work *Full House* (1996b; by which he means the full range, or normal curve of biological variation), cites variability rather than precision of adaptation, as the central characteristic of biological evolution. He writes:

> Precise adaptation, with each part finely honed to perform a definite function in an optimal way, can only lead to blind alleys, dead ends, and extinction. In our world of radically and unpredictably changing environments, an evolutionary potential for creative responses requires that organisms possess an opposite set of characteristics usually devalued in our culture: sloppiness, broad potential, quirkiness, unpredictability, and, above all, massive redundancy, The key is flexibility, not admirable precision. (p. 44)

Gould goes on to discuss three basic principles of such evolutionary variability, and although he is not talking about play, the match between his account and contemporary descriptions of play is striking. I intend here to show that the parallel between his scientific discussion of the variable processes in adaptation and the metaphors for play as a model of variability is too close to be ignored—remembering, of course, that both Gould's account of adaptive reality and my account of play are quite hypothetical. What follows, then, is my rhetoric of play "borrowed" from Gould, as it relates to his rhetoric of evolution. Gould's principles of variability as adaptation appear in italics.

1. Evolution is characterized by quirky shifts and latent potential. What could be more fundamental in talking about all forms of play than to describe them in terms of the centrality of this notion of quirky shifts? Animal play has been described by many investigators as fragmentary, disorderly, unpredictable, and exaggerated; human dreams and day-dreams are said to be bizarre and dissociative; child play has been said to be improvised, vertiginous, and nonsensical; games and sports are conflictful and unpredictable. Festivals are described as given to intensifications of action, crowds, noise, revelry, violence, inebria-tion, tricksters, clowns, hazing, and multiple other forms of inversion. The rhetorics of progress (skill uncertainty), the imaginary (mere fancy), the self (peak experience), power (unpredictable winners), identity (festival intensity), fate, (taking chances), and frivolity (non-sense) certainly lend themselves readily to this quirky metaphor.

Further support for the argument that play models the centrality of quirkiness can be found in the neurologist Gerald Edelman's account, in *Bright Air, Brilliant Fire* (1992), of the brain as a constantly diversifying, value-driven, correlator process. In his terms, this asso-ciatively quirky process is fundamental to brain activity, not derivative from it, and it applies as well to dreams as to problem solving. Contemporary theoretical play concepts, which one may read as also speaking implicitly to this quirky conception of play's variability, use such terms for play as pure assimilation, divergent thinking, indeter-minism, anarchism, dark play, inversion, the world upside down, order and disorder, transformations, dialogic imagination, the play of signifiers, paradoxical modes, tricksterism, and grotesque realism. Together, they may be interpreted as showing how multiple theorists seek to grasp the essential character of variability for their own theories of play. The variety of their concepts implies that the phe-nomenon theorists seek to model (play) is itself as centrally mercurial as Gould has suggested the variability in adaptation is.

2. Redundancy. Gould's second principle for describing variability is that of redundancy. Having produced one useful structure, imme-diately required for adaptation, the organism reproduces a series of similar structures that may have no immediate function and can be exploited for different evolutionary purposes—as occurs, for example, most obviously in the cloning processes of cellular division, where the extra copies can be used for other processes. Presumably additional "junk" genes can be used beyond the "blueprint" genes to fulfill the particular requirements in each distinct individual's emergent development. Humans do not contain anywhere near enough genes to make enough individual cells to create a fully operational brain, so an overabundance of the same or similar cells and synapses is produced, and then the brain has to use them to learn how to make itself work (Kotulak, 1996). This, Gould says, is the principle of having extra capacity or, in his jocular terms, carrying a spare tire.

This kind of proliferation of form is particularly well illustrated in all forms of play, as in the endless reproduction of games of "house" or "trucks"; or in the endless kinds of ball games played by all ages and most cultures; or in card games; or in annual celebrations, parades, parties and festivals. The most obvious modern effects of such redundancy are shown by the replications of all kinds of sports throughout the world in the past hundred years. Whatever such replicable sports are made to mean (in terms, for example, of power and bonding), they are now an international rather than a parochial concern. The same internationalizing of strategy games (chess, bridge) is also taking place. And the replicatory process now occurs with children's toys, as seen in toy lending libraries and in international consumer marketers' attempts to produce dolls and other toys that will be acceptable on all continents.

It is possible to argue from all of this that our play redundancies parallel the function of genetic redundancies in their provision of variations available for whatever uses, rhetorical or otherwise, to which the individual or the culture wishes to put them. The simplest sense of play's variability may be that it exemplifies variability and, as such, is potentially available for transfer to subsequent functions. This would be perhaps a "trickle down" theory of play's usefulness, a concept I have previously termed "adaptive potentiation" (1975a, 1975b). In what follows, however, I will outline a more central function for play's variability than this accidental one.

3. Flexibility. Third, and most important, Gould sees both quirky variability and multiple redundancy as generated by flexibility. Without flexibility's having been selected in evolution, the characteristics of quirkiness and redundancy could not have emerged. The best evidence for the natural selection of flexibility, he says, is the extent to which the length of the neonatal period is correlated with the complexity of mammal growth. Humans are the most vulnerable of species, have the longest period of dependency, and grow the most slowly of all mammals. As Gould says, "We have evolved an extended childhood, presumably for the advantages imparted by prolonged flexibility for learning. And we retain some of this crucial flexibility into an adult stage that, in most mammals, entails rigidification of behavior" (1996b, p. 54). Obviously it would not be hard to defend the position that most forms of play require similarly large amounts of flexibility, both for learning them and for performing them. If play is to be seen as some kind of adaptive variability, Gould's account provides evolutionary metaphors that certainly have some power. If quirkiness, redundancy, and flexibility are keys to evolution, then finding play to be itself quite quirky, redundant, and flexible certainly suggests that play may have a similar biological base.

My first inclination after playing this metaphoric game with Gould was to leave the matter there. Enough is enough. The notion that play itself is some kind of adaptive variability, and therefore presumably some kind of reinforcement of realistic adaptive variability, is very attractive. One can see the worth of analyzing all kinds of play data in terms of categories of variation yet to be developed. That would be a research novelty, a little bit like David Siegler's recent suggestion that Piaget's stages are just another form of essentialism and that what we really need to know is how change actually occurs. Siegler, who also bases his argument on biological evolution, says we need to identify the mechanisms that lead children to select from a variety of available responses those that will solve the problems at hand (Siegler, 1996). I could suggest, likewise, that instead of focusing only on play forms and their normative rules, we need to know what kinds of variability players actually encounter in their playing. Not that this is a new notion to those, such as Linda Hughes, who have been studying "gaming" and games in this way for some time (1983, 1988, 1989, 1991, 1993a, 1993b).

Not being able to leave well enough alone, I came to feel that this adaptive variability account, either as adaptive potentiation or as reinforcement of general adaptability, is still insufficient. I have, therefore, several other suggestions that might fill out this picture of flexibility and variability. The first is inspired by recent brain imaging technology, the second is from some recent psychological studies of the cognitive behavior of young children, and the third entails a return, finally, to the implications of Darwin's natural selection as the "struggle for survival."

Brain Imaging Technology

The key discovery in brain imaging technology, as it relates to the play rhetorics, is that in the neonatal stage, by eight months of age, the infant makes 1,000 trillion synaptic connections, but after that period the synapses attenuate if they are not actually used. By ten years of age, a child typically has only about 500 million connections. Thus the neonate has twice as many brain connections as the grown human being. It is theorized that this is to ensure enough "extra wiring" for adaptation to any kind of environment in which the child is reared. The infant brain's ability to constantly undergo physical and chemical changes as it responds to the environment is taken to suggest enormous plasticity. This synaptic information (initially presented by Peter Huttenlocher of the University of Chicago) means that humans are born with more going for them than they will ever have again, which is the very opposite of the older view that "the brain is a self contained, hard wired unit that learns from a present, unchangeable set of rules" (Kotulak, 1996, p. xii)

All of a sudden I saw in this piece of information another useful metaphor with which to understand the role of play. We could say that just as the brain begins in a state of high potentiality, so does play. The brain has these connections, but unless they are actualized in behavior, most of them will die off. Likewise in play, even when novel connections are actualized, they are still not, at first, the same as everyday reality. Actions do not become everyday reality until there is a rhetoric or practice that accounts for their use and value. Play's function in the early stages of development, therefore, may be to assist the actualization of brain potential without as yet any larger commitment to reality. In this case, its function would be to save, in both brain and behavior, more of the variability that is potentially there than would otherwise be saved if there were no play. Piaget's theory of play is, of course, the very reverse. He says that it is only after connections are established by real-life accommodation that they are consolidated in play. The present thesis would hold that another play function, perhaps the most important one, may be the actualization of novel connections, and therefore the extension of childhood's potential variability (Sutton-Smith, 1966a, 1982f).

What the imaging data suggests is that whereas Gould's triad speaks to the characteristics of play's variability, information about the evolution of the brain implies a way in which that potential variability is advanced through play. The very fact that play contains so much nonsense, so much replication, and is so flexible certainly suggests that it is a prime domain for the actualization of whatever the brain contains. And for that matter, speaking in behavioral rather than neurological terms, play is typically a primary place for the expression of anything that is humanly imaginable. After all, most fools and comedians have to first convince us that they are only playing before they lay before us their hilarious associations and nefarious interpretations.

Children's Cognitive Behavior

One can draw other lessons about the neonatal and early childhood character of human flexibility by looking at some of the cognitive work on early childhood potential. Bjorkland and Green (1992) have described the key neonatal cognitive characteristics of children, up to age five years, as those of unrealistic optimism, egocentricity, and reactivity. Children up until about five years of age overestimate their ability to function skillfully, despite continued negative feed back. Furthermore they tend, as Piaget has said, to see things rather selectively, from their own perspective. And they are highly reactive to whatever stimuli are placed before them, regardless of the relevance of those stimuli to whatever else is going on, a characteristic that Heinz Werner spoke of as their lability (1957). Here again I might argue that their persistence in the face of negative feedback, their persistence with their own concerns, and their reactivity to whatever comes their way could all contribute to the actualization of those potential neural connections. Further, while these neonatal characteristics are general in childhood, it is not hard to insist that they are especially well epitomized by play. Indeed play may be the best exemplar of such characteristics and therefore the best carrier of them and of flexibility. As a footnote, it could be argued that what I might call "neonatal ludicism," applies as well to the play of older persons, whose play can often also be described as unrealistically optimistic, egocentric, and reactive. Watching eighty-year-olds playing golf on their executive nine-hole courses illustrates the point. Being "number one" in any sport tends to require a similar foolishness.

The Struggle for Survival as the Motivation for Variability

What is lacking to this point in this account of the neonatal grounds for flexibility is much suggestion of relevant motivation. Others have talked of the motivated heart of play as optimism, intrinsic motivation, flow, empowerment, ecstatic performance, effectance, positive emotional states, and arousal, all of which suggest that there may be basic motivational accompaniments to being flexible. These are, however, all terms from this century's individualistically oriented rhetoric, as I have shown. But if play itself is to be seen as a contribution to the functioning of variability in the natural selection process, as is being touted here, then it behooves one to look deeper into evolutionary accounts of motivation. Remember that in evolutionary theory, processes of variation are supposed to be random, but selection is a matter of life or death.

   In evolutionary theory, the concept of "the struggle for survival" hovers in the background as a vague symbol for the bloody extermination and suffering that this whole topic actually requires. As Darwin put it, "Hence there will be necessarily a struggle for existence. Yet this struggle need not be entirely negative, for success is not chance. It is rather a function of the possession of various peculiar, useful features, and the nonpossession of such features by the losers" (Ruse, 1996, p. 139). The importance of variability within this scheme is that it provides alternatives when they are needed because of changes that threaten life at every level. Most of us get a fair diet of this on the Discovery Channel on television (which perhaps should be called the Darwinian Channel), where producers like to put a modern, gentle twist on these things. Having, for example, shown us a poor sick buffalo pursued for an hour by a pack of wolves and finally pulled to the ground, we are given the evolutionary euphemism; "They have made each other the best of their kind."

Everyday life for animals, it seems, requires constant concern about predation, food, sex, and exclusion. But if we are to make this natural-selection process applicable to humans in a more general way, beyond their ever-frequent wars (Keeley, 1996) and the eternal battle with the bacter (that is, the bacteria), then we would have to say that the cultural counterpart might be found in our constant struggle for safety, approval, achievement, love, and even significance, which is to invert the Maslowian scheme of things in more mundane terms. The cultural variations that impose themselves in a way that is analogous to the need for natural selection are these thoroughly familiar matters of existential anxiety that have become the obvious subject matter of psychiatry and clinical psychology throughout this century. Darwin himself is said, by the biographer Gruber, to have been in favor of some such broader view of evolution and against the presentation of struggle only in terms of the polarized life or death versions. "'Survival depends on the organism re-making itself,'" said Darwin (Gruber, 1974, p. 54). "'Variation and novelty are not chaotic or unrelated to the organism's past, but express degrees of freedom characteristic of a particular organization as it stands at one moment in its history'" (ibid., p. 249).

Though play may be most labile, it does not seem to be totally neutral. All creatures, animal and human, live with some degree of existential angst, and most of them spend some portion of their existence attempting to secure themselves from this angst by controlling their circumstances. All creatures live in a world of strong feelings and are dominated by those feelings. We constantly seek to manage the variable contingencies of our lives for success over failure, for life over death. Play itself may be a model of just this everyday existentialism. As Edelman says, the metaphor of the brain as a jungle is much more appropriate than the metaphor of the brain as a computer, which is to say that the metaphor of life as a jungle is perhaps more relevant than the metaphor of life as civilization.

Play as a Model of Adaptive Variability

The argument so far is that play variability is analogous to adaptive variability; that play potential is analogous to neural potential; that play's psychological characteristics of unrealistic optimism, egocentricity, and reactivity are analogous to the normal behavior of the very young; and finally that play's engineered predicaments model the struggle for survival. What then follows from this account of cultural natural selection in human affairs is that play, for its part, may be an invention meant to model such natural selection processes. As the renowned biologist Richard Lewontin says, as the human society "arises" out of animal societies, it "transforms" the adaptation it possesses, thereby making new needs (Lewontin, 1977). My theory, then, would be that play, as novel adaptation, may have developed in two stages: the first as a reinforcement of potential synaptic variability through the performance of variable antics (as in animals), and the second as a fuller imitation of the evolutionary process itself, in which the organism models its own biological character. In this higher development, play, as a model of evolutionary selection, engenders variable contingencies (uncertainties and risks) for the purpose of exercising selective control over them in fictive or factual terms. It is a mastery process (as Erikson said) creatively derived from the exigencies of the evolutionary predicament. Considering that Fagen, author of *Animal Play Behavior* (1980), believes that some higher animals' play resembles our games of chase and escape, king of the hill, follow the leader, tug-of-war, and keep away, it would seem that this kind of cultural invention has also occurred on the animal level.

So in conclusion, I have presented here the view that variability is the key to play, and that structurally play is characterized by quirkiness, redundancy, and flexibility. I have also presented six additional hypothetical formulations about play's biological functionality that I presume may well be complementary. Let us imagine that they proceed as follows, in a quasi-longitudinal fashion. First is the supposition that play as potential behavior may *actualize* what are otherwise only potential brain and behavior connections. Second, play subsumes those actualizations into a model of the *neonatal* processes described as unrealistic optimism, egocentricity, and reactivity, which fade in general behavior following early childhood but are encapsulated in play at all later ages. The third and simplest hypothetical interpretation of play to this point is that play functions by becoming an *exemplar* of cultural variability, an available alternative for behavior, just as are music, dance, song, and the other arts. These sustain the variability of the human condition and can be real alternatives within it, as in the case of those who become professionals, or even those who simply vitalize their leisure and recovery through the arts. A fourth and equally commonsense possibility is that there is an occasional transfer of play skills to everyday skills, which I have termed adaptive potentiation, or an example of *trickle down*. Fifth, enclosing all of these, play is conceptualized as a *model of the exigent processes of adaptation* through the induction of uncertainties and their resolution within the virtual domain. But most speculative of all is the overall claim that play's variability acts as feedback *reinforcement* of organismic adaptive variability in the real world, which is meant to maintain the flexibility of which Gould speaks. Unfortunately these six hypotheticals are just a beginning. Beyond these biological analogies one has to add a number of other fairly well established psychological characteristics of play that must have also developed along the way: namely, play's *metacommunicative characteristics*, its performance *stylizations*, its peculiar *intensifications*, its *enactive subjunctivity*, and perhaps even also its structural *dialectics*, all of which have been discussed in earlier chapters. This heteroglossia of possibilities has a postmodern ring to it, but it undoubtedly still falls far short of a full accounting.

The research implications are that we should study the variations within play in such detail as may allow us to speak more confidently of their functions than we have to date. Those who are progress minded might like to think that there is a virtual smorgasbord of ludic variations that should be available to all of us. They could also see a play socialization curriculum as necessarily providing these learning opportunities for everyone. Others of a more skeptical flavor might be inclined to think of all of this variation as a necessary precondition for having choices, but not, therefore, for predicting that the choices that are made in play, or reinforced in adaptability, will necessarily be successful. This is closer to Gould's kind of evolutionary thinking, which follows the opinion that biological progress is an accident rather than an inevitability with evolution. That is, play as an exercise in adaptive potentiation is no guarantor of actual progress, apart from that of becoming a player, though that has its satisfactions, as we all know. And most important, without such a repertoire of variations the possibility of adequate adaptation is certainly more limited. In this kind of argument progress becomes just a higher probability of the fuller repertoire of variation.

Finally, I define play as a facsimilization of the struggle for survival as this is broadly rendered by Darwin. Biologically, its function is to reinforce the organism's variability in the face of rigidifications of successful adaptation (as formulated by Gould). This variability covers the full range of behavior from the actual to the possible. Psychologically, I define play as a virtual simulation characterized by staged contingencies of variation, with opportunities for control engendered by either mastery or further chaos. Clearly the primary motive of players is the stylized performance of existential themes that mimic or mock the uncertainties and risks of survival and, in so doing, engage the propensities of mind, body, and cells in exciting forms of arousal. It is also very interesting to think of play as a lifelong simulation of the key neonatal characteristics of unrealistic optimism, egocentricity, and reactivity, all of which are guarantors of persistence in the face of adversity. I add, however, the final note that, despite my extensive criticisms of the rhetoric of progress, I have now invented yet another form of it, although this time as only the potentiation of adaptive variability.

BIBLIOGRAPHY

Abrahams, R. D. 1977. *Towards an enactment-centered theory of folklore.* American Association for the Advancement of Science. Boulder, Colo.: Westview Press, 19–120.

———. 1982. The language of festivals: Celebrating the economy. In *Celebration,* ed. V. Turner. Washington, D.C.: Smithsonian Institution Press, 161–177.

———. 1983. Performance, ritual and game: Erving Goffman on framing and other intense expressions. Address given at Brown Symposium, Southwestern University, Texas.

———. 1986. Ordinary and extraordinary experience. In *The anthropology of experience,* ed. V. W. Turner and E. M. Bruner. Urbana: University of Illinois Press, 45–72.

———. 1992. *Singing the master: The emergence of African-American culture in the plantation South.* New York: Pantheon.

Abrams, D. M., and B. Sutton-Smith. 1977. The development of the trickster in children's narratives. *Journal of American Folklore* 90:29–47.

Abt, C. C. 1981. *Serious games.* New York: Viking.

Abt, V., J. F. Smith, and E. M. Christiansen. 1985. *The business of risk.* Lawrence: University Press of Kansas.

Adams, C. R. 1980. Distinctive features in play and games: A folk model from Southern Africa. In *Play and culture,* ed. Helen S. Schwartzman. West Point, N.Y.: Leisure Press.

Aercke, K. P. 1994. *Gods of play: Baroque festive performances as rhetorical discourse.* Albany: State University of New York Press.

Aldis, O. 1975. *Play fighting.* New York: Academic Press.

Anchor, R. 1978. History and play: Johan Huizinga and his critics. *History and Theory* 17:63–94.

Angier, N. 1995. Status isn't everything, at least for monkeys. *New York Times,* Apr. 18, B1 and B8.

Appleyard, J. A. 1990. *Becoming a reader.* New York: Cambridge University Press.

Ariés, P. 1962. *Centuries of childhood.* New York: Knopf.

233

Armitage, J. 1977. *Man at play.* London: Frederick Warne.

Arnoldi, M. J. 1995. *Playing with time.* Bloomington: Indiana University Press.

Asher, S. R., and J. D. Coie. 1990. *Peer rejection in childhood.* New York: Cambridge University Press.

Avedon, E. M., and B. Sutton-Smith. 1971. *The study of games.* New York: Wiley.

Aycock, A. 1993. Virtual play: Baudrillard online. *Electronic Journal of Virtual Culture* 1(7).

———. 1995. Technologies of the self: Foucault online. *Journal of Computer Mediated Communication* 1(2).

Azoy, G. W. 1982. *Buzkashi: Game and power in Afghanistan.* Philadelphia: University of Pennsylvania Press.

Babcock, B., ed. 1978. *The reversible world.* New York: New York University Press.

Bach, G. R. 1945. Young children's play fantasies. *Psychological Monographs* 59(2):3–69.

Bachelard, G. 1960. *The poetics of reverie.* Boston: Beacon Press.

Bakhtin, M. M. 1981. *The dialogic imagination.* Austin: University of Texas Press.

———. 1984. *Rabelais and his world.* Bloomington: Indiana University Press.

Ball, D., and J. Loy. 1975. *Sport and social order.* Reading, Mass.: Addison-Wesley.

Barell, J. 1980. *Playgrounds of our minds.* New York: Teachers College Press.

Barnett, L. A., and Chick, G. E. Chips off the ol' block: Parents' leisure and their children's play. *Journal of Leisure Research* 18:266–283.

Barry, H., III, and A. Schlegel, eds. 1980. *Cross-cultural samples and codes.* Pittsburgh: University of Pittsburgh Press.

Barthes, R. 1972. *Mythologies.* New York: Hill and Wang.

Bateson, G. 1956. The message, "This is play." In *Group processes,* ed. B. Schaffner. New York: Josiah Macy.

———. 1972. *Steps to an ecology of mind.* New York: Ballantine.

Bauman, R. 1977. *Verbal art as performance.* Prospect Heights, Ill.: Waveland Press.

———. 1986. *Story, performance and event.* New York: Cambridge University Press.

———. 1992. *Folklore, cultural performances, and popular entertainments.* Oxford: Oxford University Press.

Baumeister, R. F. 1986. *Identity, cultural change and the struggle for self.* New York: Oxford University Press.

———. 1991. *Meanings of life.* New York: Guilford.

Beach, F. A. 1945. Current concepts of play in animals. *American Naturalist* 79:523–541.

Beardsley, M. C. 1981. *Aesthetics: Problems in the philosophy of criticism.* Indianapolis: Hackett.

Beaujour, M. 1984. Delayed replay: The Renaissance as "mimicry" and representation. Paper presented at the Conference on the Forms of Play in the Early Modern Period, University of Maryland, March.

Becker, H. S. 1982. *Art worlds.* Berkeley: University of California Press.

Beidelman, T. O. 1980. The moral imagination of the Kaguru: Some thoughts on tricksters, translation and comparative analysis. *American Ethnologist* (1):27–42.

Ben-Amos, D., and K. S. Goldstein. 1975. *Folklore, performance and communication.* The Hague: Mouton.

Benedict, R. 1938. Continuity and discontinuity in cultural conditioning. *Psychiatry* 1:161–167.

Beresin, A. R. 1993. The play of peer culture in a city school. Ph.D. diss., University of Pennsylvania. Ann Arbor, Mich.: UMI, order no. 9331755.

Berger, P. L. 1969. *A rumor of angels: Modern society and the rediscovery of the supernatural.* Garden City, N.Y.: Doubleday, Anchor Books.

Berger, P. L. and Luckmann, T. 1966. *The social construction of reality.* New York: Doubleday.

Bergler, E. 1957. *The psychology of gambling.* New York: Hill and Wang.

Berlyne, D. E. 1960. *Conflict, arousal, and curiosity.* New York: McGraw-Hill.

———. 1969. Laughter, humor, and play. In *The handbook of social psychology,* vol. 3, ed. G. Linzey and E. Aronson. Reading, Mass.: Addison-Wesley.

———. 1971. *Aesthetics and psychobiology,* New York: Appleton-Century-Crofts.

Berne, E. 1964. *Games people play.* New York: Grove Press.

Betcher, W. 1987. *Intimate play.* New York: Viking.

Birch, H. G. 1945. The relation of previous experience to insightful problem solving. *Journal of Comparative Physiological Psychology* 38:367–383.

Bjorklund, D. F., and B. L. Green. 1992. The adaptive nature of cognitive immaturity. *American Psychologist* 47(1)46–54.

Blake, K. 1974. *Play, games and sport: The literary works of Lewis Carroll.* Ithaca, N.Y.: Cornell University Press.

Blakeslee, S. 1996. Figuring out the brain from its acts of denial: Scientists at work. *New York Times,* Jan. 23, B1 and B7.

Blanchard, K. 1981. *The Mississippi Choctaws at play.* Urbana: University of Illinois Press.

Blanchard, K., and A. Cheska. 1985. *The anthropology of sport.* Massachusetts: Bergin and Garvey Publishers.

Bloch, M. N., and A. D. Pellegrini. 1989. *The ecological context of children's play.* New York: Academic Press.

Block, J. H., and N. R. King. 1987. *School play.* New York: Garland.

Boas, G. 1966. *The cult of childhood.* London: Warburg Institute.

Bogue, R., and M. I. Spariosu. 1994. *The playing self.* Albany: State University of New York Press.

Boocock, S. S., and E. O. Schild. 1968. *Simulation games in learning.* Beverly Hills, Calif.: Sage Publications.

Boorman, S. A. 1969. *The protracted game: A Wei-Chi interpretation of Maoist revolutionary strategy.* Oxford: Oxford University Press.

Borman, K. M., and L. A. Kurdek. 1987. Grade and gender differences in the stability and correlates of the structural complexity of childrens' playground games. *International Journal of Behavioral Development* 10(2):241–251.

Bornstein, M. H. ed. 1989. Maternal responsiveness: characteristics and consequences. New Directions for Child Development, vol. 43. San Francisco: Jossey-Bass.

Bornstein, M. H., and A. W. O'Reilly. 1993. The role of play in the development of thought. New Directions for Child Development, vol. 59. San Francisco: Jossey-Bass.

Botvin, G. J., and B. Sutton-Smith. 1977. The development of structural complexity in children's fantasy narratives. *Developmental Psychology* 13:377–388.

Brainerd, C. J. 1982. Effects of group and individualized dramatic play training on cognitive development. In *Play of children,* ed. D. J. Pepler and K. H. Rubin. *Contributions to Human Development* 6:114–129.

Brams, S. J. 1980. *Biblical games.* Cambridge, Mass.: MIT Press.

Brand, C. 1963. *Naughty children.* New York: Dutton.

Bretherton, J., ed. 1984. *Symbolic play.* New York: Academic Press.

Brewer, J. 1979. Childhood revisited: The genesis of the modern toy. In *Educational toys in America,* ed. K. Hewitt and L. Roomet. Burlington, Vt.: The Robert Hull Fleming Museum, 3–10.

Brohm, J. M. 1978. *Sport: A prison of measured time.* London: Ink Links.

Brougère, G. 1992. Le Jouet. Valeurs et paradoxes d'un petit objet secret. *Editions Autrement,* Serie Mutations n. 133.

———. 1996. From TV show to games: The Power Ranger example. International Toy Research Conference, Halmstad, Sweden.

Broughton, J. M., ed. 1987. *Critical theories of child development.* New York: Plenum Press.

Brown, C. C., and A. W. Gottfried, eds. 1986. *Play interactions: Proceedings of the eleventh Johnson and Johnson Pediatric Round Table.* Lexington, Mass.: Lexington Books.

Brown, M. F. 1996. *American spirituality in an anxious age.* Cambridge, Mass.: Harvard University Press.

Brown, S. L. 1994. Animals at play. *National Geographic* 186(6):2–35.

———. 1995. Through the lens of play: Evolution and play. *Revision* 17(2):4–13.

Browne, R. B., ed. 1973. *Popular culture and the expanding consciousness.* New York: Wiley.

Browne, R. B., and M. T. Marsden. 1994. *The cultures of celebrations.* Bowling Green, Ohio: Bowling Green State University Popular Press.

Bruner, J. S. 1972a. *Studies in cognitive growth.* New York: Wiley.

———. 1972b. The nature and uses of immaturity. *American Psychologist* 27:686–708.

———. 1990. *Acts of meaning.* Cambridge, Mass.: Harvard University Press.

Bruner, J. S., A. Jolly, and K. Sylva. 1976. *Play: Its role in development and evolution.* New York: Penguin.

Burke, K. 1950. *The rhetoric of motives.* New York: Prentice Hall.

———. 1961. *The rhetoric of religion.* Berkeley: University of California Press.

———. 1966. *Language as symbolic action.* Berkeley: University of California Press.

Burkett, W. 1996. *Creation of the sacred.* Cambridge, Mass.: Harvard University Press.

Cahan, E., J. Mechling, B. Sutton-Smith, and S. H. White. 1993. The elusive historical child. In *Children in time and place,* ed. G. G. Elder, J. Modell, and R. D. Parke. Cambridge: Cambridge University Press.

Caillois, R. 1961. *Man, play and games.* New York: Free Press.

Carlsson-Paige, N., and D. E. Levin. 1987. *The war play dilemma.* New York: Teachers College Press.

Carpenter, H., and M. Pritchard. 1984. *The Oxford companion to children's literature.* New York: Oxford University Press.

Carse, J. P. 1986. *Finite and infinite games.* New York: Free Press.

Cassirer, E. 1944. *An essay on man.* New Haven, Conn.: Yale University Press.

Caughey, J. 1984. *Imaginary source worlds: A cultural approach.* Lincoln: University of Nebraska Press.

Cavallo, P. 1981. *Muscles, morals, and team sports: Americans organize children's play.* Philadelphia: University of Pennsylvania Press.

Cherfas, J., and R. Lewin, eds. 1980. *Not work alone: A cross-cultural view of activities superfluous to survival.* Beverly Hills, Calif.: Sage Publications.

Cheska, A. T., ed. 1981. *Play as context.* West Point, N.Y.: Leisure Press.

Chick, G. 1982. The cross cultural study of games. In *Exercise and sport sciences reviews,* vol. 12, ed. R. E. Terjung. Lexington, Mass.: Colamore Press.

———. 1994. Games in culture revisited. Paper presented at the annual meeting of the Society for Cross Cultural Research, Santa Fe, New Mexico, February.

————, ed. 1991. Studies in honor of Brian Sutton-Smith. *Play and Culture* 4(2):85–193; 4(3):195–284.

Chick, G., and L. A. Barnett. 1995. Children's play and adult leisure. In *The future of play theory,* ed. A. Pellegrini. Albany: State University of New York Press.

Chick, G., J. W. Loy, and A. W. Miracle. 1994. Combat sport and war: A reappraisal of the drive discharge and culture pattern models. Paper presented at the annual meeting of the Society for Cross Cultural Research, Santa Fe, New Mexico, February.

Christie, J. F., ed. 1991. *Play and early literary development.* Albany: State University of New York Press.

Clarke-Stewart, K. A. 1973. Interactions between mothers and their young children: Characteristics and consequences. *Monographs of the Society for Research in Child Development,* serial no. 153, 38:6–7.

Clotfelter, C. T., and P. T. Cook. 1989. *Selling hope.* Cambridge, Mass.: Harvard University Press.

Cohen, D., and S. A. MacKeith. 1991. *The development of imagination: The private worlds of childhood.* London: Routledge.

Cohen, J. 1960. *Chance, skill, and luck.* Baltimore: Penguin.

Cohen, M. N. 1995. *Lewis Carroll: A biography.* New York: Knopf.

Coleman, J. S. 1961. *The adolescent society.* New York: Free Press.

Collingwood, R. G. 1958. *The principles of art.* New York: Gateway.

Colsant, S. 1991. Pilot collection of fourth grade daydreams. Unpublished manuscript, University of Pennsylvania.

Connor, K. 1991. War toys, aggression and playfighting. Ph.D. diss., University of Pennsylvania. Ann Arbor, Mich.: UMI, order no. 9125623.

Corsaro, W. A. 1985. *Friendship and peer culture in the early years.* Norwood, N.J.: Ablex.

————. 1992. Interpretive reproduction in children's peer cultures. *Social Psychology Quarterly* 55(2):160–177.

Covenay, P. 1967. *The image of childhood.* Baltimore: Penguin.

Cox, H. 1969. *The feast of fools.* New York: Harper and Row.

Csikszentmihalyi, M. 1977. *Beyond boredom and anxiety.* San Francisco: Jossey-Bass.

————. 1979. The concept of flow. In *Play and learning,* ed. B. Sutton-Smith. New York: Gardner Press.

————. 1993. *The evolving self.* New York: HarperCollins.

Csikszentmihalyi, M., and I. Csikszentmihalyi. 1988. *Optimal experience.* New York: Cambridge University Press.

Culin, S. 1895. *Games of the Orient.* Rutland, Vt.: Tuttle.

Culler, J. 1988. *Framing the sign.* Norman: Oklahoma University Press.

Curtis, H. 1915. *Education through play.* New York: Macmillan.

Damasio, A. R. 1994. *Descartes' error.* New York: Grosset-Putnam.

Dansky, J. L. 1980a. Cognitive consequences of sociodramatic play and exploratory training for economically disadvantaged preschoolers. *Journal of Child Psychology and Psychiatry* 20:47–58.

———. 1980b. Make believe: A mediator of the relationship between free play and associative fluency. *Child Development* 51:576–579.

Dansky, J. L., and I. W. Silverman. 1973. Effects of play on associative fluency in preschool-aged children. *Developmental Psychology* 9:38–43.

Davis, N. 1965. *Society and culture in early modern France.* Stanford, Calif.: Stanford University Press.

De Grazia, S. 1962. *Of time, work and leisure.* New York: Twentieth Century Fund.

De Koven, B. 1978. *The well played game.* Garden City, N.Y.: Doubleday, Anchor Books.

DeLone, R. 1979. *Small futures.* New York: Harcourt Brace Jovanovich.

DeMausse, L. 1974. *The history of childhood.* New York: Psychohistory Press.

Denney, R. 1957. *The astonished muse.* Chicago: University of Chicago Press.

Denzin, N. K. 1977. *Childhood socialization.* San Francisco: Jossey-Bass.

Derrida, J. 1970. Structure, sign and play in the discourse of the human sciences. In *The structuralist controversy,* ed. E. Macksey and E. Donato. Baltimore: Johns Hopkins University Press.

———. 1980. *The archeology of the frivolous.* Lincoln: University of Nebraska Press.

———. 1987. *The postcard from Socrates to Freud and beyond.* Chicago: University of Chicago Press.

Dewey, J. 1916. *Democracy and education.* New York: Free Press.

Dibb, M. 1982. "The fields of play." BBC television series transcript.

Donaldson, V. F. 1993. *Playing by heart.* Deerfield Beach, Fla.: Heath.

Drewal, M. T. 1992. *Yoruba ritual: Performers, play, agency.* Bloomington: Indiana University Press.

Dulles, F. A. 1940. *A history of recreation,* 2nd ed. New York: Appleton-Century-Crofts.

Duncan, M. 1988. Play discourse and the rhetorical turn: A semiological analysis of *Homo Ludens. Play and Culture,* 1(1):28–42.

Dundes, A. 1964. *The study of folklore.* Englewood Cliffs, N.J.: Prentice Hall.

———. 1979. On game morphology: A study of the structure of nonverbal folklore. In *Readings in American Folklore,* ed. J. H. Brunvand. New York: W. W. Norton.

Dunning, E. 1979. The figurational dynamics of modern sport. *Sportwissenschaft* 9:341–359.

Dunning, E., and K. Sheard. 1979. *Barbarians, gentlemen, and players.* Wellington, New Zealand: Price Milburn.

Dusinberre, J. 1987. *Alice to the lighthouse.* New York: St. Martin's Press.

Dyson, F. 1995. The scientist as rebel. *The New York Review of Books* 42(9):31–33.

Eckler, J. A., and O. Weininger. 1989. Structural parallels between pretend play and narratives. *Developmental Psychology* 25(5):736–743

Eckhardt, R. 1975. From handclap to line play. In *Black girls at play: Perspectives on child development,* ed. R. Eckhardt. Austin: Southwest Educational Development Laboratory.

Eco, Umberto. 1983. *The name of the rose.* San Diego: Harcourt Brace Jovanovich.

Edelman, G. M. 1992. *Bright air, brilliant fire.* New York: Basic Books.

Ehrmann, J., ed. 1968. *Game, play, literature.* Boston: Beacon Press.

Eifermann, R. R. 1970a. Level of children's play as expressed in group size. *The British Journal of Educational Psychology* 40(2):161–170.

––––––. 1970b. Co-operativeness and egalitarianism in kibbutz children's games. *Human Relations* 23(6):579–587.

––––––. 1971a. Social play in childhood. In *Child's play,* ed. R. Heron and B. Sutton-Smith. New York: Wiley.

––––––. 1971b. *Determinants of children's game styles.* Jerusalem: Israel Academy of Sciences and Humanities.

––––––. 1973. Rules in games. In *Artificial and human thinking,* ed. A. Elithorn and P. Jones. Amsterdam: Elsevier.

––––––. 1978. Games of physical activity. In *Physical activity and human well being,* ed. F. Landry and W. A. R. Orban. International Congress of Physical Activity Sciences. Miami: Symposia Specialists.

––––––. 1979. "It's child's play." In *Games in education and development,* ed. L. M. Shearn and E. M. Bower. Springfield, Ill.: Charles C. Thomas.

Eisen, G. 1988. *Children's play in the holocaust.* Amherst: University of Massachusetts Press.

Eisenberg, N., et al. 1985. Parental socialization of young children's play: A short-term longitudinal study. *Child Development* 56:1506–1513.

Elder, G. H., J. Modell, and R. D. Parke. 1993. *Children in time and place.* New York: Cambridge University Press.

Eldridge, N. 1995. *Reinventing Darwin: The great debate at the high table of evolutionary theory.* New York: Wiley.

Ellis, M. J. 1973. *Why people play.* Englewood Cliffs, N.J.: Prentice Hall.

––––––. 1979. The complexity of objects and peers. In *Play and learning,* ed. B. Sutton-Smith. New York: Gardner Press.

Ellis, M. J., and G. Scholtz. 1978. *Activity and play in children.* Englewood Cliffs, N.J.: Prentice Hall.

Empson, W. 1955. *Seven types of ambiguity.* New York: Meridian Books.

Endrei, W., and L. Zolnay. 1986. *Fun and games in old Europe.* Budapest: Corvina Kiadó.

Engell, J. 1981. *The creative imagination, Enlightenment to romanticism.* Cambridge, Mass.: Harvard University Press.

Erikson, E. 1950. *Childhood and society.* New York: Norton.

——. 1972. Play and actuality. In *Play and development,* ed. M. W. Piers. New York: Norton, 127–168.

——. 1977. *Toys and reasons.* New York: Norton.

Evans, J. 1986. In search of the meaning of play. *New Zealand Journal of Health, Physical Education and Recreation* 19:16–19.

Evans, J. L. 1981. Frog jumping contests. *Missouri Folklore Society Journal* 3:3–26.

Fagen, R. 1976. Modelling how and why play works. In *Play,* ed. J. S. Bruner et al. New York: Basic Books.

——. 1981. *Animal play behavior.* New York: Oxford University Press.

——. 1995. Animal play, games of angels: Biology and Brian. In *The future of play theory,* ed. A. D. Pellegrini. Albany: State University of New York Press.

Falassi, A. 1967. *Time out of time: Essays on the festival.* Albuquerque: University of New Mexico Press.

Fantuzzo, J. W., et al. 1988. Effects of adult and peer social initiations on the social behavior of withdrawn, maltreated preschool children. *Journal of Consulting and Clinical Psychology* 56(1):34–39.

——. 1995. Assessment of preschool play interaction in young low-income children: Penn interactive peer playscale. *Early Childhood Research Quarterly* 10:105–120.

Farrer, C. 1981. Contesting. In *Play as context,* ed. A. T. Cheska. West Point, N.Y.: Leisure Press.

Farver, J. A. M., Y. K. Kim, and Y. Lee. 1995. Cultural differences in Korean and Anglo-American preschoolers' social interaction and play behaviors. *Child Development* 66:1088–1099.

Fein, G. 1979. Play in the acquisition of symbols. In *Current topics in early childhood education,* ed. L. Katz. Norwood, N.J.: Ablex.

——. 1981. Pretend play in childhood: An integrative review. *Child Development* 52:1095–1118.

——. 1984. The self-building potential of pretend play as "I got a fish, all by myself." In *Child's play: Developmental and applied,* ed. T. D. Yawkey and A. D. Pellegrini. Hillsdale, N.J.: Erlbaum.

————. 1985. Learning in play: Surfaces of thinking and feeling. In *When children play*, ed. J. L. Frost and S. Sunderlin. Wheaton, Md.: Association for Childhood Education International.

————. 1987. Pretend play: Creativity and consciousness. In *Curiosity, imagination and play*, ed. D. Gorlitz and J. F. Wohlwill. Hillsdale, N.J.: Erlbaum, 281–304.

————. 1989. Mind, meaning and affect: Proposals for a theory of pretense. *Developmental Review* 9:345–406.

————. 1995. Toys and stories. In *The future of play theory*, ed. A. Pellegrini. Albany: State University of New York Press, 151–164.

Fein, G., and R. Glaubman. 1993. Commentary. *Human Development* 36(4):185–252.

Fein, G., and P. Kinney. 1994. He's a nice alligator: Observations on the affective organization of pretense. In *Children at play: Clinical and developmental studies of play*, ed. A. Slade and D. Wolf. New York: Oxford University Press, 188–204.

Feitelson, D. 1977. Cross-cultural studies of representational play. In *The biology of play*, ed. B. Tizard and D. Harvey. London: Heineman.

Feitelson, D., and G. S. Ross. 1973. The neglected factor—play. *Human Development* 16:202–223.

Fernandez, J. W. 1986. *Persuasions and performances: The play of tropes in culture.* Bloomington: Indiana University Press.

————, ed. 1991. *Beyond metaphor: The theory of tropes in anthropology.* Stanford, Calif.: Stanford University Press.

Feyerabend, P. 1995. *Killing time.* Chicago: University of Chicago Press.

Fine, G. A. 1980. Children and their culture: Exploring Newall's paradox. *Western Folklore* 39(3):170–183.

————. 1981. Rude words: Insults and narration in preadolescent obscene talk. *Maledicta* 5:61–68.

————. 1983. *Shared fantasy: Role-playing games as social worlds.* Chicago: University of Chicago Press.

————. 1988. Good children and dirty play. *Play and Culture* 1:43–56.

Fink, E. 1968. The oasis of happiness: Toward an ontology of play. In *Game, play, literature*, ed. J. Ehrmann. Boston: Beacon Press, 19–30.

Fisher, E. P. 1992. The impact of play on development: A meta-analysis. *Play and Culture* 5(2):159–181.

Flavell, J. H. 1963. *The developmental psychology of Jean Piaget.* Princeton, N.J.: Van Nostrand-Reinhold.

Fluegelman, A. 1976. *The new games book.* New York: Dolphin.

Fogel, A., E. Nwokah, and J. Karns. 1993. Parent-infant games as dynamic social systems. In *Parent-child play*, ed. K. MacDonald. Albany: State University of New York Press.

Foucault, M. 1970. *The order of things.* New York: Vintage.

———. 1972. *The archeology of knowledge.* New York: Harper and Row.

———. 1973. *Madness and civilization.* New York: Vintage.

———. 1976. *Mental illness and psychology.* Berkeley: University of California Press.

Foulkes, D. 1982. *Children's dreams: Longitudinal studies.* New York: Wiley.

Freeman, D. 1985. *Margaret Mead in Samoa.* New York: Viking.

Freud, S. 1959 (1922). Beyond the pleasure principle. In *The standard edition of the complete psychological works of Sigmund Freud,* ed. J. Strachey. London: The Institute of Psychoanalysis.

Frey, K. P. 1991. Sexual behavior in adult play. In *Adult play,* ed. J. H. Kerr and M. J. Apter. Amsterdam: Swets and Zeitlinger.

Froebel, F. 1887. *The education of man,* trans. W. N. Hailmann. New York: Appleton.

Frost, J. L., and B. Klein. 1979. *Children's play and playgrounds.* Needham Heights, Mass.: Allyn and Bacon.

Frost, J., and S. Sunderlin, eds. 1985. *When children play.* Washington, D.C.: Association for Childhood Education International.

Gadamer, H. G. 1982 (1960). *Truth and method.* New York: Crossroad.

Galda, L., and A. Pellegrini. 1985. *Play, language, and stories.* Norwood, N.J.: Ablex.

Gardner, H. 1982a. *Art, mind and brain.* New York: Basic Books.

———. 1982b. *Developmental psychology.* Boston: Little, Brown.

———. 1983. *Frames of mind.* New York: Basic Books.

Garvey, C. 1974. Some properties of social play. *Merrill-Palmer Quarterly* 20:163–180.

———. 1977. *Play.* Cambridge, Mass.: Harvard University Press.

———. 1993. Commentary. *Human Development* 36:235–240.

Gaskins, S., and A. Goncu, 1992. Cultural variations in play: A challenge to Piaget and Vygotsky. *The Quarterly Newsletter of the Laboratory for Comparative Cognition* 14(2):31–35.

Geertz, C. 1973. *The interpretation of cultures.* New York: Basic Books.

———. 1983. Blurred genres: The refiguration of social thought. In C. Geertz, *Local knowledge: Further essays in interpretative anthropology.* New York: Basic Books.

Georges, R. A. 1972. Recreations and games. In *Folklore and folklife,* ed. R. M. Dorson. Chicago: University of Chicago Press.

Gergen, K. J. 1991. *The saturated self: Dilemmas of identity in contemporary life.* New York: Basic Books.

Gerstmyer, J. S. 1991. Toward a theory of play as performance: An analysis of videotaped episodes of a toddler's play performance. Ph.D. diss., University of Pennsylvania. Ann Arbor, Mich.: UMI, order no. 9125648.

Giddens, A. 1991. *Modernity and identity: Self and society in the late modern age.* Stanford, Calif.: Stanford University Press.

Giffin, H. 1984. The coordination of meaning in the creation of a shared make-believe reality. In *Symbolic behavior,* ed. J. Bretherton. New York: Academic Press.

Gigerenzer, G., et al. 1989. *The empire of chance.* New York: Cambridge University Press.

Gillis, J. R. 1981. *Youth and history.* New York: Academic Press.

Glancy, M. 1988. The play-world setting of the auction. *Journal of Leisure Research* 20(2):135–153.

Glassford, R. G. 1976. *Application of a theory of games to the transitional Eskimo culture.* New York: Arno Press.

Gleick, J. 1987. *Chaos: Making a new science.* New York: Viking.

Glassie, H. 1982. *Passing time in Ballymenone.* Philadelphia: University of Pennsylvania Press.

Goelman, H., and E. V. Jacobs. 1994. *Children's play in childcare settings.* Albany: State University of New York Press.

Goffman, E. 1959. *The presentation of self in everyday life.* New York: Doubleday.

———. 1961a. *Encounters.* Indianapolis: Bobbs-Merrill.

———. 1961b. *Asylums.* Garden City, N.Y.: Doubleday, Anchor Books.

———. 1962. *Interaction ritual.* Garden City, N.Y.: Doubleday, Anchor Books.

———. 1963a. *Behavior in public places.* New York: Free Press.

———. 1963b. *Stigma.* Englewood Cliffs, N.J.: Prentice Hall.

———. 1969. *Strategic interaction.* Philadelphia: University of Pennsylvania Press.

———. 1974. *Frame analysis: An essay on the organization of experience.* Cambridge, Mass.: Harvard University Press.

Goldman, B. D., and H. S. Ross. 1978. Social skills in action: An analysis of early peer games. In *Studies in social and cognitive development,* vol. 1, ed. J. Glick and K. A. Clarke-Stewart. New York: Gardner Press.

Goldstein, J. H. 1979. *Sports, games and play.* Hillsdale, N.J.: Erlbaum.

———. 1994. *Toys, play and child development.* New York: Cambridge University Press.

Goleman, D. 1995. Seventy-five years later and still tracking genius. *New York Times* Mar. 7, B5 and B9.

Golumb, C. 1979. Pretense play: A cognitive perspective. In *Symbolic functioning in childhood,* ed. N. Smith and M. Franklin. New York: Wiley.

Gomme, A. B. 1894. *The traditional games of England, Scotland and Ireland.* London: Constable.

Goncu, A. 1993. Development of intersubjectivity in social pretend play. *Human Development* 36(4):185–198.

Goodall, J. 1986. *The chimpanzees of Gombe.* Cambridge, Mass.: Harvard University Press.

Goodman, G. 1979. *Choosing sides: Playground and street life on the Lower East Side.* New York: Schocken Books.

Goodwin, M. H. 1985. The serious side of jump rope: Conversational practices and social organization in the frame of play. *Journal of American Folklore* 98(389):315–330.

———. 1990. *He said, she said.* Bloomington: Indiana University Press.

Gordon, D. E. 1993. The inhibition of pretend play and its implications for development. *Human Development* 36(4):215–234.

Görwitz, D. and J. F. Wohlwill. 1987. *Curiosity, imagination, and play.* Hillsdale, N.J.: Erlbaum.

Gottfried, A. W., and C. Caldwell, eds. 1986. *Play interactions.* Lexington, Mass.: Lexington Books.

Gould, R. 1972. *Child studies through fantasy.* New York: Quadrangle.

Gould, S. J. 1982. Darwinism and the expansion of evolutionary theory. *Science* 216:380–387.

———. 1989. *Wonderful life.* New York: Norton.

———. 1996a. Creating the creators. *Discover.* 17(10):42–54.

———. 1996b. *Full house: The spread of excellence from Plato to Darwin.* New York: Harmony Books.

Greenfield, P. M., and R. R. Cocking, eds. 1994. *Cross cultural roots of minority child development.* Hillsdale, N.J.: Erlbaum.

Griffing, P. 1980. The relationship between socioeconomic status and sociodramatic play among black kindergarten children. *Genetic Psychological Monographs* 101:3–34.

Griffiths, R. 1935. *The study of imagination in early childhood.* London: Kegan Paul.

Groos, K. 1898. *The play of animals.* New York: Appleton.

———. 1901. *The play of man.* New York: Appleton.

Gross, G. 1996. *Toys in the making of American children.* Cambridge, Mass.: Harvard University Press.

Gross, M. L. 1978. *The psychological society.* New York: Simon and Schuster.

Grover, K. 1992. *Hard at play: Leisure in America, 1840–1940.* Amherst: University of Massachusetts Press.

Gruber, H. E. 1974. *Darwin on man.* New York: Dutton.

Gruneau, R. S. 1980. Freedom and constraint: The paradoxes of play, games and sport. *Journal of Sport History* 7(3):68–85.

———. 1983. *Class, sports, and social development.* Amherst: University of Massachusetts Press.

Gump, P. V., and B. Sutton-Smith. 1955a. The "it" role in children's games. *The Group* 17:3–8.

———. 1955b. Activity setting and social interaction. *American Journal of Orthopsychiatry* 25:755–760.

Guttman, A. 1978. *From ritual to record: The nature of modern sport.* New York: Columbia University Press.

———. 1994. *Games and Empires.* New York: Columbia University Press.

Haight, W. L., and P. J. Miller. 1993. *Pretending at home: Early development in sociocultural context.* Albany: State University of New York Press.

Hall, G. S. 1906. *Youth: Its education, regimen and hygiene.* New York: Appleton.

———. 1916. *Adolescence.* New York: Appleton.

———. 1921. *Aspects of child life and education.* New York: Appleton.

Halliday, J., and P. Fuller, eds. 1974. *The psychology of gambling.* New York: Harper and Row.

Handelman, D. 1990. *Models and mirrors: Toward an anthropology of public events.* Cambridge: Cambridge University Press.

———. 1992. Passages to play: Paradox and process. *Play and Culture* 5(1):1–19.

Hans, J. S. 1981. *The play of the world.* Amherst: University of Massachusetts Press.

———. 1987. *Imitation and the image of man.* Philadelphia: John Benjamins.

Harlow, H. F., and M. K. Harlow. 1966. Learning to love. *American Scientist* 54:224–272.

Harris, H. A. 1964. *Greek athletes and athletics.* London: Hutchinson.

Harris, P. L., and R. D. Kavanaugh. 1993. *Young children's understanding of pretense.* Chicago: University of Chicago Press.

Harris, W. T., ed. 1906. *The mottoes and commentaries of Friedrich Froebel's mother play.* New York: Appleton.

Hart, C. H., ed. 1993. *Children on playgrounds: Research perspectives and applications.* Albany: State University of New York Press.

Hartley, R. E., K. L. Frank, and R. M. Goldenson. 1952. *Understanding children's play.* New York: Columbia University Press.

Hartmann, W., and B. Rollett, 1994. Positive interaction in the elementary school. In *Play and intervention,* ed. J. Hellendorn et al. Albany: State University of New York Press, 195–202.

Heidegger, M. 1979 (1961). *Nietzsche,* vols. 1–4. New York: HarperCollins.

Hellendorn, J., R. Van der Kooij, and B. Sutton-Smith, eds. 1994. *Play and intervention.* Albany: State University of New York Press.

Herron, R. E., and B. Sutton-Smith. 1971. *Child's play.* New York: Wiley.

Hetherington, E. M., ed. 1983. *Handbook of child psychology,* vol. 4: *Socialization, personality and social development.* New York: Wiley.

Hindman, S. 1982. Pieter Bruegel's children's games, folly and chance. *Art Bulletin* 63:449–471.

Hirshey, G. 1994. Gambling nation. *New York Times Magazine,* July, 34–61.

Hobsbawm, T., and T. Ranger. 1983. *The invention of tradition.* Cambridge: Cambridge University Press.

Holbeck, B. 1976. Games of the powerless. *Unifol,* Arsberetring. Copenhagen: Nordic Institute of Folklore.

Horan, R. 1986. An intimate distance: Playfighting, maleness and social order at a boys' home. Ph.D. diss., University of Pennsylvania.

Holquist, M. 1969. "What is a Boojum?" In *The child's part,* ed. P. Brooks. Boston: Beacon Press.

Howes, C. 1992. *The collaborative construction of pretend.* Albany: State University of New York Press.

Hughes, L. 1983. Beyond the rules of the games: Why are Rosie rules nice? In *The world of play,* ed. F. Manning. West Point, N.Y.: Leisure Press.

———. 1988. "But that's not really mean": Competing in a cooperative mode. *Sex Roles* 9:669–687.

———. 1989. Foursquare: A glossary and "native" taxonomy of game rules. *Play and Culture* 2:102–136.

———. 1991. A conceptual framework for the study of children's gaming. *Play and Culture* 4:284–301.

———. 1993a. "You have to do it with style": Girls' games and girls' gaming. In *Feminist theory and the study of folklore,* ed. S. T. Hollis, L. Pershing, and M. J. Young. Urbana: University of Illinois Press, 130–148.

———. 1993b. Children's games and gaming. In *Children's folklore: A sourcebook,* ed. B. Sutton-Smith et al. New York: Garland, 93–120.

Hughes, R. 1993. *Culture of complaint.* New York: Oxford University Press.

———. 1994. *The shock of the new.* New York: Knopf.

Huizinga, J. 1955 (1949). *Homo ludens: A study of the play element in culture.* Boston: Beacon Press.

Humphreys, A. P., and P. K. Smith. 1987. Rough and tumble, friendships, and dominance in schoolchildren: Evidence for continuity and change with age. *Child Development* 58:201–212.

Hunt, H. T. 1989. The multiplicity of dreams. New Haven, Conn.: Yale University Press.

Hutt, C. 1971. Exploration and play in children. In *Child's play,* ed. R. E. Herron and B. Sutton-Smith. New York: Wiley.

———. 1979. Exploration and play. In *Play and learning,* ed. B. Sutton-Smith. New York: Gardner Press.

Hutt, S. J., S. Tyler, C. Hutt, and H. Christopherson. 1989. *Play, exploration and learning.* London: Routledge.

Hymes, F., ed. 1974. *Reinventing anthropology*. New York: Vintage.

———. 1984. On Erving Goffman. *Theory and Society* 13(5):621–631.

Ivic, I., and A. Marjanovic. 1986. *Traditional games and children today*. Belgrade: UNESCO, Savez drustava psihologa SR srbije.

Iwamura, S. G. 1980. *The verbal games of preschool children*. New York: St. Martin's Press.

Iwanaga, M. 1973. Development of interpersonal play structure in three-, four-, and five-year-old children. *Journal of Research and Development in Education* 6(3):71–82.

James, C. 1963. *Beyond a boundary*. London: Stanley Paul.

Johnson, J. E., J. F. Christie, and T. D. Yawkey. 1987. *Play and early childhood development*. Glenview, Ill.: Scott, Foresman.

Jones, B., and B. L. Hawes, 1972. *Step it down*. New York: Harper and Row.

Jones, J. P. 1973. *Gambling yesterday and today*. Devon, England: David and Charles.

Jones, W. T. 1952. *The twentieth century to Wittgenstein and Sartre*. New York: Harcourt Brace.

Kaarby, G. 1986. Childrens' conceptions of their own play. *Molndal*. Department of Education and Research, Göteborg University, Göteborg, Sweden.

Kane, S. R., and H. G. Furth, 1993. Children constructing social reality: A frame analysis of social pretend play. *Human Development* 36(4):199–214.

Kearney, R. 1991. *The poetics of imagining*. New York: Harper.

Keeley, L. H. 1994. *War before civilization*. New York: Oxford University Press.

Keesing, F. M. 1960. Recreative behavior and cultural change. In *Men and cultures*, ed. A. F. C. Wallace. Philadelphia: University of Pennsylvania Press.

Kelly, J. R. 1981. Leisure and sport. In *Handbook of social science of sport*, ed. R. F. Gunther and G. H. Sage. Champaign, Ill.: Stipes.

Kelly-Byrne, D. 1989. *A child's play life*. New York: Teachers College Press.

Kenyon, G. S. 1978. A conceptual model for characterizing physical activity. In *Physical activity and the social sciences*, ed. N. Widemeyer. Waterloo, Ontario: University of Waterloo, Department of Kinesiology, 2–11.

Kerr, J. H., and M. J. Apter. 1991. *Adult play*. Amsterdam: Swets and Zeitlinger.

Kessel, F. and A. Goncu, eds. 1984. *Analyzing children's play dialogues*. San Francisco: Jossey-Bass.

Kessel, F. S., and A. W. Siegel. 1981. *The child and other cultural inventions*. New York: Praeger.

Kessen, W. 1981. The child and other cultural inventions. In *The child and other cultural inventions*, ed. F. S. Kessel and A. W. Siegel. New York: Praeger.

———. 1993. A developmentalist's reflections. In *Children in time and place*, ed. G. H. Elder et al. New York: Cambridge University Press, 226–229.

King, N. R. 1979. The kindergarten perspective. *The Elementary School Journal* 80:81–87.

———. 1982. Work and play in the classroom. *Social Education* 46:110–113.

———. 1987. Elementary school play: Theory and research. In *School play*. ed. J. H. Block and N. R. King. New York: Garland, 143–165.

Kinser, S. 1990. *Carnival, American style: Mardi Gras at New Orleans and Mobile*. Chicago: University of Chicago Press.

Kirshenblatt-Gimblett, B. 1976. *Speech play*. Philadelphia: University of Pennsylvania Press.

Kinser, S., and E. Bruner. 1992. *Tourism in folklore, cultural performance and popular entertainment*. New York: Oxford University Press.

Klausner, S. Z., ed. 1968. *Why man takes chances*. New York: Doubleday, Anchor Books.

Kline, S. 1993. *Out of the garden: Children's culture in the age of advertising*. Toronto: Garamond.

Klinger, E. 1971. *Structure and functions of fantasy*. New York: Wiley.

———. 1987. The power of daydreams. *Psychology Today* 21(10):37–44.

Knapp, M., and H. Knapp. 1976. *One potato, two potato*. New York: Norton.

Koepping, K.-P. 1985. Absurdity and hidden truth: Cunning intelligence and grotesque body images as manifestations of the trickster. *History of Religion* 24:191–213.

Korkiakangas, P. 1992. The games children may not play: Improper, prophetic or dangerous. *Ethnologia Scandinavica: Journal for Nordic Ethnology* 22:95–104.

Kotulak, R. 1996. *Inside the brain*. Kansas City: Andrews and McNeel.

Krasnor, L. R., and D. J. Pepler. 1980. The study of children's play: Some suggested future directions. In *Children's play*, ed. K. Rubin. New Directions for Child Development. San Francisco: Jossey-Bass.

Kuczaj, S. A. 1983. *Crib speech and language play*. New York: Springer-Verlag.

Kuhn, T. S. 1970. The structure of scientific revolutions. Chicago: University of Chicago Press.

Kupersmidt, J. B., et al. 1995. Childhood aggression and peer relations in the context of family and neighborhood. *Child Development* 66:360–375.

Kuznets, L. R. 1994. *When toys come alive*. New Haven, Conn.: Yale University Press.

Lancy, D. F. 1996. *Playing on the mother ground*. New York: Guilford.

Lancy, D. F., and B. A. Tindall, eds. 1976. *The anthropological study of play: Problems and prospects*. West Point, N.Y.: Leisure Press.

———. 1980. Work and play: the Kpelle case. In *Play and culture*, ed. H. Schwartzman. West Point, N.Y.: Leisure Press, 324–328.

Langbaum, R. 1982. *The mysteries of identity*. Chicago: University of Chicago Press.

Langer, S. K. 1953. *Feeling and form.* New York: Scribner.

Lasch, C. 1979. *The culture of narcissism.* London: Norton.

Laurence, B., and B. Sutton-Smith. 1968. Novel responses to toys: A replication. *Merrill-Palmer Quarterly* 14:159–160.

Lavenda, R. H. 1988. Minnesota queen pageants: Play, fun and dead seriousness in a festive mode. *Journal of American Folklore* 101:168–175.

Lawrence, E. A. 1981. *Rodeo: An anthropologist looks at the wild and the tame.* Chicago: University of Chicago Press.

Leach, J. W. 1976. *Structure and message in* Trobriand Cricket: *Notes to accompany the film.* Berkeley, Calif.: Media Extension Center.

Leacock, E. 1971. At play in African villages. *Natural History,* special supplement on play, 80(10):60–65.

Leacock, S. B. 1929. *Nonsense novels.* New York: Dodd Mead.

Lear, E. 1912. *The complete nonsense book.* New York: Dodd Mead.

Lee, D. J. 1994. *Life and story.* New York: Praeger.

Lee, J. 1922. *Play in education.* New York: Macmillan.

Legman, G. 1968. *The rationale of the dirty joke.* New York: Grove.

———. 1969. *The limerick.* New York: Bell.

Leslie, A. M. 1987. Pretense and representation: The origins of a theory of mind. *Psychological Review* 94:412–426.

Lever, J. 1976. Sex differences in the games children play. *Social Problems* 23:478–487.

———. 1978. Sex differences in the complexity of children's games. *American Sociological Review* 43:471–483.

———. 1984. *Soccer madness.* Chicago: University of Chicago Press.

Levy, A. K. 1984. The language of play: the role of play in language development. *Early Child Development and Care* 17:49–62.

Levy, J. 1978. *Play behavior.* New York: Wiley.

Lewis, M. 1982. Play as whimsy. In Does play matter? Functional and evolutionary aspects of animal and human play, ed. P. K. Smith. *The Behavioral and Brain Sciences* 5(1):166.

Lewontin, R. C. 1977. Sociobiology: A caricature of Darwinism. In *Philosophy of Science Association,* ed. F. Suppe and P. Asquith, East Lansing, Mich.: Philosophy of Science Association, 22–31.

Lieberman, J. N. 1977. *Playfulness: Its relationship to imagination and creativity.* New York: Academic Press.

Lillard, A. S. 1993. Pretend play skills and the child's theory of mind. *Child Development* 64: 348–371.

Lindsay, P. L., and D. Palmer. 1981. Playground games characteristic of Brisbane primary school children. ERDC Report no. 28. Canberra: Australian Government Publishing Service.

Liss, M. 1983. *Social and cognitive skills: Sex roles and children's play.* New York: Academic Press.

Lowenfeld, M. 1967 (1935). *Play in childhood.* London: Science Editions.

Loy, J. W., ed. 1982. *The paradoxes of play.* West Point, N.Y.: Leisure Press.

———. 1995. Homo ludens revisited: A look at ludic windows of culture. Paper presented at the World Play Conference, Salzburg, Austria, June.

Loy, J. W., and G. L. Hesketh. 1995. Competitive play on the plains. In *The future of play theory,* ed. A. D. Pellegrini. Albany: State University of New York Press.

Loy, J. W., and G. Kenyon. 1969. *Sport, culture, society.* New York: Macmillan.

Loy, J. W., B. D. McPherson, and G. Kenyon. 1978. *Sport and social systems.* Reading, Mass.: Addison-Wesley.

Luke, C. 1989. *Pedagogy, printing and protestantism.* Albany: State University of New York Press.

MacAloon, J. J. 1981. *The great symbol: Pierre de Coubertin and the origins of the modern Olympic games.* Chicago: University of Chicago Press.

MacCannell, Dean. 1976. *The tourist: A new theory of the leisure class.* New York: Schocken Books.

———. 1992. *Empty meeting grounds: The tourist papers.* New York: Routledge.

Maccoby, E. 1987. The varied meanings of masculine and feminine. In *Masculinity/femininity,* ed. J. M. Reinisch. Oxford: Oxford University Press.

———. 1990. Gender and relationships, a developmental account. *American Psychologist* 45(4):513–520.

Maccoby, M. 1976. *The gamesman.* New York: Bantam.

MacDonald, K. B. 1987. Parent-child physical play with rejected, neglected and popular boys. *Developmental Psychology* 23(5):705–711.

———. 1988. *Social and personality development: An evolutionary synthesis.* New York: Plenum Press.

———, ed. 1993. *Parent-child play.* Albany: State University of New York Press.

Magee, M. A. 1987. Social play as performance. Ph.D. diss., University of Pennsylvania. Ann Arbor, Mich.: UMI, order no. 88049329.

Magill, R. A., M. J. Ash, and F. L. Smoll, eds. 1982. *Children in sport.* Champaign, Ill.: Human Kinetics Press.

Makarius, L. 1970. Ritual clowns and symbolical behavior. *Diogenes* 69:44–73.

Malinowski, B. 1944. *A scientific theory of culture.* New York: Oxford University Press.

Mangan, J. A. 1986. *The games ethic and imperialism.* New York: Viking Penguin.

Manning, F. E. 1983. *The celebration of society: perspectives on contemporary cultural performance.* Bowling Green, Ohio: Bowling Green State University Popular Press.

Marjanovic-Shane, A. 1990. Metaphor beyond play. Ph.D. diss., University of Pennsylvania.

Martens, R. 1978. *Joy and sadness in children's sports*. Champaign, Ill.: Human Kinetics Press.

Martin, P., and T. M. Caro. 1985. On the functions of play and its role in behavioral development. *Advances in the Study of Behavior* 15:59–103.

Maslow, A. H. 1968. *Toward a psychology of being*. New York: Nostrand.

Mazzotta, G. 1986. *The world at play in Boccaccio's* Decameron. Princeton, N.J.: Princeton University Press.

McCale-Small, M. 1994. Sex differences in daydreams in middle childhood. Ph.D. diss., University of Pennsylvania.

McCall, R. B. 1974. Exploratory manipulation and play in the human infant. *Monographs of the Society for Research in Child Development*, serial no. 155, 15:2.

McCarthur, T., ed. 1992. *The Oxford Companion to the English Language*. Oxford: Oxford University Press.

McCosh, S. 1979. *Children's humor*. London: Granada.

McCune, L. 1995. A normative study of representational play at the transition to language. *Developmental Psychology* 31(2):198–206.

McDougall, W. 1923. *Outline of psychology*. New York: Scribner and Sons.

McDowell, J. 1979. *Children's riddling*. Bloomington: Indiana University Press.

———. 1995. The transmission of children's folklore. In *Children's folklore: A source book*, ed. B. Sutton-Smith et al. New York: Garland, 49–62.

McFarland, 1985. *Originality and imagination*. Baltimore: Johns Hopkins University Press.

McGurrin, M., V. Abt, and J. Smith. 1984. Play as pathology: A new look at the gambler and his world. In *Masks of play*, ed. B. Sutton-Smith and D. Kelly-Byrne. West Point, N.Y.: Leisure Press.

McMahon, F. 1992. Wilderness and tradition: Power, politics and play in the Adirondacks. Ph.D. diss., University of Pennsylvania.

———. 1993a. Regional sports: Playing with politics in the Adirondacks. *New York Folklore* 19(3):55–66.

———. 1993b. The worst piece of "tale": Flaunted "hidden transcripts" in women's play. *Play Theory and Research* 1(4):251–258.

McMahon, F., and B. Sutton-Smith. 1995. The past in the present: Theoretical directions for children's folklore. In *Children's folklore: A sourcebook*, ed. B. Sutton-Smith, J. Mechling, T. W. Johnson, and F. McMahon. New York: Garland Press.

McPherson, B. D., J. E. Curtis, and J. W. Loy. 1989. The social significance of sport. Champaign, Ill.: Human Kinetics Press.

Mead, G. H. 1934. *Mind, self and society.* Chicago: University of Chicago Press.

Mechling, J. 1980. The magic of the Boy Scout campfire. *Journal of American Folklore* 93:35–56.

———. 1989. Morality play. *Play and Culture* 2(4):304–316.

Meckley, A. M. 1994. The social construction of young children's play. Ph.D. diss., University of Pennsylvania.

Meeker, J. W. 1995. Comedy and a play ethic. *Revision* 17(4):21–25.

Megill, A. 1985. *Prophets of extremity.* Berkeley: University of California Press.

Menninger, K. 1942. *Love against hate.* New York: Harcourt.

Mergen, B. 1982. *Play and playthings: A reference guide.* Westport, Conn.: Greenwood.

———. 1986. *Cultural dimensions of play, games, and sport.* West Point, N.Y.: Leisure Press.

Messenger, C. K. 1981. *Sport and the spirit of play in American fiction: Hawthorne to Faulkner.* New York: Columbia University Press.

Millar, S. 1968. *The psychology of play.* Baltimore: Penguin.

Miller, D. L. 1969. *Gods and games.* New York: World.

Miracle, A. 1977. Some functions of Aymara games and play. In *Studies in the anthropology of play,* ed. P. Stevens. West Point, N.Y.: Leisure Press, 98–104.

Mitchell, E. D. 1937. *The theory of play.* Baltimore: Penguin.

Mitchell-Kernan, C. 1973. Signifying. In *Mother wit from the laughing barrel,* ed. A. Dundes. Englewood Cliffs, N.J.: Prentice Hall, 310–328.

Moltmann, J. 1972. *Theology of play.* New York: Harper and Row.

Mouritsen, F. 1996. Project demolition. Paper presented at the International Toy Research Conference, Halmstad, Sweden, June.

Muller-Schwartze, D. 1978. *Evolution of play behavior.* Stroudsburg, Pa.: Dowden, Hutchinson and Ross.

Murphy, L. B. 1957. *Personality in young children.* New York: Basic Books.

Murray, H. J. R. 1952. *A history of board games.* Oxford: Clarendon Press.

Nachbar, J., and K. Lause. 1992. *Popular culture: An introductory text.* Bowling Green, Ohio: Bowling Green State University Popular Press.

Nardo, A. K. 1991. *The ludic self in seventeenth-century English literature.* Albany: State University of New York Press.

Nasaw, D. 1985. *Children of the city.* Garden City, N.Y.: Doubleday, Anchor Books.

Nelson, K. 1989. *Narratives from the crib.* Cambridge, Mass.: Harvard University Press.

Nemoianu, V., and R. Royal. 1992. *Play, literature and religion.* Albany: State University of New York Press.

Neulinger, J. 1974. *The psychology of leisure.* Springfield, Ill.: Charles C. Thomas.

Newall, W. W. 1963 (1883). *Games and songs of American children.* New York: Dover.

Nicolopoulou, A. 1997. Children and narratives: Toward an interpretive and sociocultural process. In *Narrative development: Six approaches,* ed. M. Bamberg. Mahwah, N.J.: Erlbaum, 179–215.

Nietzsche, F. 1954. *The portable Nietzsche,* ed. W. Kaufman. New York: Viking.

Novak, M. 1976. *The joy of sports.* New York: Basic Books.

Noyes, D. 1995. Group. *Journal of American Folklore* 108(430):449–478.

O'Flaherty, W. D. 1984. *Dreams, illusion and other realities.* Chicago: University of Chicago Press.

Olweus, D. 1993. Bullies on the playground: The role of victimization. *Children on playgrounds,* ed. C. H. Hart. Albany: State University of New York Press.

Opie, I., and P. Opie. 1959. *The lore and language of schoolchildren.* New York: Oxford University Press.

Opie, I. 1993. *The people in the playground.* New York: Oxford University Press.

———. 1969. *Children's games in the street and playground.* New York: Oxford University Press.

———. 1985. *The singing game.* New York: Oxford University Press.

Opie, P. 1963. The tentacles of tradition. *The Advancement of Science,* 20:1–10.

Oriard, M. 1991. *Sporting with the gods: The rhetoric of play and game in American culture.* Cambridge: Cambridge University Press.

Orlean, S. 1990. *Saturday night.* New York: Knopf.

Paley, V. G. 1981. *Wally's stories.* Cambridge, Mass.: Harvard University Press.

———. 1984. *Boys and girls.* Chicago: University of Chicago Press.

———. 1990. *The boy who would be a helicopter.* Cambridge, Mass.: Harvard University Press.

———. 1992. *You can't say you can't play.* Cambridge, Mass.: Harvard University Press.

Palmatier, R. A., and H. L. Ray. 1989. *Sports talk: A diet of sports metaphors.* Westport, Conn.: Greenwood Press.

Panksepp, J. 1993. *Rough and tumble play: A fundamental brain process.* In *Parent-child play,* ed. K. MacDonald. Albany: State University of New York Press.

Parke, R. D., and G. W. Ladd. 1992. *Family-peer relationships: Modes of linkage.* Hillsdale, N.J.: Erlbaum.

Parten, M. 1932. Social participation among preschool children. *Journal of Abnormal and Social Psychology* 27:243–369.

Pascal, B. 1962 (1669). *Pensées,* ed. Louis Lafuma. Paris: Editions du Seuil.

Patrick, G. T. W. 1916. *The psychology of relaxation.* Boston: Houghton Mifflin.

Pavlov, I. P. 1927. *Conditioned reflexes.* Oxford: Clarendon Press.

Peckham, M. 1967. *Man's rage for chaos.* New York: Schocken Books.

Pellegrini, A. D. 1988. Elementary school children's rough and tumble play and social competence. *Developmental Psychology* 24(6):802–806.

——. 1989. So what about recess, really? *Play and Culture* 2(4):354–356.

Pellegrini, A. D., ed. 1995a. *The future of play theory: A multidisciplinary inquiry into the contribution of Brian Sutton-Smith.* Albany: State University of New York Press.

——. 1995b. *School recess and playground behavior.* Albany: State University of New York Press.

Pellegrini, A. D. and J. C. Perimutter. 1987. A re-examination of the Smilansky-Parten matrix of play behavior. *Journal of Research in Childhood Education* 2:89–96.

Pepler, D. J. 1982. Play and divergent thinking. In *The play of children: Current theory and research,* D. J. Pepler and K. Rubin. New York: S. Karger.

Pepler, D. J., and H. S. Ross. 1981. The effects of play on convergent and divergent problem solving. *Child Development* 52:1202–1210.

Pepler, D. J., and K. Rubin. 1982. *The play of children: Current theory and research.* New York: S. Karger.

Pepper, S. 1961. *World hypotheses.* Berkeley: University of California Press.

Peterson, C., and A. McCabe. 1983. *Three ways of looking at children's narrative.* London: Plenum.

Peterson, I. 1995. The promise of gambling. *New York Times,* Dec. 26, A1 and C3.

Phillips, R. 1977. *Aspects of Alice.* New York: Vintage.

Piaget, J. 1951. *Play, dreams and imitation in childhood.* New York: Norton.

——. 1952. *The origins of intelligence in children.* New York: International University Press.

——. 1965 (1948). *The moral judgement of the child.* New York: Macmillan.

——. 1976. *Structuralism.* New York: Basic Books.

Pitcher, E. G., and E. Prelinger. 1963. *Children tell stories.* New York: International University Press.

Pitcher, E. G., and L. H. Schultz. 1983. *Boys and girls at play.* New York: Praeger.

Pocock, J. G. A. 1975. *The Machiavellian moment.* Princeton, N.J.: Princeton University Press.

Polgar, S. K. 1976. The social context of games, or when is play not play. *Sociology of Education* 49:265–271.

Portnoy, J., and S. Portnoy. 1983. *How to take trips with your kids.* Boston, Mass.: Harvard Common Press.

Poster, M. 1990. *The mode of information.* Chicago: University of Chicago Press.

Postman, N. 1982. *The disappearance of childhood.* New York: Dell.

Pulaski, M. A. 1973. Toys and imaginative play. In *The child's world of make-believe,* ed. J. L. Singer. New York: Academic Press.

Rabelais, F. 1955 (1562). *Gargantua and Pantagruel.* London: Penguin.

Radin, P. 1956. *The trickster.* New York: Schocken Books.

Rapoport, A. 1960. *Fights, games and debates.* Ann Arbor: University of Michigan Press.

Rath, S. P., ed. 1986. Game, play, literature: An introduction. *South Central Review* 3:4.

Ratner, N., and J. S. Bruner. 1978. Games, social exchange, and the acquisition of language. *Journal of Child Language* 5:391–401.

Read, H. 1944. *Education through art.* London: Faber and Faber.

Redekop, P. 1988. *Sociology of sport: An annotated bibliography.* New York: Garland.

Redl, F., P. Gump, and B. Sutton-Smith. 1971. The dimensions of games. In *The study of games,* ed. E. M. Avedon and B. Sutton-Smith. New York: Wiley.

Reiff, P. 1966. *The triumph of the therapeutic.* Chicago: Chicago University Press.

Renson, R. 1991. *The promotion of traditional games: The Flemish approach.* Proceedings of the Second European Seminar on Traditional Games. Louvain, Belgium: Vlaamse Volkssport Centrale, 55–58.

Rescher, N. 1995. Luck. In *The brilliant randomness of everyday life.* New York: Farrar, Straus and Giroux.

Reynolds, P. 1976. Play language and human evolution. In *Play,* ed. J. S. Bruner, A. Jolly, and K. Sylva. New York: Basic Books.

Roberts, J. M. 1979. Comment on "Games of strategy" by P. H. Townshend. *Newsletter of the Association for the Anthropological Study of Play* 6:10–11.

Roberts, J. M., M. J. Arth, and R. R. Bush. 1959. Games in culture. *American Anthropologist* 61:597–605.

Roberts, J. M., and H. C. Barry III. 1976. Inculcated traits and game-type combinations. In *The humanistic and health aspects of sports, exercise and recreation,* ed. T. T. Craig. Chicago: American Medical Association, 5–11.

Roberts, J. M., and M. L. Forman. 1972. Riddles: Models of interrogation. *Ethnology* 10:509–533.

Roberts, J. M., H. Hoffman, and B. Sutton-Smith. 1965. Pattern and competence: A consideration of tick tack toe. *El Palacio* 72:17–30.

Roberts, J. M., and B. Sutton-Smith. 1962. Child training and game involvement. *Ethnology* 1(2):166–185.

Roberts, J. M., B. Sutton-Smith, and A. Kendon. 1963. Strategy in folktales and games. *Journal of Social Psychology* 61:185–199.

Roberts, J. M., W. E. Thompson, and B. Sutton-Smith. 1966. Expressive self-testing and driving. *Human Organization* 25:54–55.

Roberts, R., and J. Olson. 1993. *Winning is the only thing: Sports in America since 1945.* Baltimore: Johns Hopkins University Press.

Roberts, R. H., and Good, J. M. M. 1993. *The recovery of rhetoric.* Charlottesville: University Press of Virginia.

Robinson-Finnan, C. L. 1982. The ethnography of children's spontaneous play. In *Doing the ethnography of schooling,* ed. G. Spindler. New York: Holt, Rinehart and Winston.

Rojek, C. 1995. *Decentering leisure: Rethinking leisure theory,* London: Sage Publications.

Roopnarine, J. L., J. E. Johnson, and Frank H. Hooper, eds. 1994. *Children's play in diverse cultures.* Albany: State University of New York Press.

Roopnarine, J. L. and N. S. Mounts. 1985. Mother-child and father-child play. *Early Child Development and Care* 20:157–169.

Rose, J. 1993. *The case of Peter Pan,* Philadelphia: University of Pennsylvania Press.

Rosen, C. E. 1974. The effects of sociodramatic play on problem solving among culturally disadvantaged children. *Child Development* 45:920–927.

Rosenberg, B. G., and B. Sutton-Smith. 1959. The development of masculinity and femininity in children. *Child Development* 30:373–380.

———. 1960. A revised conception of masculine-feminine differences in play activities. *Journal of Genetic Psychology* 96:165–170.

———. 1964. The measurement of masculinity and femininity in children: An extension and revalidation. *Journal of Genetic Psychology* 194:259–264.

Ross, H. S., and S. P. Lollis. 1987. Communication with infant social games. *American Psychologist* 23(2):241–248.

Rubin, K. H., ed. 1980. *Children's play.* New Directions for Child Development, vol. 9. San Francisco: Jossey-Bass.

Rubin, K. H., G. G. Fein, and B. Vandenberg. 1983. Play. In *Handbook of child psychology: Social development,* vol. 4, ed. E. M. Hetherington. New York: Wiley.

Rubin, K. H., T. Maloni, and M. Hornung. 1976. Free play behaviors in middle-and lower-class preschoolers: Parten and Piaget revisited. *Child Development* 47:414–419.

Rubin, K. H., and L. Marioni. 1975. Play preference and its relationship to egocentrism, popularity and classification skills in preschoolers. *Merrill-Palmer Quarterly* 21:171–179.

Rubin, K. H., and D. J. Pepler. 1980. The relationship of child's play to social-cognitive development. In *Friendship and childhood relationships,* ed. H. C. Foot, A. J. Chapman, and J. R. Smith. London: Wiley.

Rubin, K. H., K. S. Watson, and T. W. Jambour. 1978. Free play behaviors in preschool and kindergarten children. *Child Development* 49:534–546.

Rubin, W., ed. 1984. *Primitivism in twentieth-century art.* New York: Museum of Modern Art.

Ruse, M. 1996. *Monad to man: The concept of progress in evolutionary biology.* Cambridge, Mass.: Harvard University Press.

Rushkoff, D. 1996. *Playing the future.* New York: HarperCollins.

Sacks, O. 1995. *An anthropologist on Mars.* New York: Knopf.

Saler, M. A. 1977. Meteorological play forms of the eastern woodlands. In *Studies in the anthropology of play,* ed. P. Stevens Jr. West Point, N.Y.: Leisure Press.

Salter, M. A., ed. 1977. *Play: Anthropological perspectives.* West Point, N.Y.: Leisure Press.

———. 1983. Classic game, classic people: Ball games of the lowland Maya. In *The celebration of society: Perspectives on contemporary cultural performance,* ed. F. E. Manning. Bowling Green, Ohio: Bowling Green State University Popular Press.

Saltz, E., and J. Brodie. 1982. Pretend-play in childhood: A review and critique. *Contributions to Human Development* 6:1–158.

Saltz, E., D. Dixon, and J. Johnson. 1977. Training disadvantaged preschoolers on various fantasy activities: Effects on cognitive functioning and impulse control. *Child Development* 48:367–368.

Sapora, A. V., and E. D. Mitchell. 1948. *The theory of play and recreation.* New York: Ronald Press.

Savasta, M. L., and B. Sutton-Smith. 1979. Sex differences in play and power. In *Die dialektik des spiel,* ed. B. Sutton-Smith. Schorndorf, Germany: Verlag Karl Hoffman.

Sawyer, K. 1996. *Pretend play as improvisation: Conversation in the preschool classroom.* Hillsdale, N.J.: Erlbaum.

Scarborough, V. L., and D. R. Wilcox. 1991. *The Mesoamerican ball game.* Tucson: University of Arizona Press.

Schaefer, C. E. 1970. *Therapeutic use of child's play.* New York: Jason Aronsen.

Schaefer, C. E., and O'Connor. 1983. *Handbook of play therapy.* New York: Wiley.

Schechner, R. 1988. Playing. *Play and Culture* 1(1):3–27.

———. 1993. *The future of ritual.* New York: Routledge.

Schechner, R., and M. Schuman, eds. 1976. *Ritual, play and performance.* New York: Seabury Press.

Schele, L., and M. E. Miller. 1986. *The blood of kings.* New York: Braziller.

Schelling, T. C. 1960. *The strategy of conflict.* Oxford: Oxford University Press.

Schiller, F. 1965 (1795). *On the aesthetic education of man,* trans. R. Snell. New York: Frederick Ungar.

Schlosberg, H. 1947. The concept of play. *Psychological Review* 54:229–231.

Schudson, M. 1984. Embarrassment and Erving Goffman's idea of human nature. *Theory and Society* 13(5):633–648.

Schultz, T. R. 1979. Play as arousal modulation. In *Play and learning*, ed. B. Sutton-Smith. New York: Gardner Press.

Schwartzman, H. B. 1978. *Transformations: The anthropology of children's play.* New York: Plenum.

———. 1979. The sociocultural context of play. In *Play and learning*, ed. B. Sutton-Smith. New York: Gardner Press.

———, ed. 1980. *Play and culture.* West Point, N.Y.: Leisure Press.

Schwartzman, J. 1980. Paradox, play and postmodern fiction. In *Play and culture*, ed. H. B. Schwartzman. West Point, N.Y.: Leisure Press, 38–48.

Scott, J. C. 1990. *Domination and the arts of resistance.* New Haven, Conn.: Yale University Press.

Seagoe, M. Y. 1970. An instrument for the analysis of children's play in an index of degree of socialization. *Journal of School Psychology* 8(2):139–144.

———. 1971. A comparison of children's play in six modern cultures. *Journal of School Psychology* 9:61–72.

Sheehan, K. 1993. Two childhoods. Ph.D. diss., University of Pennsylvania.

Siegler, R. S. 1996. *Emerging minds: The process of change in children's thinking.* New York: Oxford University Press.

Silvey, R., and S. MacKeith. 1988. The paracosm: A special form of fantasy. In *Organizing early experience*, ed. D. C. Morrison. Amityville, N.Y.: Baywood Publishing.

Simon, T., and P. K. Smith. 1985. Play and problem solving: A paradigm questioned. *Merrill-Palmer Quarterly* 31(3):265–277.

Singer, D., and J. L. Singer. 1977. *Partners in play.* New York: Random House.

———. 1981. *Television, imagination and aggression.* Hillsdale, N.J.: Erlbaum.

———. 1992. *The house of make-believe.* Cambridge, Mass.: Harvard University Press.

Singer, J. L. 1966. *Daydreaming: An introduction to the experimental study of inner experience.* New York: Random House.

———. 1973. *The child's world of make believe.* New York: Academic Press.

———. 1975. *The inner world of daydreaming.* New York: Harper and Row.

Sipes, R. G. 1973. War, sports and aggression: An empirical test of two rival theories. *American Anthropologist* 75:64–86.

Slade, A., and D. P. Wolf. 1994. *Children at play.* Oxford: Oxford University Press.

Slukin, A. 1981. *Growing up in the playground.* London: Routledge and Kegan Paul.

Smilansky, S. 1968. *The effects of sociodramatic play on disadvantaged preschool children.* New York: Wiley.

Smith, E. O., ed. 1978. *Social play in primates.* New York: Academic Press.

Smith, P. K. 1982. Does play matter? Functional and evolutionary aspects of animal and human play. *The Behavioral and Brain Sciences* 5:139–184.

———. 1995. Play, ethology, and education: A personal account. In *The future of play theory,* ed. A. T. Pellegrini. Albany: State University of New York Press, 1–22.

———, ed. 1984. *Play in animals and humans.* London: Blackwell.

———, ed. 1986. *Children's play: Research developments and practical applications.* London: Gordon and Breach.

Smith, P. K., and K. J. Connolly. 1980. *The ecology of preschool behavior.* Cambridge: Cambridge University Press.

Smith, P. K., and S. Dutton. 1979. Play and training in direct and innovative problem solving. *Child Development* 50:830–836.

Smith, P. K., and S. Syddall. 1978. Play and non-play tutoring in preschool children: Is it play or tutoring which matters? *British Journal of Educational Psychology* 48:315–325.

Smith, P. K., and R. Vollstedt. 1985. On defining play: An empirical study of the relationship between play and various play criteria. *Child Development* 56:1042–1050.

Smith, V. L., ed. 1977. *Hosts and guests: The anthropology of tourism.* Philadelphia: University of Pennsylvania Press.

Solnit, A. J., D. J. Cohen, and P. B. Neubauer. 1993. *The many meanings of play.* New Haven, Conn.: Yale University Press.

Snow-Dockser, L. 1989. *Mothers in children's museums: A neglected dynamic.* Ph.D. diss., University of Pennsylvania.

Solnit, A. J., D. J. Cohen, and P. B. Neubauer. 1993. *The many meanings of play: A psychoanalytic perspective.* New Haven, Conn.: Yale University Press.

Spack, P. 1986. *Gossip.* Chicago: University of Chicago Press.

Spariosu, M. 1982. *Literature, mimesis, play.* Tübingen: Gunter Narr Verlag.

———. 1984. *Mimesis in contemporary theory.* Philadelphia: John Benjamin.

———. 1989. *Dionysus reborn.* Ithaca, N.Y.: Cornell University Press.

———. 1991. *God of many names.* Durham, N.C.: Duke University Press.

Spencer, H. 1896 (1855). *Principles of psychology.* New York: Appleton.

Stallybrass, P., and A. White. 1986. *The politics and poetics of transgression.* Ithaca, N.Y.: Cornell University Press.

Stanton, D. 1997. South of the border, upside down Mexico way. *Outside* February 70–105.

Starobinski, J. 1988 (1957). *Jean Jacques Rousseau: Transparency and obstruction.* Chicago: University of Chicago Press.

Staten, H. 1984. *Wittgenstein and Derrida*. Lincoln: University of Nebraska Press.

Steiner, W. 1995. *The scandal of pleasure*. Chicago: University of Chicago Press.

Stephenson, W. 1967. *The play theory of mass communication*. Chicago: University of Chicago Press.

Stevens, P. 1972. Towards a history of childhood. *History of Education Quarterly* Summer:198–209.

———. 1980. Play and work: A false dichotomy. In *Play and culture*, ed. H. B. Schwartzman. West Point, N.Y.: Leisure Press.

———, ed. 1977. *Studies in the anthropology of play*. West Point, N.Y.: Leisure Press.

Stewart, S. 1978. *Nonsense: Aspects of intertextuality in folklore literature*. Baltimore: Johns Hopkins University Press.

———. 1984. *On longing: Narratives of the miniature, the gigantic, the souvenir, the collection*. Baltimore: Johns Hopkins University Press.

———. 1991. *Crimes of writing*. New York: Oxford University Press.

Stoeltje, B. 1978. *Children's handclaps: Informal learning in play*. Austin: Southwest Educational Development Laboratory.

Stone, L. 1979. *The family, sex and marriage in England, 1500–1800*. New York: Harper.

Strutt, J. 1801. *The sports and pastimes of the people of England*. London: Methuen.

Suits, B. 1978. *The grasshopper: Games, Life, and Utopia*. Toronto: University of Toronto Press.

Sutton-Smith, B. 1951. The meeting of Maori and European cultures and its effects upon the unorganized games of Maori children. *Journal of Polynesian Society* 60:93–107.

———. 1952. New Zealand variants of the game Buck. *Folklore* 63:329–333.

———. 1953a. Seasonal games. *Western Folklore* 12:186–193.

———. 1953b. The traditional games of New Zealand children. *Folklore* 64:411–423.

———. 1959a. A formal analysis of game meaning. *Western Folklore* 18:13–24.

———. 1959b. *Games of New Zealand children*. Berkeley: University of California Press.

———. 1959c. The kissing games of adolescents in Ohio. *Midwestern Folklore* 9:189–211.

———. 1960. The cruel joke series. *Midwestern Folklore* 10:11–12.

———. 1961. Cross-cultural study of children's games. *American Philosophical Society Yearbook*, 426–429 (grant no. 2716, 1960).

———. 1964. Review of *The encounter* by E. Goffman. *American Journal of Psychology* 106:13–37.

———. 1965. Play preferences and play behavior: A validity study. *Psychological Reports* 16:65–66.

———. 1966a. Piaget on play: A critique. *Psychological Review* 73:104–110.

———. 1966b. Review of *Song games from Trinidad and Tobago* by J. D. Elder. *Western Folklore* 25:265–266.

———. 1966c. Role replication and reversal in play. *Merrill-Palmer Quarterly* 12:285–298.

———. 1967a. Games, play, daydreams. *Quest* 10:47–58.

———. 1967b. The role of play in cognitive development. *Young Children* 6:361–370.

———. 1968. Novel responses to toys. *Merrill-Palmer Quarterly* 14:151–158.

———. 1969a. Review of *The psychology of play*, by S. Millar. *Child Development Abstracts* 43:146.

———. 1969b. The two cultures of games. In *Aspects of contemporary sport sociology*, ed. G. Kenyon. Chicago: Athletic Institute.

———. 1970a. The cross-cultural study of games. In *A cross-cultural analysis of sports and games*, ed. G. Luschen. Champaign, Ill.: Stipes.

———. 1970b. A psychologist looks at playgrounds. *The Educational Product Reports* Fall 3(8–9):13–15.

———. 1970c. Review of *The effects of sociodramatic play on disadvantaged preschool children*. *The Record* 71:529–531.

———. 1970d. The psychology of childlore. *Western Folklore* 29:1–8.

———. 1971a. Children at play. *The Journal of the American Museum of Natural History* 80:54–59.

———. 1971b. Child's play. *Psychology Today* 5:55–59.

———. 1971c. The expressive profile. *Journal of American Folklore* 84:80–92.

———. 1971d. Play, games and controls. In *Social control*, ed. J. P. Scott. Chicago: University of Chicago Press.

———. 1971e. The playful modes of knowing. In *Play: The child strives towards self-realization*. Special monograph. Washington, D.C.: National Association for the Education of Young Children.

———. 1971f. Review of *The question of play* by Joyce McCelland. *Young Children* January:191.

———. 1972a. The expressive profile. In *Towards new perspectives in folklore*, ed. A. Parades. Austin: University of Texas Press.

———. 1972b. *The folkgames of children*. Austin: University of Texas Press.

———. 1972c. Research in play. *Leisure Today* 1(2):6–7.

———. 1973a. Comment on play. *Forum for Contemporary History*, Dec. 14, 23.

———. 1973b. A developmental approach to play, games and sports. *Proceedings of the Second World Symposium on the History of Sport*. Banff: University of Alberta, 75–83.

———. 1973c. Games: The socialization of conflict. *Sportswissenschaft* 3:41–46.

———. 1973d. Play as the mediation of novelty, games as the socialization of conflict. In *Sport in the modern world: Chances and problems*, ed. O. Grupe. Berlin: Springer-Verlag.

———. 1973e. Review of *Step it down: games, plays, songs*. *Journal of American Folklore* 86:307–308.

———. 1974a. The anthropology of play. *Association for the Anthropological Study of Play* 2:8–12.

———. 1974b. Developmental structural aspects of play and games. *Proceedings of the British Commonwealth and International Conference on Health, Physical Education and Recreation*. Christchurch, New Zealand.

———. 1974c. Play as novelty training. In *One child indivisible:* Washington, D.C.: National Association for the Education of Young Children, *NAEYC conference proceedings*. 227–258.

———. 1974d. Review of *Play and development* ed. M. W. Piers. *Teachers College Record* 74 (Spring):444.

———. 1974e. Review of *Play as exploratory learning* by M. Reilly. *Opening Education* 2(1):25–26.

———. 1974f. Review of *Word play* by Peter Farb. *Natural History* 84:81–83.

———. 1975a. Play as adaptive potentiation. *Sportswissenschaft* 5:103–118.

———. 1975b. Play: The useless made useful. *School Review* 83:197–214.

———. 1976a. Current research in play, games and sports. In *Human movement*, ed. T. T. Craig. Schorndorf, Germany: Verlag Karl Hoffman.

———. 1976b. A developmental structural account of riddles. In *Speech play*, ed. B. Kirschblatt-Gimblett. Philadelphia: University of Pennsylvania Press.

———. 1976c. The psychology of childlore: A theory of ludic models. *Resources of Education* ERIC (July).

———. 1976d. A structural grammar of games and sports. *International Journal of Sports Sociology* 2(11):117–138.

———, ed. 1976e. *Studies in play and games*, vols. 1–3. New York: Arno Press.

———. 1977a. Games of order and disorder. *Newsletter of the Association for the Anthropological Study of Play* 4:119–126.

———. 1977b. Play and curiosity. *International encyclopedia of neurology, psychiatry, psychoanalysis and psychology*, vol. 8.

———. 1977c. A sociolinguistic approach to ludic action. In *Handlungen theories interdisziplinar*, vol 4, ed. H. Lenk. Munich: Wilhem Fink Verlag.

———. 1977d. Structural approaches to play: Towards an anthropology of play; Play as adaptive potentiation: A footnote to the 1976 keynote address. In *Studies in the anthropology of play*, ed. P. Stevens. West Point, N.Y.: Leisure Press.

———. 1977e. The world of play, sport and leisure. *Bulletin of the American Society for Information Science* 4:12–13.

———. 1978a. The dialectics of play. In *Physical activity and human well-being,* ed. F. Landry and W. Oban. Miami: Symposia Specialists.

———. 1978b. *Die dialektik des spiels.* Schorndorf, Germany: Verlag Karl Hoffman.

———. 1979a. The development of folklore and games in the Pacific. *Proceedings of the International Conference on the History of Sport and Physical Education in the Pacific Region.* Otago, New Zealand: School of Physical Education.

———. 1979b. Folkgames. In *American Folklore Series,* ed. H. Cohen. Delanda, Fla.: Cassette Curriculum.

———. 1979c. The meanings of play. *The Newsletter of the Association for the Anthropological Study of Play* 6:12–18.

———. 1979d. *Play and learning.* New York: Gardner Press.

———. 1979e. Play as innovation. In *Taking early childhood seriously,* The Evangeline Burgess Memorial Lectures, ed. M. Wolman. Pasadena, Calif.: Pacific Oaks College and Children's School.

———. 1979f. The play of girls. In *Becoming females: Perspectives on development,* ed. C. B. Kopp and M. Kirkpatrick. New York: Plenum.

———. 1979g. Presentation and representation in fictional narrative. In *Fact, fiction and fantasy in childhood,* ed. E. Winner and H. Gardner. San Francisco: Jossey-Bass.

———. 1979h. Toys for object and role mastery. In *Educational toys in America: 1800 to the present* ed. K. Hewitt and L. Roomet. Burlington, Vt.: Robert Hull Fleming Museum.

———. 1980a. Children's play: Some sources of play theorizing. In *Children's play,* ed. K. H. Rubin. New Direction for Child Development, vol. 9. San Francisco: Jossey-Bass.

———. 1980b. The social psychology and anthropology of play and games. In *Handbook of social science of sport,* ed. G. R. F. Luschen and G. H. Sage. In Reading, Mass.: Addison-Wesley.

———. 1980c. A sportive theory of play. In *Play and culture,* ed. H. B. Schwartzman. West Point, N.Y.: Leisure Press.

———. 1981. *The folkstories of children.* Philadelphia: University of Pennsylvania Press.

———. 1981b. *A history of children's play.* Philadelphia: University of Pennsylvania Press.

———. 1981c. The new meanings of play. In *Recreation Reconsidered into the eighties,* ed. J. Shallcrass. Auckland, New Zealand: New Zealand Council for Recreation and Sport.

————. 1982a. Die idealisierung des spiels. In *Spiel, spiele, spielen,* ed. O. Grupe, H. Gabler, and U. Gohner. Schorndorf, Germany: Verlag Karl Hoffman.

————. 1982b. Een prastatie-theories over relaties met leeftijdgenoen. In *Motorisch gedrag en ontwikkeling,* ed. N. H. A. van Rossum. Nijmegen, The Netherlands: dekker and van de Vagt.

————. 1982c. One hundred years of change in play research. *Newsletter of TAASP* 9(2):13–17.

————. 1982d. A performance theory of peer relationships. In *The social life of children in a changing society,* ed. K. M. Borman. Hillsdale, N.J.: Erlbaum.

————. 1982e. Piaget on play: Revisited. In *The relationship between social and cognitive development,* ed. W. F. Overton. Hillsdale, N.J.: Erlbaum.

————. 1982f. Play theory and the cruel play of the nineteenth century. In *The world of play,* ed. F. E. Manning. West Point, N.Y.: Leisure Press.

————. 1982g. Play theory of the rich and the poor. In *Children in and out of school,* ed. P. Gilmore and A. Glathorn. Washington, D.C.: Center for Applied Linguistics.

————. 1982h. Review of *Growing up in the playground* by Andy Slukin. *Contemporary Psychology* 27(9):729–730.

————. 1982i. Review of *Children's riddling* by John McDowell. *Language and Society* 11:150–151.

————. 1983a. Child's play: Idealizing the savage. Paper presented at the Miquon Conference on Progressive Education, Philadelphia, April 7–9.

————. 1983b. Commentary on social class differences in sociodramatic play in historical context: A reply to McLoyd. *Developmental Review* 3:1–5.

————. 1984a. From narcissism to charisma: the vicissitudes of central person games. *Newsletter of TAASP* (The Anthropological Association for the Study of Play) 10(1):10–19.

————. 1984b. Recreation as folly's parody. *Newsletter of TAASP* 9(4):4–13.

————. 1984c. Text and context in imaginative play. In *Analysing children's play dialogues: New directions for child development,* no. 25, ed. F. Kessel and A. Goncu. San Francisco: Jossey-Bass.

————. 1984d. A toy semiotics. *Children's Environmental Quarterly* 50(1):19–22.

————. 1985a. Introduction: The history and meaning of children's play; Projection: The future of play. In *Children's play, past, present and future.* Philadelphia: Please Touch Museum.

————. 1985b. Play research: State of the art. In *When children play,* ed. J. L. Frost and S. Sunderlin. Washington, D.C.: Association for Childhood Education International.

———. 1985c. Spel doorprikt: Over de idealerising van der recreation. *Inboud* 13(5):pr.a.

———. 1986a. Review of *Symbolic play* by I. Bretherton, ed. *American Journal of Education* 94(2):265–267.

———. 1986b. *Toys as culture.* New York: Gardner Press.

———. 1986c. The metaphor of games in social science research. In *Play: Play therapy, play research,* ed. R. van der Kooij and J. Hellendorn. Lisse, The Netherlands: Swets and Zeitlinger.

———. 1987b. In search of the imagination. In *Education and the imagination,* ed. D. Nadaner and K. Egan. New York: Teachers College Press.

———. 1987c. Introduction. In *The play theory of mass communication,* ed. W. Stephenson. New Brunswick, N.J.: Transaction Publishers.

———. 1987d. Review of *The singing game* by Iona and Peter Opie. *Journal of American Folklore* 99(392):239–240.

———. 1987e. School play: A commentary. In *School play,* ed. J. H. Block and N. R. King. New York: Garland Press.

———. 1987f. The spirit of play. In *The young child at play,* ed. G. Fein and M. Rivkin. Washington, D.C.: National Association for the Education of Young Children.

———. 1987g. The struggle between sacred play and festival play. In *Play as a learning medium,* ed. D. Berger. New York: Heineman.

———. 1988a. Children's play. In *Leaders in education,* ed. M. A. Johnson. New York: University Press of America.

———. 1988b. Creativity and vicissitudes of play. *Annals of Adolescent Psychiatry* 15:307–318.

———. 1988c. Jouets et culture. *L'Education par le Jeu et l'Environment,* 3eme trimestre, 3–7.

———. 1988d. Les jouets comme fonction d'isolement dans la societie moderne. *L'Education par le Jeu et l'Environment.* 4eme trimester:3–8.

———. 1988e. Play and creativity. In *Creativity through play,* ed. P. J. Heseltine. Report of the tenth conference of the International Association for the Child's Right to Play. Cambridge, England: University Printing Service.

———. 1988f. Republication of "Spiel und sport als potential der erneuerung." In *Das Kinderspiel,* ed. A. Flitner. Munich: Piper.

———. 1988g. War toys and childhood aggression. *Play and Culture* 1(1):57–69.

———. 1989a. Childhood: The multi-vocal mind. In *Proceedings defining the field of early childhood education,* ed. L. R. Williams and D. P. Fromberg. Charlottesville, Virginia: The A. W. Alton Jones Foundation.

———. 1989b. Childrens' folkgames as customs. *Western Folklore* 47(1):33–42.

————. 1989c. Forward to *A child's play: An ethnographic study*, D. Kelly-Byrne. New York: Teachers College Press.

————. 1989d. Introduction to play as performance, rhetoric and metaphor. *Play and Culture* 2(3):189–192.

————. 1989e. Models of power. In *The content of culture constants and variants: Studies in honor of John M. Roberts*, ed. R. Bolton. New Haven, Conn.: Human Relations Area Files Press.

————. 1989f. Review of *Captain Cook chased a chook* by June Factor. *Children's Folklore Newsletter* 12:2.

————. 1989g. Review of *Fun and games* by W. Andrei and L. Zoknay. *Journal of American Folklore* 102:503–505.

————. 1990a. The future agenda of child study and the implications for the study of children's folklore. *Children's Folklore Review* 1(1):17–21.

————. 1990b. The school playground as festival. *Children's Environments Quarterly* 7(2):3–7.

————. 1991. Preface to *Play and playscapes* by J. L. Frost. Albany, N.Y.: Delmar.

————. 1992a. Commentary: At play in the public arena. *Early Education and Development* 3(4):390–400.

————. 1992b. Les rhetoriques du jeu au 20eme siecle. *L'Education par le Jeu.* 46(Summer):9–13.

————. 1992c. Notes towards a critique of twentieth-century play theory. In *Homo ludens,* vol. 2. Salzburg: Verlag Emil Katzbichler, 95–107.

————. 1992d. Response to Handleman. *Play and Culture* 5:20–21.

————. 1992e. Review of *Dionysus reborn* by M. Spariosu. *Play and Culture* 5:314–322.

————. 1992f. Tradition from the perspective of children's games. *Children's Folklore Quarterly* 14(2):3–16.

————. 1993a. Dilemmas in adult play with children. In *Parent-child play: descriptions and implications,* ed. K. McDonald, Albany: New York State University Press.

————. 1993b. Play rhetorics and toy rhetorics. *Play Theory and Research* 1(4):239–250.

————. 1993c. Suggested rhetorics in adult play theories. *Play Theory and Research* 1(2):102–116.

————. 1994a. The future of toys. In *Toys and child development,* ed. J. Goldstein. New York: Cambridge University Press.

————. 1994b. Memory of games and some games of memory. In *Life and story: Autobiographies for a narrative psychology,* ed. D. John Lee. Westport, Conn.: Praeger.

————. 1994c. Paradigms of intervention. In *Play and intervention,* ed. J. Hellendorn et al. Albany: State University of New York Press.

————. 1995a. Conclusion: The persuasive rhetorics of play. In *The future of play*, ed. A. Pellegrini. Albany: State University of New York Press.

————. 1995b. Radicalizing childhood: The multivocal mind. In *Narrative in teaching, learning*, ed. H. McEwan and K. Eagan. New York: Teachers College Press.

Sutton-Smith, B., and D. Abrams. 1978. Psychosexual material in the stories told by children. *Archives of Sexual Behavior* 7(6):521–543.

Sutton-Smith, B., J. Gerstmyer, and A. Mechley. 1988. Playfighting as folkplay amongst preschool children. *Western Folklore* 47:161–176.

Sutton-Smith, B., and S. B. Heath, 1981. Paradigms of play. *The Quarterly Newsletter of the Laboratory of Comparative Human Cognition* 3(3):41–45.

Sutton-Smith, B., and D. Kelly-Byrne. 1982. The phenomenon of bipolarity in play theories. In *Child's play: Developmental and applied*, ed. T. D. Yawkey and A. D. Pellegrini. Hillsdale, N.J.: Erlbaum.

————. 1984. *The masks of play*. West Point, N.Y.: Leisure Press.

Sutton-Smith, B. and M. A. Magee. 1989. Reversible childhood. *Play and Culture*, 2(1):52–63.

Sutton-Smith, B., J. Mechling, T. Johnson, and F. McMahon. 1995. *Children's folklore: A sourcebook*. New York: Garland.

Sutton-Smith, B. and J. M. Roberts. 1963. Game involvement in adults. *Journal of Social Psychology* 60:15–30.

————. 1964. Rubrics of competitive behavior. *Journal of Genetic Psychology* 105:13–37.

————. 1979. Play, toys, games and sports. In *Handbook of cross-cultural psychology: Developmental psychology*, vol. 4, ed. A. Heron and E. Kroeger. New York: Allyn and Bacon.

Sutton-Smith, B., and B. G. Rosenberg. 1960. Manifest anxiety and game preference in children. *Child Development* 31:307–311.

————. 1961. Sixty years of historical change in the game preferences of American children. *Journal of American Folklore* 74:17–46.

————. 1965. Age changes in the effects of ordinal position on sex role identification. *Journal of Genetic Psychology* 107:61–73.

Sutton-Smith, B., B. G. Rosenberg, and E. Morgan. 1963. The development of sex differences in play choices during preadolescence. *Child Development* 34:119–126.

Sutton-Smith, B., and S. Sutton-Smith. 1974. *How to play with your children*. New York: Hawthorne.

Sutton-Smith, B., et al., 1967. Studies in an elementary game of strategy. *Genetic Psychology Monographs* 75:3–42.

Swiderski, R. M. 1986. *Voices: An anthropologist's dialogue with an Italian-American festival*. Bowling Green, Ohio: Bowling Green State University Popular Press.

Talbot, M. 1988. *Relative freedoms: Women and leisure.* Philadelphia: Open University Press.

Taylor, C. 1989. *Sources of the self: The making of modern identity.* Cambridge, Mass: Harvard University Press.

Tedeschi, J. T., B. R. Schlenker, and T. V. Bonoma, eds. 1973. *Conflict, power and games.* Chicago: Aldine Publishing.

Textor, R. B. 1967. *A cross cultural summary.* New Haven, Conn.: Human Relations Area Files Press.

Thorne, B. 1993. *Gender play: Girls and boys in school.* New Brunswick, N.J.: Rutgers University Press.

Tizard, B. and D. Harvey, eds. 1977. *The biology of play.* Philadelphia: Lippincott.

Tokofsky, P. I. 1992. The rules of fools: carnival in southwest Germany. Ph.D. diss., University of Pennsylvania. Ann Arbor, Mich.: UMI, order no. 9308671.

Tolman, E. C. 1967 (1932). *Purposive behavior in animals and man.* New York: Meredith.

Townshend, P. 1978. Games of strategy: a new look at correlates. *Newsletter of the Association for the Anthropological Study of Play* 4(4):3–7. Reprinted, 1993, in *Play Theory and Research* 1(3):225–230.

Trevarthen, C. 1989. Origins and directions for the concept of infant subjectivity. In *Society for Research in Child Development Newsletter,* ed. B. Rogoff. Chicago: University of Chicago Press, 1–4.

Triandis, H. C. 1996. The psychological measurement of cultural syndromes. *American Psychologist* 51(4):407–415.

Trilling, L. 1971. *Sincerity and authenticity.* Cambridge, Mass.: Harvard University Press.

Trudeau, G. 1995. Out of the crayons of babes. *New York Time Magazine,* Jan. 22, 34–35.

Turkle, S. 1995. *Life on the screen.* New York: Simon and Schuster.

Turner, E. S. 1948. *Boys will be boys.* London: Michael Joseph.

Turner, V. 1969. *The ritual process.* New York: Aldine.

———. 1974a. *Drama, fields and metaphors.* Ithaca, N.Y.: Cornell University Press.

———. 1974b. Liminal to liminoid in play, flow and ritual: An essay in comparative symbology. *Rice University Studies* 60:53–92.

———. 1978. Comments and conclusions. In *The reversible world,* ed. B. Babcock. New York: New York University Press.

———. 1982a. *From ritual to theater.* New York: Performing Arts Journal Publications.

———, ed. 1982b. *Celebration: Studies in festivity and ritual.* Washington, D.C.: Smithsonian Press.

Turner, V. W., and E. M. Bruner. 1986. *The anthropology of experience.* Urbana: University of Illinois Press.

Vaihinger, H. 1924. *The philosophy of "as if"* London: C. K. Ogden.

Vandenberg, B. 1980. *Play, problem-solving and creativity.* New Directions for Child Development, vol. 9. San Francisco: Jossey-Bass.

————. 1981. The role of play in the development of insightful tool-using strategies. *Merrill-Palmer Quarterly* 27:97–109.

————. 1988. The realities of play. In *Organizing early experience,* ed. D. C. Morrison. Amityville, N.Y.: Baywood Publishing.

————. 1993. Developmental psychology, God and the good. *Theory and Psychology* 3(2):191–205.

Van der Kooij, R., and R. de Groot. 1977. *That's all in the game.* Groningen, Netherlands: Schindele Verlag.

Veblen, T. 1899. *The theory of conspicuous consumption.* New York: Macmillan.

Von Glascoe, C. A. 1980. The work of playing "redlight." In *Play and culture,* ed. H. B. Schwartzman. West Point, N.Y.: Leisure Press.

Von Neumann, J., and O. Morgenstern. 1944. *Theory of games and economic behavior.* New York: Wiley.

Vygotsky, L. S. 1967. Play and its role in the mental development of the child. *Soviet Psychology* 12:62–76.

————. 1978 (1930). *Mind in society.* Cambridge, Mass.: Harvard University Press.

Walder, R. 1933. The psychoanalytical theory of play. *Psychoanalytic Quarterly* 2:208–224.

Wapner, S., and B. Kaplan. 1983. *Toward a holistic developmental psychology.* Hillsdale, N.J.: Erlbaum Press.

Warnock, M. 1976. *Imagination.* Berkeley: University of California Press.

Weber, M. 1930. *The protestant ethic and the spirit of capitalism.* London: Allen and Unwin.

Wegener-Sphoring, G. 1989. War toys and aggressive games. *Play and Culture* 2(1):35–47.

Weiner, A. B. 1988. *The Trobrianders of Papua New Guinea.* New York: Holt, Rinehart and Winston.

Weir, R. 1962. *Language in the crib.* The Hague: Mouton.

Welsford, E. 1961 (1935). *The fool.* Garden City, N.Y.: Doubleday, Anchor Books.

Werner, H. 1957. *The comparative psychology of mental development.* New York: International University Press.

Werner, H., and B. Kaplan. 1963. *Symbol formation.* New York: Wiley.

West, M. I. 1988. *Children's culture and controversy.* Hampden, Conn.: Archon Books.

White, R. W. 1959. Motivation reconsidered: The concept of competence. *Psychological Review* 66:197–333.

Whitehead, A. N. 1946. *Science and the modern world.* Cambridge: Cambridge University Press.

Whiting, B. B., ed. 1963. *Six cultures: Studies of child rearing.* New York: Wiley.

Whiting, B. B., and C. P. Edwards. 1988. *Children of different worlds.* Cambridge, Mass.: Harvard University Press.

Whiting, B. B., and J. W. M. Whiting. 1975. *Children of six cultures.* Cambridge, Mass.: Harvard University Press.

Whyte, W. F. 1943. *Street corner society.* Chicago: University of Chicago Press.

Wilcox, B. L., and H. Naimark. 1991. The rights of the child: Progress toward human dignity. *American Psychologist* 46(1):49.

Wilkinson, P. F. 1980. *In celebration of play.* New York: St. Martin's Press.

Willis, P. 1977. *Learning to labour.* London: Gower.

Wilson, A. 1980. The infancy of early childhood: An appraisal of Phillipe Ariés. *History and Theory* 19:132–153.

Wilson, S. 1984. The myth of mother a myth: A historical view of European child rearing. *Social History* 9:181–199.

Winner, E., and H. Gardner, eds. 1979. *Fact, fiction and fantasy in childhood.* New directions for child development, vol. 6. San Francisco: Jossey-Bass.

Winnicott, D. W. 1971. *Playing and reality.* New York: Basic Books.

Wolf, D. P., and S. H. Grollman. 1982. Ways of playing: Individual differences in imaginative style. *Contributions to Human Development* 6:46–63.

Wolfe, T. 1975. *The painted word.* New York: Bantam Books.

Wordsworth, J., M. C. Jaye, and R. Woof. 1987. *William Wordsworth and the age of English romanticism.* New Brunswick, N.J.: Rutgers University Press.

Wright, B. 1994. *Clowns of the Hopi: Tradition keepers and delight makers.* Flagstaff, Ariz.: Northland Publishing.

WuDunn, S. 1996. Sumo wrestles with outsized scandal. *International Herald Tribune,* June 22, 1 and 4.

Wullschlager, J. 1996. *Inventing wonderland.* New York: Free Press.

Yawkey, T. D., and A. D. Pellegrini, eds. 1984. *Child's play: Developmental and applied.* Hillsdale, N.J.: Erlbaum.

Young, D. C. 1984. *The Olympic myth of Greek amateur athletics.* Chicago: Ares Publishers.

Zelizer, V. 1985. *Pricing the priceless child: The changing social value of children.* New York: Basic Books.

Zingell, J. 1981. *The creative imagination: enlightenment in romanticism.* Cambridge, Mass.: Harvard University Press.

Zuckerman, M. 1976. Children's rights: The failure of reform. *Policy Analysis* 2(3):371–385.

———. 1985. Suburban play. In *Children's play: Past, present and future,* ed. B. Sutton-Smith. Philadelphia: Please Touch Museum.

INDEX